SPANISH
at a Glance
Phrase Book & Dictionary for Travelers

Fifth Edition

BY HEYWOOD WALD, Ph.D.
Former Chairman, Department of Foreign Languages
Martin Van Buren High School, New York

All inquiries should be addressed to:
Barron's Educational Series, Inc.
250 Wireless Boulevard
Hauppauge, New York 11788
www.barronseduc.com

ISBN: 978-0-7641-4773-9

Library of Congress Control Number: 2011944080

PRINTED IN CHINA
9 8 7 6 5 4 3 2 1

CONTENTS

PREFACE

This book will enable you to communicate quickly and confidently in colloquial terms. It is intended not only for beginners with no knowledge of the language, but also for those who have already studied it and have some familiarity with it.

Some of the unique features and highlights of the Barron's series are:

- Easy-to-follow *pronunciation keys* and complete phonetic transcriptions for all words and phrases in the book.
- Compact *dictionary* of commonly used words and phrases—built right into this phrase book so there's no need to carry a separate dictionary.
- Useful phrases for the *tourist*, grouped together by subject matter in a logical way so that the appropriate phrase is easy to locate when you need it.
- Special phrases for the *business traveler*, including banking terms, trade and contract negotiations, and secretarial services.
- Thorough section on *food and drink*, with comprehensive food terms you will find on menus.
- *Emergency phrases* and terms you hope you won't need: legal complications, medical problems, theft or loss of valuables, replacement or repair of watches, camera, etc.
- *Sightseeing itineraries*, with shopping tips, practical travel tips, and regional food specialties to help you get off the beaten path and into the countryside, to the small towns and cities, and to the neighboring areas.
- A *reference section* providing important signs, conversion tables, holidays, abbreviations, telling time, days of week, and months of year.
- A brief *grammar section*, with the basic elements of the language quickly explained.

Enjoy your vacation and travel with confidence. You have a, friend by your side.

Travel Tips There are many theories on how to survive jet lag—the adjustment to a long trip into a different time zone. Some multinational corporations take jet lag so seriously that they do not allow employees to make business decisions on the first day abroad. Most experts agree on several techniques: Eat lightly for several days before departing, avoid dehydration while flying by drinking plenty of nonalcoholic liquids; take frequent strolls around the plane to keep your blood circulating; if possible, get some rest on the flight; use ear plugs, an eye mask, and an inflatable neck collar to make sleep easier. If you arrive early in the morning, take an after-lunch nap, get up for some exercise and dinner, then go to bed at the regular new time. If you arrive at your destination in the afternoon or later, skip the nap and try to sleep late the next morning. In countries where massage or saunas are standard hotel service, indulge yourself on the evening of arrival to help you sleep soundly that night.

ACKNOWLEDGMENTS

We would like to thank the following individuals and organizations for their assistance on this project: Patricia Brooks, author, *Fisher's Guide to Spain and Portugal;* René Campos, Director, Spanish Institute, New York City; Mercedes Garcia-Rodriguez, Spanish Institute, New York City; George Lange, George Lang, Inc., New York City; Professor Robert Piluso, SUC New Paltz, NY; Professor Henry Urbanski, Chairman, Department of Foreign Languages, SUC New Paltz, NY; Pilar Vico, Spanish National Tourist Office, New York City; Professor Lynn Winget, Wichita State University, KS; Herta Erville; Fernando Pfannl; Alfonso Hernández.

Also, the Association of American Travel Writers; *The New York Times; Signature* magazine; the Spanish Institute; the Spanish National Tourist Office; *Travel-Holiday* magazine; *Travel and Leisure* magazine; U.S. Tour Operators; and U.S. Travel Data Center.

QUICK PRONUNCIATION GUIDE

Although all the phrases in this book are presented with an easy-to-use key to pronunciation, you will find speaking Spanish quite a bit easier if you learn a few simple rules. Many letters in Spanish are pronounced approximately as they would be in English. There are some differences, however, which are given below. Since these sounds rarely vary, you can follow these guidelines in pronouncing all Spanish words.

All letters are pronounced, with the exception of *h;* the letters *v* and *b* are most often both pronounced like the English *b*. Words ending in a vowel, an *n*, or an *s* are stressed on the next-to-last syllable—**casa** *(KAH-sah)*. Words ending in a consonant (other than *n* or *s*) are stressed on the last syllable—**general** *(hehn-eh-RAHL)*. A written accent is required on any words that break either of these rules—**lápiz** *(LAH-pees)*.

Note: When pronouncing the words in the following examples, stress the vowels that appear in CAPITAL letters.

VOWELS

Spanish Letter(s)	Sound in English	Examples
a	ah (y<u>a</u>cht)	taco *(TAH-koh)*
e	ay (d<u>ay</u>)	mesa *(MAY-sah)*
	eh (p<u>e</u>t)	perro *(PEH-roh)*
i	ee (m<u>ee</u>t)	libro *(LEE-broh)*
o	oh (<u>o</u>pen)	foto *(FOH-toh)*
u	oo (t<u>oo</u>th)	mucho *(MOO-choh)*

COMMON VOWEL COMBINATIONS (DIPHTHONGS)

Spanish Letter(s)	Sound in English	Examples
au	ow (c<u>ow</u>)	causa *(COW-sah)*
		auto *(OW-toh)*
ei	ay (d<u>ay</u>)	aceite *(ah-SAY-tay)*
ai	y (t<u>y</u>pe)	baile *(BY-lay)*
ie	yeh (<u>ye</u>t)	abierto *(ah-BYEHR-toh)*
ue	weh (<u>we</u>t)	bueno *(BWEH-noh)*

CONSONANTS

Spanish Letter(s)	Sound in English	Examples
c (before *a, o, u*)	hard k sound (<u>c</u>at)	campo *(KAHM-poh)*
		cosa *(KOH-sah)*
		Cuba *(KOO-bah)*
c (before *e, i*)	soft s sound (<u>c</u>ent)	central *(sehn-TRAHL)*
		cinco *(SEEN-koh)*
cc	hard and soft cc (ks sound) (a<u>cc</u>ept)	acción *(ahk-see-OHN)*
ch	hard ch sound (<u>ch</u>air)	muchacho *(moo-CHAH-choh)*
g (before *a, o, u*)	hard g (<u>g</u>o)	gafas *(GAH-fahs)*
		goma *(GOH-mah)*
g (before *e, i*)	breathy h (<u>h</u>ot)	general *(hehn-eh-RAHL)*
h	always silent	hasta *(AHS-tah)*
j	breathy as in h sound (<u>h</u>ot)	José *(ho-SAY)*
l	English l sound (<u>l</u>amp)	lámpara *(LAHM-pahr-ah)*
ll	as in English y (<u>y</u>es)	pollo *(POH-yoh)*
n	English n (<u>n</u>o)	naranja *(nah-RAHN-ha)*
ñ	English ny (can-<u>y</u>on)	señorita *(seh-nyoh-REE-tah)*
qu	English k (<u>k</u>eep)	que *(kay)*
r	trilled once	caro *(KAH-roh)*

Spanish Letter(s)	Sound in English	Examples
rr (or r at beginning of word)	trilled strongly (operator, three)	rico (*RREE-koh*) perro (*PEH-rroh*)
s	English s (<u>s</u>ee)	rosa (*ROH-sah*)
v	Approximately as in English b (<u>b</u>ook)	primavera (*pree-mah-BEHR-ah*)
x	English s, ks (<u>s</u>ign, so<u>cks</u>)	extra (*ES-trah*) examinar (*ek-sah-mee-NAHR*)
y	English y (<u>y</u>es) (by itself y = i)	yo (*yoh*) y (*ee*)
z	English s	zapato (*sah-PAH-toh*)

The above pronunciations apply to the Spanish that is spoken in Central and South America, and that is also spoken in parts of southern Spain. The remaining areas of Spain use the Castilian pronunciation, which differs mostly in the sound of the letters *ll* and of the *z* and the *c* before *e* and *i*. For example, the Castilian pronunciations are as follows:

Spanish Letter(s)	Sound in English	Examples
ll	ly sound as in million	llamo (*LYAH-moh*)
c (before *e* or *i*) }	a <u>th</u> sound instead of an s sound	gracias (*GRAH-thee-ahs*)
z }		lápiz (*LAH-peeth*)

THE BASICS FOR GETTING BY

MOST FREQUENTLY USED EXPRESSIONS

The following are expressions you'll use over and over—the fundamentals of polite conversation, the way to express what you want or need, and some simple question tags that you can use to construct all sorts of questions. We suggest you become very familiar with these phrases.

Hello!	**¡Hola!** *OH-lah*
Yes	**Sí** *see*
No	**No** *noh*
Maybe	**Quizás** *kee-SAHS*
Please	**Por favor** *pohr-fah-BOHR*
Thank you (very much).	**(Muchas) gracias.** *(MOO-chahs) GRAH-see-ahs*
You're welcome.	**De nada.** *day NAH-dah*
Excuse me	
■ (having disturbed or bumped into someone)	**Perdón** *pehr-DOHN*
■ (leaving a group or walking in front of a person)	**Con permiso** *kohn pehr-MEE-soh*
■ (getting one's attention)	**Por favor** *pohr fah-BOHR*
I'm sorry.	**Lo siento.** *loh see-EHN-toh*
Just a second.	**Un momento.** *oon moh-MEN-toh*

That's all right, okay.	**Está bien.**	*eh-STAH bee-ehn*
It doesn't matter.	**No importa.**	*noh eem-PORT-ah*
Good morning.	**Buenos días.**	*bway-nohs DEE-ahs*
Good afternoon.	**Buenas tardes.**	*bway-nahs TAHR-dehs*
Good evening (night).	**Buenas noches.**	*bway-nahs NOH-chehs*
Sir	**Señor**	*seh-NYOHR*
Madame	**Señora**	*seh-NYOHR-ah*
Miss	**Señorita**	*seh-nyohr-EE-tah*
Good-bye.	**Adiós.**	*ah-DYOHS*
See you later (so long).	**Hasta la vista (Hasta luego).**	*AH-stah lah BEE-stah (AH-stah loo-EH-goh)*
See you tomorrow.	**Hasta mañana.**	*AH-stah mah-NYAH-nah*

COMMUNICATIONS

Do you speak English?	**¿Habla usted inglés?**	*ah-blah oos-TEHD een-GLAYS*
I speak (a little) Spanish.	**Hablo español (un poco).**	*AH-bloh ehs-pah-NYOHL (oon POH-koh)*
I don't speak Spanish.	**No hablo español.**	*noh AH-bloh ehs-pah-NYOHL*
Is there anyone here who speaks English?	**¿Hay alguien aquí que hable inglés?**	*AH-ee AHL-ghee-ehn ah-KEE kay AH-blay een-GLAYS*
Do you understand?	**¿Comprende usted?**	*kohm-PREHN-day oos-tehd*

I understand.	**Comprendo.** *kohm-PREHN-doh*
I don't understand.	**No comprendo.** *noh kohm-PREHN-doh*
What? What did you say?	**¿Cómo?** *KOH-moh*
How do you say ____ in Spanish?	**¿Cómo se dice ____ en español?** *KOH-moh say DEE-say ____ ehn ehs-pah-NYOHL*
What do you call this (that) in Spanish?	**¿Cómo se llama esto (eso) en español?** *KOH-moh say YAH-mah EHS-toh (EHS-oh) ehn ehs-pahn-YOHL*
Please speak slowly.	**Hable despacio, por favor.** *AH-blay dehs-PAH-see-oh pohr fah-BOHR*
Please repeat.	**Repita, por favor.** *ray-PEE-tah pohr fah-BOHR*

INTRODUCTIONS

I'm American (English) (Australian) (Canadian).	**Soy norteamericano(a), (inglés, inglesa), (australiano, australiana), (canadiense).** *soy nohr-tay-ah-mehr-ee-KAH-noh (nah) (een-GLAYS een-GLAY-sah) (ow-strahl-YAH-noh nah) (kah-nah-DYEHN-say)*
My name is ____.	**Me llamo ____.** *may YAH-moh*
What's your name?	**¿Cómo se llama usted?** *KOH-moh say YAH-mah oos-TEHD*
How are you?	**¿Cómo está usted?** *KOH-moh ehs-TAH oos-TEHD*
How's everything?	**¿Qué tal?** *kay tahl*

Very well, thanks. And you?	**Muy bien, gracias. ¿Y usted?** *mwee bee-EHN GRAH-see-ahs ee oos-TEHD*

GETTING AROUND

Where is ____?	**¿Dónde está ____?** *DOHN-day ehs-TAH*
the bathroom	**el baño** *ehl BAH-nyoh*
the bus stop	**la parada de autobuses** *lah pahr-AH-dah day ow-tow-BOOS-ehs*
the dining room	**el comedor** *ehl koh-meh-DOHR*
the entrance	**la entrada** *lah ehn-TRAH-dah*
the exit	**la salida** *lah sahl-EE-dah*
the subway	**el metro** *ehl MEH-troh*
the taxi stand	**la parada de taxis** *lah pah-RAH-dah day TAHK-sees*
the telephone	**el teléfono** *ehl tehl-EHF-oh-noh*
the train station	**la estación de trenes** *lah esh-tah-SYOHN day TREH-nehs*
I'm lost.	**Me he perdido.** *may heh pehr-DEE-doh*

We're lost.	**Nos hemos perdido.** *nohs HEH-mohs pehr-DEE-doh*
Where are _____?	**¿Dónde están _____?** *dohn-day ehs-TAHN*

SHOPPING

How much is it?	**¿Cuánto es?** *KWAHN-toh ehs*
I'd like _____.	**Quisiera _____.** *kee-see-YEHR-ah*
Please bring me _____.	**Tráigame, por favor _____.** *TRAH-ee-gah-may pohr fah-BOHR*
Please show me _____.	**Muéstreme, por favor _____.** *MWEHS-treh-may pohr fah-BOHR*
Here it is.	**Aquí está.** *ah-KEE eh-STAH*

MISCELLANEOUS

I'm hungry.	**Tengo hambre.** *TEHN-goh AHM-bray*
I'm thirsty.	**Tengo sed.** *tehn-goh SEHD*
I'm tired.	**Estoy cansado (m.) Estoy cansada (f.)** *eh-stoy kahn-SAH-doh (dah)*
What's that?	**¿Qué es eso?** *kay ehs EHS-oh*
What's up?	**¿Qué hay?** *kay AH-ee*
I (don't) know.	**Yo (no) sé.** *yoh (noh) say*

QUESTIONS

Where is (are) _____?	**¿Dónde está (están) _____?** *DOHN-day eh-STAH (STAHN)*
When?	**¿Cuándo?** *KWAHN-doh*

How?	**¿Cómo?** *KOH-moh*
How much?	**¿Cuánto?** *KWAHN-toh*
Who?	**¿Quién?** *key-EN*
Why?	**¿Por qué?** *pohr KAY*
Which?	**¿Cuál?** *kwal*
What?	**¿Qué?** *kay*

EXCLAMATIONS, SLANG, COLLOQUIALISMS

Ouch!	**¡Ay!** *AH-ee*
Wow! Gosh!	**¡Caramba!** *kah-RAHM-bah*
How pretty!	**¡Qué bonito! (m.)** *kay boh-NEE-toh* **¡Qué bonita! (f.)** *kay boh-NEE-tah*
That's awful!	**¡Es horrible!** *ehs ohr-EE-blay*
Great! Wonderful!	**¡Estupendo!** *ehs-too-PEHN-doh* **¡Magnífico!** *mahg-NEE-fee-koh*
That's it!	**¡Eso es!** *ehs-oh EHS*
My goodness!	**¡Dios mío!** *dyohs MEE-oh*
Bottoms up, cheers.	**¡Salud!** *sah-LOOD*
Quiet!	**¡Silencio!** *see-LEHN-see-oh*
Shut up!	**¡Cállese!** *KAH-yeh-say*
That's enough!	**¡Basta!** *BAHS-tah*
Never mind!	**¡No importa!** *noh eem-POHR-tah*

Of course!	**¡Claro!** _KLAH-roh_
With pleasure.	**¡Con mucho gusto!** _kohn MOO-choh GOOS-toh_
Let's go!	**¡Vamos!** _BAH-mohs_
What a shame (pity)!	**¡Qué lástima!** _kay LAH-stee-mah_
What a nuisance! (showing annoyance)	**¡Qué lata!** _kay LAH-tah_
Good luck!	**¡Buena suerte!** _bweh-nah SWEHR-tay_

PROBLEMS, PROBLEMS, PROBLEMS (EMERGENCIES)

Watch out!	**¡Cuidado!** _kwee-DAH-doh_
Hurry up!	**¡Dése prisa!** _day-say PREE-sah_
Look!	**¡Mire!** _MEE-reh_
Listen!	**¡Escuche!** _ehs-KOO-cheh_
Wait!	**¡Espere!** _ehs-PEHR-eh_
Fire!	**¡Fuego!** _FWAY-goh_

ANNOYANCES

What's the matter with you?	**¿Qué le pasa?** _kay lay PAH-sah_
What (the devil) do you want?	**¿Qué (diablos) quiere usted?** _kay (dee-AH-blohs) kee-EHR-eh oos-TEHD_

Stop bothering me!	**¡No me moleste más!** *noh meh moh-LEHS-tay mahs*
Go away!	**¡Váyase!** *BAH-yah-say*
I'm going to call a cop!	**¡Voy a llamar a un policía!** *boy ah yah-MAHR ah oon pohl-ee-SEE-yah*
Help, police!	**¡Socorro, policía!** *soh-KOH-roh poh-lee-SEE-yah*
That guy is a thief!	**¡Ese tipo es un ladrón!** *ehs-eh tee-poh ehs oon lah-DROHN*
He has stolen ____.	**Me ha robado ____.** *may ah roh-BAH-doh*
my car	**el coche** *ehl KOH-chay*
my passport	**el pasaporte** *ehl pah-sah-POHR-tay*
my purse	**la bolsa** *lah BOHL-sah*
my suitcase	**la maleta** *lah mahl-EH-tah*
my wallet	**la cartera** *lah kahr-TEHR-ah*

| This young man is annoying me. | **Este joven me está molestando.** *ehs-teh HOH-behn may ehs-TAH moh-lehs-TAHN-doh* |

He keeps following me.	**Me está siguiendo.**	*may ehs-TAH see-ghee-YEHN-doh*
Stop that boy!	**¡Paren a ese muchacho!**	*PAH-rehn ah ehs-eh moo-CHAH-choh*

COMPLICATIONS

I haven't done anything.	**No he hecho nada.**	*noh eh EH-choh NAH-dah*
It's not true.	**No es verdad.**	*noh ehs behr-DAHD*
I'm innocent.	**Soy inocente.**	*soy een-oh-SEHN-teh*
I want a lawyer.	**Quiero un abogado.**	*kee-YEHR-oh oon ah-boh-GAH-doh*
I want to go ____.	**Quiero ir ____.**	*kee-YEHR-oh eer*
to the American (British) (Australian) (Canadian) Consulate	**al consulado norteamericano (inglés), (australiano), (canadiense)**	*ahl kohn-soo-LAH-doh nohr-tay-ah-mehr-ee-KAH-noh (een-GLAYS) (ow-strahl-YAH-noh) (kah-nah-DYEHN-say)*
to the police station	**al cuartel de policía**	*ahl kwahr-TEHL day poh-lee-SEE-ah*
I need help, quick.	**Necesito ayuda, pronto.**	*nehs-ehs-EE-toh ah-YOO-dah PROHN-toh*
Can you help me, please?	**¿Puede usted ayudarme, por favor?**	*pweh-day oos-TEHD ah-yoo-DAHR-may pohr fah-BOHR*
I have lost ____.	**He perdido ____.**	*ay pehr-DEE-doh*
Does anyone here speak English?	**¿Hay alguien aquí que hable inglés?**	*AHl-ee AHL-ghee-yehn ah-KEE kay AH-blay een-GLEHS*
I need an interpreter.	**Necesito un intérprete.**	*neh-seh-SEE-toh oon een-TEHR-preh-tay*

NUMBERS AND QUANTITIES

CARDINAL NUMBERS

0	**cero**	*SEHR-oh*
1	**uno**	*OO-noh*
2	**dos**	*dohs*
3	**tres**	*trehs*
4	**cuatro**	*KWAH-troh*
5	**cinco**	*SEEN-koh*
6	**seis**	*sayss*
7	**siete**	*SYEH-tay*
8	**ocho**	*OH-choh*
9	**nueve**	*NWEH-bay*
10	**diez**	*dyehs*
11	**once**	*OHN-say*
12	**doce**	*DOH-say*
13	**trece**	*TREH-say*
14	**catorce**	*kah-TOHR-say*
15	**quince**	*KEEN-say*
16	**diez y seis (dieciséis)**	*dyeh-see-SAYSS*
17	**diez y siete (diecisiete)**	*dyeh-see-SYEH-tay*
18	**diez y ocho (dieciocho)**	*dyeh-see-OH-choh*

19	**diez y nueve (diecinueve)** *dyeh-see-NWEH-bay*
20	**veinte** *BAYN-tay*
21	**veintiuno** *bayn-tee-OO-noh*
22	**veintidós** *bayn-tee-DOHS*
23	**veintitrés** *bayn-tee-TREHS*
24	**veinticuatro** *bayn-tee-KWAH-troh*
25	**veinticinco** *bayn-tee-SEEN-koh*
26	**veintiséis** *bayn-tee-SAYSS*
27	**veintisiete** *bayn-tee-SYEH-tay*
28	**veintiocho** *bayn-tee-OH-choh*
29	**veintinueve** *bayn-tee-NWEH-bay*
30	**treinta** *TRAYN-tah*
40	**cuarenta** *kwahr-EHN-tah*
50	**cincuenta** *seen-KWEHN-tah*
60	**sesenta** *seh-SEHN-tah*
70	**setenta** *seh-TEHN-tah*
80	**ochenta** *oh-CHEHN-tah*
90	**noventa** *noh-BEHN-tah*
100	**cien(to)** *syehn(toh)*
101	**ciento uno** *SYEHN-toh OO-noh*
102	**ciento dos** *SYEHN-toh DOHS*
200	**doscientos (as)** *dohs-SYEHN-tohs (tahs)*
300	**trescientos (as)** *trehs-SYEHN-tohs (tahs)*

400	**cuatrocientos (as)** *kwah-troh-SYEHN-tohs (tahs)*
500	**quinientos (as)** *kee-NYEHN-tohs (tahs)*
600	**seiscientos (as)** *sayss-SYEHN-tohs (tahs)*
700	**setecientos (as)** *seh-teh-SYEHN-tohs (tahs)*
800	**ochocientos (as)** *oh-choh-SYEHN-tohs (tahs)*
900	**novecientos (as)** *noh-beh-SYEHN-tohs (tahs)*
1.000	**mil** *meel*
2.000	**dos mil** *dohs meel*
1.000.000	**un millón** *oon mee-YOHN*
2.000.000	**dos millones** *dohs mee-YOHN-ays*

Note: In Spanish, thousands are separated by periods, not commas.

ORDINAL NUMBERS

first	**primero (primer, -a)** *pree-MEH-roh (rah)*
second	**segundo (a)** *seh-GOON-doh (dah)*
third	**tercero (tercer,-a)** *tehr-SEH-roh (rah)*
fourth	**cuarto (a)** *KWAHR-toh (tah)*
fifth	**quinto (a)** *KEEN-toh (tah)*
sixth	**sexto (a)** *SEHS-toh (tah)*
seventh	**séptimo (a)** *SEHT-tee-moh (mah)*

eighth	**octavo (a)**	*ohk-TAH-boh (bah)*
ninth	**noveno (a)**	*noh-BAY-noh (nah)*
tenth	**décimo (a)**	*DEH-see-moh (mah)*
last	**último (a)**	*OOL-tee-moh (mah)*
once	**una vez**	*OO-nah behs*
twice	**dos veces**	*dohs BEH-sehs*
three times	**tres veces**	*trehs BEH-sehs*

FRACTIONS

half of ____.   **la mitad de ____.**   *lah mee-TAHD day*

■ half (of) the money   **la mitad del dinero**   *lah mee-TAHD del dee-NEH-row*

half a ____.   **medio ____.**   *MEH-dyoh*

■ half a kilo   **medio kilo**   *MEH-dyoh KEE-loh*

a fourth (quarter)   **un cuarto**   *oon KWAHR-toh*

a dozen ____.   **una docena de ____.**   *OO-nah doh-SAY-nah day*

■ a dozen oranges   **una docena de naranjas**   *OO-nah doh-SAY-nah day nah-RAHN-hahs*

100 grams   **cien gramos**   *syehn GRAH-mohs*

200 grams   **doscientos gramos**   *dohs-SYEHN-tohs GRAH-mos*

350 grams   **trescientos cincuenta gramos**   *trey-SYEHN-tohs seen-KWEHN-tah GRAH-mos*

a pair (of) ____.   **un par de ____.**   *oon pahr day*

a pair of shoes   **un par de zapatos**   *oon pahr day sah-PAH-tohs*

QUANTITIES

I want ____.	**Quiero** ____. *KEE-eh-roh*
a bag of	**una bolsa de** *OO-nah BOHL-say day*
a bottle of	**una botella de** *OO-nah boh-TEH-yah day*
a box of	**una caja de** *OO-nah KAH-hah day*
a can of	**una lata de** *OO-nah LAH-tah day*
a dozen of	**una docena de** *OO-nah doh-SEH-nah day*
a kilo of	**un kilo de** *oon KEE-loh day*

a liter of	**un litro de** *oon LEE-troh day*
a package of	**un paquete de** *oon pah-KEH-teh day*
a pair of	**un par de** *oon PAHR day*
a pound of	**una libra de** *OO-nah LEE-brah day*
a slice of	**una tajada de** *OO-nah tah-HA-dah day*
a bit of	**un poco de** *oon POH-ko day*
a lot of	**mucho** *MOO-choh*
enough of	**suficiente** *soo-fee-SYEHN-tay*
too much	**demasiado** *deh-mah-SYAH-doh*

WHEN YOU ARRIVE

PASSPORT AND CUSTOMS

Customs is usually a routine procedure in Spain. Items that can be brought in duty-free include clothing, jewelry, and personal effects needed for a visit; 200 cigarettes or 50 cigars; 2 liters of wine or 1 liter of spirits (above 22 percent alcohol); 1/4 liter of cologne. Sums of money in excess of 10,000 euros must be declared.

Customs in other Spanish-speaking countries vary greatly, although crossing the border into Mexico is usually a very casual affair. We suggest you check ahead, should you be entering any country in Central or South America.

My name is ____.	**Me llamo ____.** *may YAH-moh*
I'm American (British) (Australian) (Canadian).	**Soy norteamericano(a), (inglés, a), (australiano, a), (canadiense).** *soy nohr-tay-ah-mehr-ee-KAH-noh(nah) (een-GLAYS ah) (ow-strahl-YAH-noh nah) (kah-nah-DYEHN-say)*
My address is ____.	**Mi dirección es ____.** *mee dee-rehk-SYOHN ehs*
I'm staying at ____.	**Estoy en el hotel ____.** *ehs-TOY ehn ehl oh-TEHL*
Here is (are) ____.	**Aquí tiene ____.** *ah-KEE TYEHN-ay*
▩ my documents	**mis documentos** *mees doh-koo-MEHN-tohs*
▩ my passport	**mi pasaporte** *mee pah-sah-POHR-tay*
▩ my tourist card	**mi tarjeta de turista** *mee tahr-HAY-tah day toor-EES-tah*

I'm ____.	**Estoy ____.** *ehs-TOY*
■ on a business trip	**en un viaje de negocios** *ehn oon bee-AH-hay day neh-GOH-see-ohs*
■ on vacation	**de vacaciones** *day bah-kah-SYOHN-ays*
■ visiting relatives	**visitando a mis familiares** *bee-see-TAHN-doh ah mees fah-meel-YAHR-ays*
■ just passing through	**solamente de paso** *soh-lah-MEHN-tay day PAH-soh*
I'll be staying here ____.	**Me quedaré aquí ____.** *may kay-dahr-AY ah-KEE*
■ a few days	**unos días** *OON-ohs DEE-ahs*
■ a few weeks	**unas semanas** *OON-ahs seh-MAH-nahs*
■ a week	**una semana** *OON-ah seh-MAH-nah*
■ a month	**un mes** *oon mehs*
I'm traveling ____.	**Viajo ____.** *bee-AH-hoh*
■ alone	**solo(a)** *SOH-loh(lah)*
■ with my husband	**con mi marido** *kohn mee mah-REE-doh*
■ with my wife	**con mi mujer** *kohn mee moo-HAIR*
■ with my family	**con mi familia** *kohn mee fah-MEEL-yah*
■ with my friend	**con mi amigo(a)** *kohn mee ah-MEE-go(ah)*

Customs in the major ports of entry is a simple affair. As you pass through the gates, you'll see signs dividing the path in two directions: Follow the green arrow if you have nothing to declare (**nada que declarar**), or head for the red arrow if you have items to declare (**artículos para declarar**).

NADA QUE DECLARAR	ARTICULOS PARA DECLARAR

These are my bags.	**Estas son mis maletas.** *EHS-tahs sohn mees mah-LAY-tahs*
I have nothing to declare.	**No tengo nada que declarar.** *noh tehn-goh NAH-dah kay day-klahr-AHR*
I only have ____.	**Sólo tengo ____.** *SOH-loh tehn-goh*
▪ a carton of cigarettes	**un cartón de cigarrillos** *oon kahr-TOHN day see-gahr-EE-yohs*
▪ a bottle of whisky	**una botella de whisky** *OON-nah boh-TEH-yah day WEE-skee*
What's the problem?	**¿Hay algún problema?** *AH-ee ahl-GOON proh-BLAY-mah*
They're gifts (for my personal use).	**Son regalos (para mi uso personal).** *sohn ray-GAH-lohs (pah-rah mee OO-soh pehr-sohn-AHL)*
Do I have to pay duty?	**¿Tengo que pagar impuestos?** *ten-goh kay pah-GAHR eem-PWEHS-tohs*
May I close my bag now?	**¿Puedo cerrar la maleta ahora?** *pweh-doh sehr-AHR lah mah-LEH-tah ah-OHR-ah*

IDENTITY CARD (TARJETA DE IDENTIDAD)

Upon entering the country (or on your flight into the country), you will be required to complete an identity card, usually with the following information.

Apellidos: (Surname) _____

Nombre: (First Name) _____

Nacionalidad: (Nationality) _____

Fecha de nacimiento: (Date of Birth) _____

Profesión: (Profession) _____

Dirección: (Address) _____

Pasaporte expedido en: (Passport Issued in) _____

BAGGAGE AND PORTERS

You will find carts for your baggage at virtually all airports. After you have retrieved your bags, push your cart through the "Nothing to Declare" doors. After customs, you can carry your bags to the taxi or bus stand—or ask a porter for help. Porters are readily available.

Where can I find a baggage cart?	**¿Dónde está un carrito para-maletas?** *DOHN-day eh-STAH oon kahr-REE-toh pah-rah mah-LEH-tahs*
I need a porter!	**¡Necesito un maletero!** *neh-seh-SEE-toh oon mah-leh-TEH-roh*
These are our (my) bags.	**Estas son nuestras (mis) maletas.** *EHS-tahs sohn NWEHS-trahs (mees) mah-LEH-tahs*
Put them here (there).	**Póngalas aquí (allí).** *POHN-gah-lahs ah-KEE (ah-YEE)*
Be careful with that one!	**¡Cuidado con ésa!** *kwee-DAH-doh kohn EH-sah*

I'll carry this one myself.	**Yo me llevo ésta.** *yoh may YEH-boh EHS-tah*
I'm missing a suitcase.	**Me falta una maleta.** *may FAHL-tah oo-nah mah-LEH-tah*
How much do I owe you?	**¿Cuánto le debo?** *KWAHN-toh lay DEHB-oh*
Thank you (very much). This is for you.	**(Muchas) gracias. Esto es para usted.** *(moo-chahs) GRAHS-yahs EHS-toh ehs pah-rah oos-TEHD*

AIRPORT TRANSPORTATION

Where can I get a taxi?	**¿Dónde puedo tomar un taxi?** *DOHN-deh PWEH-doh toh-MAHR oon TAHK-see*
How much is the taxi ride into the city?	**¿Cuánto cuesta el viaje en taxi a la ciudad?** *KWAHN-toh KWEHS-tah ehl BYAH-heh ehn TAHK-see ah lah see-yoo-DAHD*
What buses go into the city?	**¿Qué autobuses van a la ciudad?** *KAY ow-toh-BOOS-ehs bahn ah lah see-you-DAHD*
Where is the bus stop?	**¿Dónde está la parada del autobús?** *DOHN-deh ehs-TAH lah pah-RAH-dah del ow-toh-BOOS*
How much is the fare?	**¿Cuánto cuesta el viaje?** *KWAHN-toh KWEHS-tah ehl BYAH-heh*
Where can I rent a car?	**¿Donde puedo arrendar un coche?** *DOHN-deh PWEH-doh ah-ren-DAHR oon KOH-cheh*

Travel Tips   There was a time when buying an airline ticket was simple. Since the airline industry was deregulated, however, travelers must shop and compare prices, buy charter or discount tickets far in advance and join frequent flier clubs to become eligible for free tickets. Read the fine print in ads and ask questions when making reservations. Often, discount fare tickets cannot be exchanged for cash or another ticket if travel plans must be changed. If you must change plans en route, talk to an airline ticket agent. Sometimes they have soft hearts!

It's a sad fact that airlines become more miserly with each passing year. You should shop around and see which company will feed you for free and not charge extra for your second suticase. Also, most airlines nowadays will lose your luggage and do little or nothing about compensation. Keep all your valuables in your hand luggage!

BANKING AND MONEY MATTERS

The **euro** is the currency of Spain, with 100 **cents** in each **euro**. Best exchange rates are usually offered at banks, of which there are dozens. Banco Exterior has an office at the airport in Madrid.

The euro is the official monetary currency not only of Spain but of the entire European Union, which means that you can use the same currency throughout most of Western Europe. The euro is issued in the following denominations: notes—5, 10, 20, 50, 100, 200, and 500; coins—1, 2, 5, 10, 20, 50 cents, 1 and 2 euros.

In Mexico and many countries in Central and South America the **peso** is the currency, with 100 **centavos** equaling one peso. In recent years, devaluations and value fluctuations have had profound effects on the peso's exchange value. You will get a very favorable exchange for pounds or dollars.

Major credit cards are widely accepted, as are all major travelers checks.

Banking hours are generally from 9 A.M. to 3 P.M., Monday through Friday, plus Saturday morning. Business hours are usually from 9 A.M. to 1:30 P.M., then 4:30 P.M. to 8 P.M., Monday through Friday. Many businesses keep Saturday morning hours too. "Morning" in Spain or Mexico generally means until it is time for the lunch break—i.e., 1 or 1:30 P.M.

CURRENCIES OF
SPANISH-SPEAKING COUNTRIES

Argentina	**peso**	*PEH-soh*
Bolivia	**peso**	*PEH-soh*
Chile	**peso**	*PEH-soh*
Colombia	**peso**	*PEH-soh*
Costa Rica	**colón**	*koh-LOHN*
Cuba	**peso**	*PEH-soh*
Ecuador	**US dollar**	
Guatemala	**quetzal**	*kayt-SAHL*
Honduras	**lempira**	*lem-PEER-ah*

México	**peso** *PEH-soh*
Nicaragua	**córdoba** *KOHR-doh-bah*
Panamá	**balboa** *bahl-BOH-ah*
Paraguay	**guaraní** *gwahr-ah-NEE*
Perú	**sol** *sohl*
República Dominicana	**peso** *PEH-soh*
El Salvador	**colón** *koh-LOHN*
Spain (España)	**euro** *EW-roh*
Uruguay	**peso** *PEH-soh*
Venezuela	**bolívar** *boh-LEE-bahr*

Note: 1. When writing numbers, Spanish uses a comma where English uses a decimal point, and vice versa. One thousand euros in Spanish is 1.000 euros. 2. Pesos from different countries have different values depending on the current rate of exchange in that country.

EXCHANGING MONEY

Where can I find an ATM machine?	**¿Dónde hay un cajero automático?** *DOHN-day AH-ee oon kah-HEHR-oh ow-toh-MAH-tee-koh*
Where is the currency exchange (bank)?	**¿Dónde hay un banco para cambiar moneda extranjera?** *DOHN-day AH-ee oon BAHN-koh pah-rah kahm-bee-AHR moh-NAY-dah ehs-trahn-HEHR-ah*
I wish to change ____.	**Quiero cambiar ____.** *kee-YEHR-oh kahm-bee-YAHR*
■ money	**dinero** *dee-NEHR-oh*

■ dollars (pounds) **dólares (libras)** *DOH-lahr-ays (LEE-brahs)*

■ travelers checks **cheques de viajero** *CHEH-kays day bee-ah-HAIR-oh*

Can I cash a personal check? **¿Puedo cambiar un cheque personal?** *PWEH-doh kahm-bee-YAHR oon CHEH-kay pehr-sohn-AHL*

At what time do they open (close)? **¿A qué hora abren (cierran)?** *ah kay ohra AH-brehn (SYEHR-ahn)*

Where is the cashier's window? **¿Dónde está la caja, por favor?** *DOHN-day eh-STAH lah KAH-hah pohr fah-BOHR*

The current exchange rates are posted in those banks that exchange money and are also published daily in the newspapers. Since the rates fluctuate from day to day, it may be useful to convert the common amounts here for your quick reference.

EURO	YOUR OWN CURRENCY	OTHER	YOUR OWN CURRENCY
1	_____	1	_____
5	_____	10	_____
10	_____	50	_____
20	_____	100	_____
50	_____	1000	_____
100	_____	10,000	_____

What's the current exchange rate for dollars (pounds)? **¿A cómo está el cambio hoy del dólar (de la libra)?** *ah KOH-moh ehs-TAH ehl KAHM-bee-oh oy del DOH-lahr (day lah LEE-brah)*

What commission do you charge? **¿Cuál es el interés que ustedes cobran?** *kwahl ehs ehl een-tehr-AYS kay oos-TEHD-ays KOH-brahn*

I'd like to cash this check.	**Quisiera cobrar este cheque.** *kee-SYEHR-ah koh-BRAHR EHS-teh CHEH-kay*
Where do I sign?	**¿Dónde debo firmar?** *DOHN-day DEH-boh feer-MAHR*
I'd like the money ____.	**Quisiera el dinero ____.** *kee-SYEHR-ah ehl dee-NEHR-oh*
▨ in (large) bills	**en billetes (grandes)** *ehn bee-YEH-tehs (GRAHN-days)*
▨ in small change	**en suelto** *ehn SWEHL-toh*
Give me two twenty-peso bills.	**Déme dos billetes de a veinte pesos.** *DEH-may dohs bee-YEH-tays day ah BAYN-tay PAY-sohs*
▨ fifty-peso bills	**cincuenta** *seen-KWEHN-tah*
▨ one hundred-peso bills	**cien** *see-YEHN*
Do you accept credit cards?	**¿Acepta usted tarjetas de crédito?** *a-SEHP-tah oo-STEHD tahr-HAY-tahs day KREHD-ee-toh*

BUSINESS AND BANKING TERMS

ATM	**el cajero automático** *ehl kah-HEHR-oh ow-toh-MAH-tee-koh*
account	**la cuenta** *lah KWEHN-tah*
amount	**la cantidad** *lah kahn-tee-DAHD*
bad check	**un cheque sin fondos** *oon CHEH-kay seen FOHN-dohs*
bank	**el banco** *ehl BAHN-koh*
banker	**el banquero** *ehl bahn-KEH-roh*
bill	**el billete** *ehl bee-YEH-tay*

borrow (to)	**pedir prestado** *peh-DEER prehs-TAH-doh*
cashier	**el (la) cajero(a)** *ehl (lah) kah-HEHR-oh(ah)*
capital	**el capital** *ehl kah-pee-TAHL*
cashier's office	**la caja** *lah KAH-hah*

check	**el cheque** *ehl CHEH-kay*
checkbook	**el libreto de cheques** *ehl lee-BREH-toh day CHEH-kays*
credit card	**la tarjeta de crédito** *lah tahr-HAY-tah deh KREHD-ee-toh*
debit card	**la tarjeta de débito** *lah tahr-HAY-tah deh DEH-bee-toh*
endorse (to)	**endosar** *ehn-doh-SAHR*
income	**el ingreso** *ehl een-GREHS-oh*
interest rate	**el tipo de interés** *ehl TEE-poh day een-tehr-AYS*
investment	**la inversión** *lah een-behr-SYOHN*
to lend	**prestar** *prehs-TAHR*
loss	**la pérdida** *lah PEHR-dee-dah*
make change (to)	**dar (el) cambio** *dahr (ehl) KAHM-bee-oh*

money	**el dinero** *ehl dee-NEHR-oh*
mortgage	**la hipoteca** *lah eep-oh-TEH-kah*
open an account (to)	**abrir una cuenta** *ah-BREER oo-nah KWEHN-tah*
premium	**el premio** *ehl PRAY-mee-oh*
profit	**la ganancia** *la gah-NAHN-see-ah*
safe	**la caja fuerte** *lah KAH-ha FWEHR-tay*
savings account	**la cuenta de ahorros** *lah KWEHN-tah day ah-OHR-ohs*
savings book	**la libreta de ahorros** *la lee-BREH-tah day ah-OHR-ohs*
signature	**la firma** *lah FEER-mah*
window	**la ventanilla** *lah ben-tah-NEE-yah*

TIPPING

In many areas, service charges are often included in the price of the service rendered. These usually come to about 10 to 15% and should be indicated on the bill.

Usually a customer will leave some small change in addition to any charge that has been included if the service has been satisfactory. At times, a set amount should be given.

Tips will vary from country to country and from time to time due to inflation and other factors. It is therefore advisable to ask some knowledgeable person (hotel manager, tour director, etc.) once you get to the country, or to check the current rate of exchange.

Travel Tips Touring on a budget? Then it pays to do your homework. Look for hotels or bed-and-breakfast establishments that include a morning meal in the price of a room. Often the breakfast is hearty enough to allow a light lunch. Carry nutrition bars from home in your tote bag for snacking when only expensive airport or restaurant food is available. Use public transportation whenever possible. Rail and air passes are sold for Europe and other regions but often can only be purchased in the U.S. before departure. If you must rent a car and have booked one from home, double-check local prices and make sure to check all taxes and surcharges. Sometimes better deals can be arranged on the spot. When you first arrive in a country, check with a visitors' bureau. Agents there will explain discount cards or money-saving packets offered by local governments or merchants. The discount plans often cover transportation, food, lodging, museums, concerts, and other entertainment.

AT THE HOTEL

If you are unfamiliar with the city to which you are going, you'll probably find it best to make a hotel reservation in advance from home. It is possible that you would do better on prices for a room in some Mexican hotels, however, if you bargain for your room once you get there.

You can buy a *Guía de Hoteles* at a Spanish National Tourist Office, which gives official government listings of hotels in Spain by category. Ratings run from 5-star deluxe to plain 1-star. Every hotel has a plaque outside with an "H" (for hotel) on it and the star rating it has been allocated. "HS" on the plaque stands for Hostal; "HR" signifies Hotel-residencia, which means the hotel serves breakfast only. "P" stands for Pensión.

The following is a listing of the types of hotels you will encounter in Spain.

Hoteles   hotels

Hostales   small hotels or inns with no restaurant

Pensiones	guesthouses providing full board only
Paradores	first-class hotels run by the state located in places of historical interest and attractive surroundings. Many are converted castles, palaces, or monasteries
Refugios	retreats or rustic lodges, which are located in scenic mountain areas and are popular with hunters, hikers, and fishermen
Albergues Nacionales de Carretera	state-run roadside inns (period of stay is restricted). They also provide gas station and car repair services
Albergues Juveniles	youth hostels provide cheap accommodations for young people who are members of the international Youth Hostels Association; maximum length of stay at any one hostel is 3 nights

Note: Paradores are extremely popular with tourists. There are more than 80 located throughout Spain, but because they have relatively few rooms, they are often booked far in advance. Brochures on paradores, albergues, and refugios are available free from the Spanish National Tourist Office.

Hotels include a service charge in the bill. It is customary, though, to tip the porter carrying your luggage, maids, room service, and the doorman who summons your cab. A helpful concierge might receive a tip for doing special favors, such as securing theater tickets or making phone calls and reservations.

GETTING TO YOUR HOTEL

I'd like to go to the ____ Hotel.	**Quisiera ir al Hotel ____.** *kee-SYEH-rah eer ahl oh-TEL*
Is it near (far)?	**¿Está cerca (lejos) de aquí?** *ehs-TAH SEHR-kah (LAY-hohs) day ah-KEE*
Where can I get a taxi?	**¿Dónde puedo tomar un taxi?** *DOHN-day PWEH-doh toh-MAHR oon TAHK-see*
What buses go into town?	**¿Qué autobuses van al centro?** *kay ow-toh-BOOS-ehs bahn ahl SEHN-troh*
Where is the bus stop?	**¿Dónde está la parada?** *DOHN-day ehs-TAH lah pah-RAH-dah*
How much is the fare?	**¿Cuánto cuesta el billete?** *KWAHN-toh KWEHS-tah ehl bee-YEH-tay*

CHECKING IN

Most first-class or deluxe hotels will have personnel who speak English. If you are checking in to a smaller hotel, you might find these phrases useful in getting what you want. In Spain, all visitors are required to fill out a registration form *(una ficha de identidad)* requiring certain information.

Apellido _____	
(Surname)	
Nombre _____	
(First name)	
Fecha de Nacimiento _____	
(Date of birth)	
Nacionalidad _____	
(Nationality)	
Lugar de Nacimiento _____	
(Place of birth)	
Dirección _____	
(Address)	
No. de Pasaporte _____	
(Passport number)	
Exp. en _____	
(Issued at)	
Firma del Viajero _____	
(Signature)	

I'd like a single (double) room for tonight.	**Quisiera una habitación con una sola cama (con dos camas) para esta noche.** *kee-SYEHR-ah OO-nah ah-bee-tah-SYOHN kohn OO-nah SOH-lah KAH-mah (kohn dohs KAH-mahs) pah-rah EHS-tah NOH-chay*
How much is the room ____?	**¿Cuánto cuesta el cuarto ____?** *KWAHN-toh KWEHS-tah ehl KWAHR-toh*
▪ with a balcony	**con balcón** *kohn bahl-KOHN*
▪ facing the ocean	**con vista al mar** *kohn bees-tah ahl mahr*

facing the street	**que dé a la calle** *kay day ah lah KAH-yeh*
facing the courtyard	**que dé al patio** *kay day ahl PAH-tee-oh*
in the back	**al fondo** *ahl FOHN-doh*

Does it have ___?	**¿Tiene ___?** *tee-YEH-neh*
air-conditioning	**aire acondicionado** *AH-ee-ray ah-kohn-dee-syohn-AH-doh*
television	**televisión** *teh-lay-bee-SYOHN*
a hair dryer	**un secador de pelo** *oon seh-kah-DOHR day PEH-loh*
a mini-bar	**un minibar** *oon mee-nee-BAHR*
Is there ___ at the hotel?	**¿Hay ___ en el hotel?** *AH-ee ehn ehl oh-TEL*
a fitness center	**un gimnasio** *oon heem-NAH-see-yoh*
a restaurant	**un restaurante** *oon rest-ow-RAHN-teh*
a swimming pool	**una piscina** *oo-nah pee-SEE-nah*

■ a gift shop — **una tienda de regalos** *oo-nah TYEHN-dah day reh-GAH-lohs*

■ valet parking — **personal de estacionamiento** *pehr-sohn-AHL day es-tah-syohn-ah-MYEHN-toh*

■ a laundry — **una lavandería** *oo-nah lah-bahn-dehr-EE-ah*

■ dry cleaning service — **servicio de limpiado en seco** *sehr-BEE-syoh day leem-PYAH-doh en SEH-koh*

I (don't) have a reservation. — **(No) tengo reserva.** *(noh) ten-goh reh-SEHR-bah*

Could you call another hotel to see if they have something? — **¿Podría llamar a otro hotel para ver si tienen algo?** *poh-DREE-ah yah-MAHR ah OH-troh O-TEL pah-rah behr see tee-YEN-ehn AHL-goh*

May I see the room? — **¿Podría ver la habitación?** *poh-DREE-ah behr lah ah-bee-tah-SYOHN*

I (don't) like it. — **(No) me gusta.** *(noh) may GOOS-tah*

Do you have something ____? — **¿Hay algo ____?** *AH-ee ahl-goh*

■ better — **mejor** *may-HOHR*

■ larger — **más grande** *mahs GRAHN-day*

■ smaller — **más pequeño** *mahs peh-KAYN-yo*

■ cheaper — **más barato** *mahs bah-RAH-toh*

■ quieter — **donde no se oigan ruidos** *DOHN-day noh say OY-gahn RWEE-dohs*

What floor is it on? — **¿En qué piso está?** *ehn kay PEE-soh ehs-TAH*

Where is the elevator? — **¿Dónde está el ascensor?** *DOHN-day ehs-TAH ehl ah-sen-SOHR*

Is everything included?	**¿Está todo incluído?** *eh-STAH toh-doh een-kloo-EE-doh*
How much is the room with ____?	**¿Cuánto cobra usted por la habitación ____?** *KWAHN-toh KOH-brah oos-TEHD pohr lah ah-bee-tah-SYOHN*
▓ the American plan (2 meals a day)	**con media pensión** *kohn MEH-dee-yah pen-SYOHN*
▓ bed and breakfast	**con desayuno** *kohn dehs-ah-YOO-noh*
▓ no meals	**sin la comida** *seen lah koh-MEE-dah*
The room is very nice. I'll take it.	**La habitación es muy bonita. Me quedo con ella.** *lah ah-bee-tah-SYOHN ehs mwee boh-NEE-tah may KAY-doh kohn EH-ya*
We'll be staying ____.	**Nos quedamos ____.** *nohs kay-DAH-mohs*
▓ one night	**una noche** *oo-nah NOH-chay*
▓ a few nights	**unas noches** *oo-nahs NOH-chays*
▓ one week	**una semana** *oo-nah seh-MAH-nah*
How much do you charge for children?	**¿Cuánto cobra por los niños?** *kwahn-toh KOH-brah pohr lohs NEEN-yohs*
Could you put another bed in the room?	**¿Podría poner otra cama en la habitación?** *poh-DREE-ah poh-NEHR oh-trah KAH-mah ehn lah ah-bee-tah-SYOHN*
Is there a charge? How much?	**¿Hay que pagar más? ¿Cuánto?** *AH-ee kay pah-GAHR mahs? KWAHN-toh*
Do you have a crib for the baby?	**¿Tiene una cuna para el nene (la nena)?** *TYEHN-eh oo-nah COO-nah pah-rah el NEH-neh (lah NEH-nah)*

Do you know someone who baby-sits? (a sitter)	**¿Conoce a alguien que pueda cuidar a los niños? (un síter)** *coh-NOH-say AHL-ghee-ehn kay PWEH-day kwee-DAHR ah lohs NEE-nyohs (oon SEE-tehr)*
Is there Internet service in the room (hotel)?	**¿Hay servicio de internet en la habitación (el hotel)?** *AH-ee sehr-VEE-see-oh deh een-tehr-NEHT enh lah ah-bee-tah-SYOHN (ehl oh-TEL)*
Does the room have T.V.?	**¿Hay televisión en la habitación?** *AH-ee tel-eh-bee-SYOHN en lah ah-bee-tah-SYOHN*
Do you receive satellite programs (cable, CNN, programs in English)?	**¿Recibe programas de satélite (cable, CNN, en inglés)?** *reh-SEE-beh pro-GRAH-mahs deh sah-TEL-ee-tay (KAH-blay seh ehn-eh ehn-eh ehn een-GLEHS)*
Are there porno programs?	**¿Hay espectáculos pornográficos?** *AH-ee es-pec-TAH-koo-lohs por-no-GRAHF-ee-kohs*
On what channels? At what time?	**¿En qué canales? ¿A qué hora?** *En kay kah-NAH-lehs Ah kay OR-ah*
Can they be blocked?	**¿Hay bloqueo de canales?** *AH-ee bloh-KAY-oh deh kah-NAH-lehs*
Is there a sports (cartoon, news, movie) channel?	**¿Hay un canal de deportes (dibujos animados, noticias, películas)?** *AH-ee oon kah-NAHL deh deh-POR-tehs (dee-BOO-hohs ah-nee-MAH-dos no-TEE-see-yahs pel-EE-koo-lahs)*
Is there automatic checkout?	**¿Hay horario de salida automático?** *AH-ee or-AH-ree-oh day sah-LEE-dah ow-toh-MAH-tee-coh*

OTHER ACCOMMODATIONS

I'm looking for ____.	**Busco ____.** *BOOS-koh*
▓ a boardinghouse	**una pensión (una casa de huéspedes)** *oo-nah pen-SYOHN (oo-nah kah-sah day WES-pehd-ays)*
▓ a private house	**una casa particular** *oo-na kah-sah pahr-teek-oo-LAHR*
I want to rent an apartment.	**Quiero alquilar un apartamento.** *kee-YEHR-oh ahl-kee-LAHR oon ah-pahr-tah-MEHN-toh*
I need a living room, bedroom, and kitchen	**Necesito una sala, un dormitorio, y una cocina.** *neh-seh-SEE-toh oon-nah SAH-lah oon dohr-mee-TOHR-ee-oh ee oo-nah koh-SEE-nah*
Do you have a furnished room?	**¿Tiene un cuarto amueblado?** *tee-YEN-ay oon KWAHR-toh ah-mway-BLAH-doh*
How much is the rent?	**¿Cuánto es el alquiler?** *KWAHN-toh ehs ehl ahl-kee-LEHR*
I'll be staying here for ____.	**Me quedaré aquí ____.** *may kay-dahr-AY ah-KEY*
▓ two weeks	**dos semanas** *dohs seh-MAH-nahs*
▓ one month	**un mes** *oon mehs*
▓ the whole summer	**todo el verano** *toh-doh ehl behr-AH-noh*
I want a place that's ____.	**Quiero un sitio ____.** *kee-yehr-oh oon SEE-tee-yo*
▓ centrally located	**en el centro de la ciudad** *ehn ehl SEHN-troh day lah syoo-DAHD*
▓ near public transportation	**cerca del transporte público** *SEHR-kah del trahns-POHR-tay POOB-lee-koh*

in a quiet, safe neighborhood	**en un barrio tranquilo y seguro** *en oon BAH-ree-oh trahn-KEE-loh ee seh-GOOR-oh*
Is there a youth hostel around here?	**¿Hay un albergue juvenil por aquí?** *AH-ee oon ahl-BEHR-gay hoo-ben-EEL pohr ah-KEE*

TRAVELERS WITH SPECIAL NEEDS

The following organizations provide advice and referrals to travelers with disabilities:

Moss Rehab Hospital—(215) 456-9600

American Foundation for the Blind—(800) 232-5463

Society for the Advancement of Travel for the Handicapped (SATH)—(212) 447-7284

Mobility International—(541) 343-1284

Information Center for Individuals with Disabilities—(800) 462-5015

Do you have facilities for the disabled?	**¿Tienen facilidades para los incapacitados?** *tee-EH-nen fah-see-lee-DAH-dehs PAH-rah lohs een-kah-pah-see-TAH-dohs*
Is there a reduced rate?	**¿Hay un precio rebajado?** *AH-ee oon PRAY-see-oh ray-bah-HAH-doh*
Do you have a toilet equipped for the handicapped?	**¿Tienen baños equipados para gente incapacitada?** *tee-YEN-en BAHN-yohs eh-kee-PAH-dos par-rah HEN-teh een-kah-pah-see-TAH-dah*
Can you provide a wheelchair?	**¿Podría facilitar una silla de ruedas?** *po-DREE-ah fah-see-lee-TAHR oo-nah SEE-yah day RWAY-dahs*

Is there room in the elevator for a wheelchair?	**¿Tiene espacio el ascensor para una silla de ruedas?** *tee-YEN-eh es-PAH-see-oh el ah-sen-SOHR pah-rah oo-nah SEE-yah day RWAY-dahs*
I cannot climb stairs/walk by myself.	**No puedo subir las escaleras/caminar por mí mismo.** *noh PWAY-doh soo-BEER lahs es-cah-LEHR-ahs/kah-mee-NAHR por mee MEES-moh*
I need a ground floor room.	**Necesito una habitación en la planta baja.** *Neh-seh-SEE-toh OO-nah ah-bee-tah-SYOHN ehn lah PLAHN-tah BAH-hah*
Is there a doctor in the hotel?	**¿Hay un médico en el hotel?** *AH-ee oon MED-ee-ko en ehl oh-TEL*
How can we get a doctor in an emergency?	**¿Cómo podemos conseguir un médico en caso de emergencia?** *KOH-moh poh-day-mohs kohn-say-GEER oon MED-ee-koh en KAH-soh day ehm-ehr-HEN-syah*
Do you allow seeing-eye dogs?	**¿Se permiten perros de guía?** *say pehr-MEE-ten PEH-rohs day GHEE-ah*
I have asthma/heart problems.	**Padezco de asma/de problemas del corazón.** *pah-DES-coh deh AHS-mah/dey pro-BLAY-mahs dehl cohr-ah-SOHN*
My father (mother) is elderly (blind, deaf).	**Mi padre (madre) es un anciano (una anciana) (ciego(a), sordo(a)).** *mee PAH-dray (MAH-dray) es oon ahn-SYAH-no (ahn-SYAH-nah) (see-AY-goh(ah) SOHR-doh(ah)*
Are there access ramps for wheelchairs?	**¿Hay rampas de acceso para sillas de ruedas?** *AH-ee RAHM-pahs day ahk-SES-oh pah-rah SEE-yahs day RWAY-das*

In case of emergency, are there agencies (overnight drugstores, emergency rooms) we can contact?	**En caso de emergencia, ¿hay agencias (farmacias de guardia, salas de emergencia) que podemos notificar?** *en KAH-soh day em-her-HEN-syah, AH-ee ah-HEN-syahs (far-MAH-syahs day GWAR-dee-yah, SAH-lahs day em-her-HEN-syah) kay poh-DAY-mohs noh-tee-fee-KAHR*

ORDERING BREAKFAST

Larger hotels will offer breakfast. The Spanish breakfast is a simple one—**café con leche** (hot coffee mixed half and half with steaming milk), with a sweet roll or **churro** (fried pastry). Mexican breakfasts tend to be a little more elaborate, usually **café con leche** and perhaps a tortilla topped with fried eggs, tomatoes and spices or toasted **bollitos** (small boat-shaped yeast rolls). At hotels that cater to American and British tourists, you will also be able to order an English breakfast (juice, eggs, bacon, and toast). Larger hotels will have a dining room where you can eat breakfast, but the usual procedure is to have breakfast sent up to your room or to go out to a café or chocolatería (the hot chocolate in Spain is marvelous) or, in Mexico, to a street vendor who fries up your breakfast at her curbside stand.

I'll eat breakfast downstairs.	**Voy a desayunar abajo.** *boy ah dehs-ah-yoo-NAHR ah-BAH-ho*
We'll have breakfast in the room.	**Queremos desayunar en nuestra habitación.** *keh-RAY-mohs dehs-ah-yoo-NAHR ehn NWEHS-trah ah-bee-tah-SYOHN*

We'd like ____.	**Quisiéramos ____.** *kee-SYEHR-ah-mohs*
Please send up ____.	**Haga el favor de mandarnos.** *AH-gah ehl fah-BOHR day mahn-DAHR-nohs*
one (two) coffee(s)	**una taza (dos tazas) de café** *oo-nah TAH-sah (dohs TAH-sahs) day kah-FAY*
butter	**mantequilla** *mahn-teh-KEE-yah*
cold cuts	**fiambres** *fee-AHM-brehs*
cereal	**cereal** *sehr-eh-AHL*
grapefruit	**toronja (pomelo)** *tohr-OHN-ha (poh-MEH-loh)*
white bread	**pan blanco** *pahn BLAHN-koh*
black bread	**pan moreno (pan negro)** *pahn morh-EH-noh (pan NEH-groh)*
rye bread	**pan de centeno** *pahn day sehn-TEH-noh*
margarine	**margarina** *mahr-gahr-EE-nah*
tea	**una taza de té** *oo-nah TAH-sah day teh*
hot chocolate	**una taza de chocolate** *oo-nah TAH-sah day cho-koh-LAH-tay*
a sweet roll	**un pan dulce** *oon pahn DOOL-say*
fruit (juice)	**un jugo (de fruta)** *oon HOO-goh day FROO-tah*
bacon and eggs	**huevos con tocino** *WEH-bohs kohn toh-SEE-noh*
scrambled (fried, boiled) eggs	**huevos revueltos (fritos, pasados por agua)** *WEH-bohs ray-BWEHL-tohs (FREE-tohs pah-SAH-dohs pohr AH-gwah)*
toast	**pan tostado** *pahn tohs-TAH-doh*
jam (marmalade)	**mermelada** *mehr-may-LAH-dah*

Please don't make it too spicy.	**No lo haga muy picante.**	*noh loh AH-gah mwee pee-KAHN-tay*

NOTE: See the food section (pages 120–159) for more phrases dealing with ordering meals.

HOTEL SERVICES

Where is ____?	**¿Dónde está ____?**	*dohn-day ehs-TAH*
the dining room	**el comedor**	*ehl koh-meh-DOHR*
the bathroom	**el baño**	*ehl BAHN-yo*
the elevator (lift)	**el ascensor**	*ehl ah-sen-SOHR*
the phone	**el teléfono**	*ehl tel-EF-oh-no*
What is my room number?	**¿Cuál es el número de mi cuarto?**	*kwahl ehs ehl NOO-mehr-oh day mee KWAR-toh*
May I please have my key?	**Mi llave, por favor.**	*mee YAH-bay pohr fah-BOHR*
I've lost my key.	**He perdido mi llave.**	*eh pehr-DEE-doh mee YAH-bay*
I need ____.	**Necesito ____.**	*neh-seh-SEE-toh*
a bellhop	**un botones**	*oon boh-TOH-nays*
housekeeping (maid)	**una camarera**	*oo-nah kah-mah-REHR-ah*
Please send ____ to my room.	**Haga el favor de mandar ____ a mi habitación.**	*AH-gah ehl fah-BOHR day mahn-DAHR ah mee ah-bee-tah-SYOHN*
a towel	**una toalla**	*oo-nah toh-AH-yah*
a bar of soap	**una pastilla de jabón**	*oo-nah pahs-TEE-yah day hah-BOHN*

▨ some hangers	**unas perchas**	*oo-nahs PEHR-chahs*
▨ a pillow	**una almohada**	*oo-nah ahl-moh-AH-dah*
▨ a blanket	**una manta**	*oo-nah MAHN-tah*
▨ some ice cubes	**cubitos de hielo**	*koo-BEE-tohs day YEH-loh*
▨ some ice water	**agua helada**	*ah-guah eh-LAH-dah*
▨ a bottle of mineral water	**una botella de agua mineral**	*oo-nah boh-TEH yah day AH-guah mee-nehr-AHL*
▨ toilet paper	**papel higiénico**	*pah-PEHL ee-HYEHN-ee-koh*
▨ an electric adapter	**un adaptador eléctrico**	*oon ah-dahp-tah-DOHR eh-LEK-tree-koh*

AT THE DOOR

Who is it?	**¿Quién es?**	*kee-EHN ehs*
Just a minute.	**Un momento.**	*oon moh-MEN-toh*
Come in.	**Adelante.**	*ah-del-AHN-tay*
Put it on the table.	**Póngalo en la mesa.**	*POHN-gah-loh ehn lah MAY-sah*
Please wake me tomorrow at ____.	**¿Puede despertarme mañana a ____?**	*PWEH-day dehs-pehr-TAHR-may mahn-YAH-nah ah*

COMPLAINTS

There is no ____.	**No hay ____.**	*noh AH-ee*
▨ running water	**agua corriente**	*AH-gwah kohr-YEN-tay*
▨ hot water	**agua caliente**	*AH-gwah kahl-YEN-tay*
▨ electricity	**electricidad**	*eh-lek-tree-see-DAHD*

The ____ doesn't work.	**No funciona ____.** *noh foon-SYOHN-ah*
air-conditioning	**el aire acondicionado** *ehl AH-ee-ray ah-kohn-dees-yohn-AH-doh*
fan	**el ventilador** *ehl ben-tee-lah-DOHR*
faucet	**el grifo** *ehl GREE-foh*
lamp	**la lámpara** *lah LAHM-pah-rah*
light	**la luz** *lah loos*
radio	**la radio** *lah RAH-dee-oh*
electric socket	**el enchufe** *ehl ehn-CHOO-fay*
light switch	**el interruptor** *ehl een-tehr-oop-TOHR*
television	**el televisor** *ehl tel-eh-bee-SOHR*
Can you fix it ____?	**¿Puede arreglarlo ____?** *PWEH-day ah-ray-GLAHR-loh*
now	**ahora** *ah-OH-rah*
as soon as possible	**lo más pronto posible** *loh mahs PROHN-toh poh-SEE-blay*

AT THE DESK

Are there any ____ for me?	**¿Hay ____ para mí?** *AH-ee pah-rah MEE*
letters	**cartas** *KAHR-tahs*
messages	**recados** *ray-KAH-dohs*
packages	**paquetes** *pah-KEH-tays*
postcards	**postales** *pohs-TAH-lays*

Did anyone call for me?	**¿Preguntó alguien por mí?** *preh-goon-TOH AHL-ghee-ehn pohr MEE*
I'd like to leave this in your safe.	**Quisiera dejar esto en su caja fuerte.** *kee-SYEHR-ah day-HAHR EHS-toh ehn soo KAH-ha FWEHR-tay*

| Will you make this call for me? | **¿Podría usted hacerme esta llamada?** *poh-DREE-ah oos-TEHD ah-SEHR-may EHS-tah yah-MAH-dah* |

CHECKING OUT

I'd like the bill, please.	**Quisiera la cuenta, por favor.** *kee-SYEHR-ah lah KWEHN-tah pohr fah-BOHR*
I'll be checking out today (tomorrow).	**Pienso marcharme hoy (mañana).** *PYEHN-soh mahr-CHAR-may oy (mahn-YA-nah)*
Please send someone up for our baggage.	**Haga el favor de mandar a alguien para recoger nuestro equipaje.** *AH-gah ehl fah-BOHR day mahn-DAHR ah AHL-ghy-ehn pah-rah ray-koh-HEHR NWEHS-troh AY-kee-PAH-hay*

GETTING AROUND TOWN

In most cities, you will find that getting around town to sightsee is an easy affair. You'll get more of the flavor of a city if you use public transportation, but oftentimes a taxi will be the quicker way to go somewhere, and usually they are not too expensive. For information on train or plane travel, see pages 76–81.

THE BUS

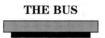

Public transportation in most large cities is cheap, efficient, and frequent. In Spain, bus stops are clearly marked by number, and each number's stops are clearly delineated. Be sure to signal when you want the bus to stop, as the driver doesn't stop automatically at every stop on the route. Free bus maps often are available at the hotels (if not, ask the concierge about getting one). Most bus routes run from 6 A.M. to midnight, though some have 24-hour service. There are no free transfers.

There are two types of buses—the standard red bus and the yellow microbus. Both operate between 6 A.M. and midnight, and charge €1 for each one-way ride in the city, though the *bono* or Metrobus ticket giving 10 rides costs €7.

Night buses (known locally as *buhos*, meaning owls) operate from Plaza de Cibeles to many suburbs between midnight and 6 A.M. and the tickets cost the same as during the day.

Bus information offices are located in Plaza de Cibeles and Puerta del Sol, where you can pick up route maps and schedules.

For full bus information see *www.emtmadrid.es*

In Mexico City, an unusually large urban area, there are bus routes that crisscross the entire town. Bus routes are at times confusing, so it is best to obtain specific instructions from your hotel concierge. Buses are more expensive than the subway (underground), but since both are so cheap in comparison to other cities' systems, the difference is negligible.

Where is the bus stop (terminal)?	**¿Dónde esta la parada (la terminal) de autobús?** *DOHN-day ehs-TAH lah pah-RAH-dah (lah tehr-mee-NAHL) day AH-oo-toh-BOOS*
Which bus do I take to get to ____?	**¿Qué autobús hay que tomar para ir a ____?** *kay AH-oo-toh-BOOS AH-ee kay toh-MAHR PAH-rah eer ah*
Do I need exact change?	**¿Necesito tener cambio exacto?** *neh-seh-SEE-toh ten-EHR KAHM-bee-oh ehk-SAHK-toh*
In which direction do I have to go?	**¿Qué rumbo tengo que tomar?** *kay ROOM-boh TEN-goh kay toh-MAHR*
How often do the buses run?	**¿Con qué frecuencia salen los autobuses?** *kohn kay freh-KWEHN-see-ah SAH-lehn lohs AH-oo-toh-BOOS-ehs*
Do you go to ____?	**¿Va usted a ____?** *bah oos-TEHD ah*
Is it far from here?	**¿Está lejos de aquí?** *eh-STAH LAY-hos day ah-KEE*

How many stops are there?	**¿Cuántas paradas hay?** *KWAHN-tahs pah-RAH-dahs AH-ee*
Do I have to change?	**¿Tengo que cambiar?** *TEN-goh kay kahm-bee-AHR*
How much is the fare?	**¿Cuánto es el billete?** *KWAHN-toh ehs ehl bee-YEH-tay*
Where do I have to get off?	**¿Dónde tengo que bajarme?** *DOHN-day ten-goh kay bah-HAHR-may*
Please tell me where to get off.	**Dígame, por favor, dónde debo bajarme.** *DEE-gah-may pohr fa-BOHR DOHN-day deh-boh bah-HAHR-may*

THE SUBWAY (UNDERGROUND)

The subways (metros) in Madrid and Barcelona are clean, cheap, safe, and comfortable. And graffiti-free. There are nine lines in Madrid with interchange points.

The subway (metro) in Mexico City is a very busy one and often too crowded for most tourists, although the system itself is clean and efficient. Best to avoid it during peak hours. There are also subways in several Latin American cities; such as the Santiago and Buenos Aires Metro, which are modern and well run.

Is there a subway (underground) in this city?

¿Hay un metro en esta ciudad?
AH-ee oon MEHT-roh ehn EHS-tah syoo-DAHD

Where is the closest subway (underground) station?

¿Dónde está la estación más cercana? *DOHN-day eh-STAH lah ehs-tah-SYOHN mahs sehr-KAH-nah*

How much is the fare?

¿Cuánto es la tarifa? *KWAHN-toh ehs lah tah-REE-fah*

Where can I buy a token (a ticket)?

¿Dónde puedo comprar una ficha (un billete)? *DOHN-day PWEH-doh kohm-PRAHR oo-nah FEE-chah (oon bee-YEH-teh)*

Which is the line that goes to _____?

¿Cuál es la línea que va a _____? *kwahl ehs lah LEEN-eh-ah kay bah ah*

Does this train go to _____?

¿Va este tren a _____? *bah ehs-teh trehn ah*

Do you have a map showing the stops?

¿Tiene un mapa que indique las paradas? *TYEH-nay oon MAH-pah kay een-DEE-kay lahs pahr-AH-dahs*

How many more stops?

¿Cuántas paradas más? *KWAHN-tahs pah-RAH-dahs mahs*

What's the next station?

¿Cuál es la próxima estación? *kwahl ehs lah PROHK-see-mah ehs-tah-SYOHN*

Where should I get off?

¿Dónde debo bajarme? *DOHN-day deh-boh bah-HAHR-may*

Do I have to change?

¿Tengo que hacer trasbordo? *ten-goh kay ah-SEHR trahs-BOHRD-oh*

Please tell me when we get there.

Haga el favor de avisarme cuando lleguemos. *AH-gah ehl fah-BOHR day ah-bee-SAHR-may kwahn-doh yeh-GAY-mohs*

TAXIS

In Spain, taxis are plentiful, metered, and, generally speaking, cheap. Official taxis are white with a diagonal red stripe. A green light on the roof shows when they are free. The standard base taxi fare is €2.05, with a charge of €0.98 for every further kilometer.

Few are the countries where you can take a taxi and be certain that the driver is absolutely honest. If you plan to take a taxi from the airport, be sure to check with the information desk at the airport and ask for the distance to the city as well as the average price of a taxi ride. For intercity travel, watch the taximeter like a hawk and be careful with the unfamiliar bills and coins when you pay.

The custom of tipping changes from country to country (in some places no tipping is customary), so it is best to inquire with the hotel concierge.

Is there a taxi stand near here?	**¿Hay una parada de taxis por aquí?** *AH-ee oo-nah pah-RAH-dah day TAHK-sees pohr ah-KEE*
Please get me a taxi.	**¿Puede usted conseguirme un taxi, por favor?** *PWEH-day oos-TEHD kohn-say-GHEER-may oon TAHK-see pohr fah-BOHR*
Where can I get a taxi?	**¿Dónde puedo tomar un taxi?** *DOHN-day PWEH-doh toh-MAHR oon TAHK-see*
Taxi! Are you free (available)?	**¡Taxi! ¿Está libre?** *TAHK-see ehs-TAH LEE-bray*
Take me (I want to go) _____.	**Lléveme (Quiero ir) _____.** *YEHV-eh-may (kee-EHR-oh eer)*
■ to the airport	**al aeropuerto** *ahl ah-ehr-oh-PWEHR-toh*

■ to this address	**a esta dirección** *ah ehs-tah dee-rehk-SYOHN*
■ to the ____ hotel	**al hotel ____** *ahl o-TEL*
■ to the station	**a la estación** *ah lah ehs-tah-SYOHN*
■ to ____ street	**a la calle ____** *ah lah KAH-yeh*
Do you know where it is?	**¿Sabe dónde está?** *sah-bay DOHN-day ehs-TAH*
How much is it to ____?	**¿Cuánto cuesta hasta ____?** *KWAHN-toh KWEHS-tah AHS-tah*
Faster! I'm in a hurry.	**¡Más rápido, tengo prisa!** *mahs RAH-pee-doh ten-goh PREE-sah*
Please drive slower.	**Por favor, conduzca más despacio.** *pohr fah-BOHR kohn-DOOS-kah mahs dehs-PAH-see-oh*
Stop here ____.	**Pare aquí ____.** *PAH-ray ah-KEE*
■ at the corner	**en la esquina** *ehn lah ehs-KEE-nah*
■ at the next block	**en la otra calle** *ehn lah OH-trah KAH-yeh*

Wait for me. I'll be right back.	**Espéreme. Vuelvo pronto.** *ehs-PEHR-eh-may BWEHL-boh PROHN-toh*
I think you are going the wrong way.	**Creo que me está llevando por una dirección equivocada.** *KRAY-oh kay may ehs-TAH yeh-BAHN-doh pohr oo-nah dee-rek-SYOHN eh-kee-boh-KAH-dah*
How much do I owe you?	**¿Cuánto le debo?** *KWAHN-toh lay DEHB-oh*
This is for you.	**Esto es para usted.** *ehs-toh ehs PAH-rah oos-TEHD*

SIGHTSEEING AND TOURS

You'll want to visit a variety of sights—cathedrals, plazas, shopping areas, parks, and museums—and we give you here some phrases to help you locate the English-language tours, when available.

Where is the Tourist Information Office?	**¿Dónde está la oficina de turismo?** *DOHN-day ehs-TAH lah of-fee-SEEN-ah day toor-EES-moh*
I need an English-speaking guide.	**Necesito un guía de habla inglesa.** *neh-seh-SEE-toh oon GHEE-ah day AH-blah een-GLAY-sah*
How much does he/she charge ____?	**¿Cuánto cobra ____?** *KWAHN-toh KOH-brah*
■ per hour	**por hora** *pohr OHR-ah*
■ per day	**por día** *pohr DEE-ah*
There are two (four, six) of us.	**Somos dos (cuatro, seis).** *soh-mohs dohs (KWAHT-roh sayss)*

Where can I buy a guidebook (map)?	**¿Dónde puedo comprar una guía (un mapa)?** *DOHN-day PWEH-doh kohm-PRAHR oo-nah GHEE-ah (oon MAH-pah)*
What are the main attractions?	**¿Cuáles son los puntos principales de interés?** *KWAHL-ehs sohn lohs poon-tohs preen-see-PAHL-ays day een-tehr-AYS*
What are the things of interest here?	**¿Qué cosas interesantes hay aquí?** *kay KOH-sahs een-tehr-ehs-AHN-tays AH-ee ah-KEE*
Are there trips through the city?	**¿Hay excursiones por la ciudad?** *AH-ee ehs-koor-SYOHN-ehs pohr lah see-oo-DAHD*

BOOKING A TOUR

When does the tour begin?	**¿Cuando empieza la excursión?** *KWAHN-doh ehm-PYEH-sah lah ehs-koor-SOYHN*
How long is the tour?	**¿Cuánto tiempo dura?** *KWAHN-toh TYEHM-poh DOOR-ah*
Where do they leave from?	**¿De dónde salen?** *day DOHN-day SAHL-ehn*
We want to see ____.	**Queremos ver ____.** *kehr-EHM-ohs behr*
■ the botanical garden	**el jardín botánico** *ehl har-DEEN boh-TAHN-ee-koh*
■ the bullring	**la plaza de toros** *lah plah-sah day TOHR-ohs*
■ the business center	**el centro comercial** *ehl SEN-troh koh-mehr-SYAHL*
■ the castle	**el castillo** *ehl kahs-TEE-yoh*
■ the cathedral	**la catedral** *lah kah-tay-DRAHL*
■ the church	**la iglesia** *lah eeg-LEHS-ee-ah*

■ the concert hall	**la sala de conciertos** *lah SAH-lah day kohn-see-EHR-tohs*
■ the downtown area	**el centro de la ciudad** *ehl SEN-troh day lah see-oo-DAHD*
■ the fountains	**las fuentes** *lahs FWEHN-tays*
■ the library	**la biblioteca** *lah beeb-lee-oh-TAY-kah*
■ the main park	**el parque central** *ehl pahr-kay sen-TRAHL*
■ the main square	**la plaza mayor** *lah plah-sah my-YOR*
■ the market	**el mercado** *ehl mehr-KAH-doh*
■ the mosque	**la mezquita** *lah mehs-KEE-tah*
■ the museum (of fine arts)	**el museo (de bellas artes)** *ehl moo-SAY-oh (day bel-yahs AHR-tays)*
■ a nightclub	**un club nocturno** *oon kloob nohk-TOOR-noh*
■ the old part of town	**la ciudad vieja** *lah see-oo-DAHD BYEH-ha*
■ the opera	**la ópera** *lah OH-pehr-ah*
■ the palace	**el palacio** *ehl pah-LAH-see-oh*
■ the stadium	**el estadio** *ehl ehs-TAHD-ee-oh*
■ the synagogue	**la sinagoga** *lah seen-ah-GOH-gah*
■ the university	**la universidad** *lah oon-ee-behr-see-DAHD*
■ the zoo	**el parque zoológico** *ehl PAHR-kay soh-oh-LOH-hee-koh*

ADMISSIONS

Is it all right to go in now?	**¿Se puede entrar ahora?** *say PWEH-day ehn-TRAHR ah-OHR-ah*
Is it open (closed)?	**¿Está abierto (cerrado)?** *ehs-TAH ah-bee-YEHR-toh (sehr-AH-doh)*

At what time does it open (close)?	**¿A qué hora se abre (cierra)?** *ah kay OHR-ah say AH-bray (see-YEHR-ah)*
What's the admission price?	**¿Cuánto es la entrada?** *KWAHN-toh ehs lah ehn-TRAH-dah*
How much do children pay?	**¿Cuánto pagan los niños?** *KWAHN-toh pah-GAHN lohs NEEN-yohs*
Can they go in free? Until what age?	**¿Pueden entrar gratis? ¿Hasta qué edad?** *PWEH-dehn ehn-TRAHR GRAH-tees ah-stah kay eh-DAHD*
Is it all right to take pictures?	**¿Se puede sacar fotos?** *say PWEH-deh sah-KAHR FOH-tohs*
How much extra does it cost to take pictures?	**¿Hay que pagar para poder sacar fotos?** *AH-ee kay pah-GAHR pah-rah poh-DEHR sah-KAHR FOH-tohs*
I do (not) use a flash.	**(No) uso flash.** *(noh) oo-soh flahsh*

Prohibido Tomar Fotografías	(no picture-taking allowed)

A SIGHTSEEING ITINERARY—SPAIN

Spain is one of the great tourist destinations in the world today, and deservedly so. Many visitors from northern Europe view the country primarily as a place where they can escape the rigors of the cold by relaxing on the beaches of the Costa del Sol while soaking up the hot sun and swimming in the warm, clear-blue waters of the southern Mediterranean.

Spain does offer this, but also much more. Spain is a land of startling contrasts, offering the traveler large modern cities with urban amenities: department stores, museums, theaters, restaurants, high-fashion boutiques, and nightlife.

In addition, the country is full of charming tiny villages with ancient churches, palaces, and looming castles that recall other eras.

Here are some of the highlights:

MADRID

The capital and largest city (3.7 million inhabitants), Madrid offers a vast variety of things to see and do.

■ *The Prado Museum* Houses one of the most magnificent art collections in the world, particularly strong in Spanish, Flemish, and Italian art.

■ *La Puerta del Sol* Considered the center of the city. It is a major transportation hub.

■ *La Plaza Mayor* A beautiful seventeenth-century square lined with shops and a couple of outdoor cafés. One of the entrances to the plaza is the Arco de Cuchilleros, which leads into Old Madrid, one of the most intriguing tourist areas of the city. Crowds throng the narrow streets with their many bars or *tascas* to sample *tapas* (snacks), drink wine, and listen to music.

■ *Retiro Park* A former palace grounds, this popular park near the Prado has tree-shaded paths, fountains, rose gardens, an enormous artificial lake for boating, two nightclubs, and over a dozen outdoor cafés.

■ *Calle Serrano* Madrid's best shopping street—blocks and blocks of chic shops and small restaurants.

■ *Museum of Lázaro Galdiano* A superb art collection displayed in the home of the collector, a writer and scholar.

■ *Museum of Decorative Arts*   Five floors of an old mansion filled with ceramics, tiles, silver, crystal.

■ *Botanical Gardens (El Jardín Botánico)*   Has a huge number of species of trees and plants from throughout the world.

■ *La Calle de Alcalá* and *La Gran Vía (Avenida de San José)*   Wide boulevards which are two of Madrid's main thoroughfares.

■ *El Palacio Real* (Royal Palace)   Used nowadays for important state functions. You can visit the luxurious throne room and see the collections of tapestries, porcelain, crystal, clocks, and fine art. The Royal Armory and Carriage Museum are also well worth a visit.

■ *El Rastro* (flea market)   Located on Ribera de Curtidores Street, this fascinating open-air market is a place where on Sunday morning one can buy anything from antiques, junk, old clothes, toys and trinkets to furniture and art work. The rest of the week you can visit antique shops in the area. Bargaining is expected here.

■ *Teatro de la Zarzuela*   Located behind the Spanish Parliament building (Las Cortes), this theater offers operas, ballets, and authentic Spanish zarzuelas (light operas).

■ *Museum of the Americas*   Has a collection of dolls, toys, masks, and other Indian items brought back from pre-Columbian America.

■ *Archeological Museum*   Features a reconstruction of the thirty-thousand-year-old prehistoric Altamira cave, paintings of Altamira, more than 2,000 archeological objects, and the rare statues called *Dama de Elche* and *Dama de Baza*.

■ *Casa de Campo*   The largest park in Madrid, with a zoo, a wooded area, a lake, and an amusement park which can be reached by cable car from Paseo del Pintor Rosales. The car passes over the Manzarlares River and affords a spectacular view of the city.

■ *Museo del Pueblo Español*   This unusual museum contains dress and household items from the different regions of Spain.

■ *Plaza de España* A spacious plaza with two skyscrapers. (El Edificio España—the tallest building in Spain—and the Torre de Madrid.) Note the small park with statues of Miguel de Cervantes, Don Quixote, and Sancho Panza.

■ *Temple of Debod* An Egyptian temple of the fourth century, transported from Aswan to rescue it from the flooded dam area.

■ *Centro de Arte Reina Sofía* Madrid's museum of modern art. Filled with the works of Dalí, Gris, Miró and Picasso, including the famous *Guérnica*.

■ *Thyssen-Bornemisza Museum* Madrid's newest art museum. It contains an extensive collection of works of the great masters including El Greco, Velázquez, Rembrandt, Goya, Manet, Monet, Dalí, Tintoretto, Caravaggio, and many others.

PLACES NEAR MADRID

■ *El Escorial* An enormous monastery, mausoleum, and palace constructed by King Felipe II.

■ *El Valle de los Caídos* (Valley of the Fallen) General Francisco Franco's tomb and monument dedicated to the memory of those who fell in the Spanish Civil War.

EASY DAY TRIPS FROM MADRID

■ *Segovia* Known for its first-century Roman aqueduct and its fairytalelike *Alcázar* on a hilltop overlooking the medieval town.

■ *Avila* A medieval city of churches, with the oldest, best-preserved city walls in Spain, possibly in all of Europe.

■ *Aranjuez* With its eighteenth-century Royal Palace and fabulous gardens.

■ *Toledo* A jewel of a city, still medieval in feeling, famous for its many El Greco paintings and for its mix of Moorish, Jewish, and Christian legacies. Don't miss the cathedral; El Greco's house and museum; Church of Santo Tomé with one of El Greco's masterpieces; and the Museum of Santa Cruz.

BARCELONA

Spain's principal seaport and industrial heart has a population of approximately two million people. Among its many attractions are:

- *The Ramblas* A wide, tree-lined boulevard that goes from the center of the city to the waterfront, where one can stroll past flower stalls, caged birds, newspaper and magazine stands, and book shops.

- *The Pueblo Español* Located on top of Montjuic (reachable by cable railway), is a model village, featuring buildings from the various regions of the country. In the village the visitors can see pottery making, glass blowing, and other arts and crafts.

- *The Plaza de Cataluña* A beautiful and spacious plaza located in the center of the city.

- *The Catedral* A Gothic monument located in the *barrio gótico* (the Gothic quarter), the old part of the city; this is the site of sardana dancing on weekends.

- *The Picasso Museum* Contains one of the world's largest collections of the famous modern Spanish artist, installed in a thirteenth-century palace.

- *Museum of Catalonian Art* A rare collection of eleventh- and twelfth-century Romanesque art, as well as works by El Greco, Tintoretto, and others.

■ *Museum of Federico Marés* An unusual and rare sculpture collection located in a palace near the Cathedral.

■ *The Church of the Sagrada Familia* (Holy Family) The spectacular unfinished work of the architect Antonio Gaudí.

■ *Parque Güell* The whimsical park designed by Gaudí.

SEVILLA

One of the most picturesque and romantic of all Spanish cities. In Sevilla, you can see:

■ *Museo Provincial de Bellas Artes* A collection of Spanish paintings, lodged in an old convent.

■ *La Catedral* The largest cathedral in all of Spain.

■ *La Giralda* The bell tower of the cathedral which was constructed originally as the minaret of a mosque. City views from the top are extraordinary.

■ *El Alcázar* A Christian and Moorish fortress with beautiful gardens.

■ *Barrio Santa Cruz* Onetime Jewish quarter of narrow, winding streets.

■ *La Calle de las Sierpes* (Snake Street) The principal business thoroughfare of the city, lined with sidewalk cafés, restaurants, and shops.

■ *Itálica* Remains of a Roman city just outside Sevilla.

GRANADA

When in Granada, don't miss the following:

■ *The Alhambra* Exquisitely beautiful Moorish palace, one of the major sights of Spain.

■ *El Albaicín* The gypsy quarter whose inhabitants dwell in furnished caves with electricity.

■ *El Generalife* Summer palace of the Moorish kings, famous for its beautiful gardens.

CORDOBA

One can visit the imposing Mezquita (the Great Mosque), with its beautiful marble columns and intricate mosaics and its superimposed Christian church inside. Also visit *Judería*, the old Jewish quarter of Cordova with a tiny synagogue, the only one left in town.

MARBELLA AND TORREMOLINOS

Fashionable resort areas on the Costa del Sol, with its Mediterranean beaches, luxurious hotels, and fine restaurants.

IN THE NEW WORLD: MEXICO

During the last decade Mexico has been plagued by wars between the drug cartels, and the violence has significantly reduced tourist traffic. This is a shame, because Mexico is a beautiful country that has a lot to offer at prices that are unequalled elsewhere.

Be prudent and try to stay as part of a group in order to minimize difficulties and avoid possible problems.

In Mexico City and its vicinity, be sure not to miss these:

- *Chapultepec Castle and Park*   A magnificent park containing a zoo, museums, lakes, and concert halls. One of the largest parks in the world.

- *The Palacio de Bellas Artes* (Palace of Fine Arts)   Contains the famous murals of Rivera, Siqueiros, and Orozco.

- *La Ciudad Universitaria* (University City)   An architectural and artistic wonder, the site of the past Olympic Games. The library building is completely covered with brilliantly colored mosaic tiles depicting the history of Mexico.

- *La Torre Latinoamericana*   The tallest building in Mexico. The magnificent view from the top lets you see the entire city.

- *El Zócalo*   The main square of the city. Here one finds the National Palace with its magnificent Diego Rivera murals.
- *The Plaza de Garibaldi*   The center for the mariachis, strolling musicians who rent themselves out for tips.
- *Floating Gardens of Xochimilco*   The Venice of the Americas. Boats can be rented to travel through the flower-lined canals.
- *Teotihuacán*   Famous Toltec ruins, which include the Pyramids of the Sun and of the Moon and the Temple of Quetzalcoatl.

BEACHES AND RESORTS

With over 6,000 miles of beaches along Mexico's coastlines, on four different seas, no other country in the world offers vacationers such a variety of beaches and resorts.

All of Mexico's beaches are open to the public, with free access for all. You may sunbathe, swim, and use the watersport facilities of any beach you'd like, including those of the beachfront hotels.

Though peak time for vacationers generally runs from October through May, Mexico's coastal sun is in season all year round.

THE CARIBBEAN AND GULF COAST

Many regard the Caribbean beaches of the Yucatan's east coast as the most beautiful in all of Mexico. The fine, powdery white sand, derived from limestone, is unique to the area.

The Caribbean coast is ideal beach vacation territory. The weather is warm and temperate, and waters are excellent for snorkeling, diving, boating, and waterskiing.

■ *Cancún* Cancun is actually an island—a thin stretch of sand connected to the mainland by two bridges. The beaches are exquisite everywhere. There are boating, fishing, and diving charters available from its pier. The numerous beachfront hotels also offer watersports. In addition, there are many tennis courts, a Robert Trent Jones golf course, and a host of restaurants, shops, and discos.

No Cancun vacation is complete without a visit to the Mayan ruins that dot the Yucatan—including two of the most famous sites in Mexico: Chichén-Itzá and Uxmal.

South of Cancun, along the coast to Tulum, is the village of Xel-Ha. Xel-Ha boasts a beautiful swimming beach, and the best snorkeling on the mainland.

■ *Cozumel* First to be discovered by the international jet set, Cozumel has still managed to be virtually unspoiled. Most of the land is still in its natural state.

Cozumel's main attraction is Palancar Reef—the world's second largest coral reef—which surrounds the island. Scuba enthusiasts rate Cozumel as one of the world's best diving areas, and there are many diving shops and schools on the island. Chancnab Lagoon, on the southern end of the island, is the best spot for snorkeling. The island's beaches are lovely, but take care to swim at beaches that are free of sharp underwater coral.

Cozumel offers a full range of resort hotels, restaurants, and night spots. It is 12 miles off the Yucatan coast and easily accessible by air or hydrofoil from Cancun.

■ *Veracruz* The coastal city is Mexico's principal port. The water is calm, warm, and shallow for a long wade into the Gulf, and you can rent beach chairs and umbrellas from seaside vendors.

Mocambo Beach, five miles south of the city, is the most beautiful in Veracruz. Villa del Mar and Hornos Costa are nearer town and are both good swimming beaches. Fishing charters can be arranged at any number of piers in the city.

While in Veracruz, visit the Plaza de Armas, the old center of town surrounded by a high wall, and the fort of San Juan de Ulloa, both dating back to the sixteenth century.

You may want to plan your trip to coincide with the Carnival of Veracruz in March—Mexico's own Mardi Gras celebration.

THE PACIFIC COAST

This is a stretch of coastline with 2,000 miles of spectacular and varied beaches.

■ *Mazatlán* The original lure of Mazatlan was deep-sea sport fishing, with marlin and sailfish the prize catches. But beach lovers now predominate, and there are plenty of beaches to accommodate all of them.

North Beach, which extends some six miles beyond the city's oceanfront boulevard, is the largest. Farther north is the Playa Sabalo, probably the most beautiful of all Mazatlan beaches. Las Gaviotas is the beach nearest town, whereas the island beach of Venados offers exceptionally calm and clear waters.

For a break from sunbathing, Mazatlan offers plenty of golf, tennis, sailing, and surfing. Horseback riding is popular at Playa Sabalo.

■ *Puerto Vallarta* This once sleepy fishing village is now one of the most popular resorts in the world. Puerto Vallarta boasts luxurious hotels, colorful restaurants and nightclubs, and nearly every popular resort pastime imaginable.

The town's main beach, the Playa del Sol, is the center of action. There are also several quieter alternatives nearby, such as Chino Beach, Playa de Oro, and Playa Las Estacas. From any of these beaches you can enjoy the spectacular Puerto Vallarta scenery.

■ *Manzanillo* The docks of this port city provide Mexico with a vital link to Asia, while its thick jungle, tropical fruit plantations, and deserted beaches make a lush setting for vacationers. Land and water sports, golf, tennis, hunting and deep-sea fishing are available at the beachfront hotels.

The Playa Azul is a curving, seven-mile-long beach that extends from Manzanillo city. Most of the beachfront hotels in the area are built along this spectacular beach, and the smaller but equally lovely Playa Las Brisas.

Nearby is the famous Mexican resort, Las Hadas. The brainchild of a South American millionaire, Las Hadas is most notable for its unusual architecture, with domed roofs that give the development a North African feeling.

■ *Ixtapa/Zihuantanejo* Luxurious Ixtapa was carved from the jungle by the Mexican government for development into a tourist resort. It is sparkling clean and elegant, featuring first-class hotels, a Robert Trent Jones 18-hole golf course, inviting shops, gourmet restaurants, and an exciting nightlife. Visitors enjoy waterskiing, diving, snorkeling, windsurfing, and sailing. Excursions to nearby beaches such as Playa Quieta, Playa Linda, and Ixtapa Island are also available.

Just a few miles north of Ixtapa is the picturesque fishing village of Zihuantanejo. Here is a place where you can still see fisherman mending nets on the beaches. The village has several small but very attractive hotels, including the world-class Villa del Sol, and the popular Las Gatas Beach, where you can swim with the sea turtles and enjoy a lunch of freshly caught fish.

■ *Acapulco* Known as the "Pearl of the Pacific" and the "Riviera de las Americas," Acapulco is Mexico's most famous beach resort. There are over 20 beaches on and around Acapulco Bay: Playa Condesa, Caleta-Caletilla (the "morning beach"), Hornos (the "afternoon beach"), are some of the most popular. La Roqueta, located on an uninhabited island across Boca Chica Channel, offers the calmest waters for swimming.

A must-see for anyone visiting Acapulco are the world-renowned cliff divers. From the top of La Quebrada they dive 136 feet to the shallow inlet below, timing their dives so that they enter the water at the exact time the wave pours into the inlet.

BAJA

Jutting a thousand miles out of San Diego, the Baja Peninsula offers vacationers a coastline of rugged desert mountain ranges and sunny beaches.

■ *Los Cabos*   Twenty miles of secluded beaches with an average of 360 sunny days per year, located at the very tip of the Baja peninsula.

At the western end of the Los Cabos area is the town of Cabo San Lucas, whose surrounding waters may have the finest marlin fishing in the world.

■ *La Paz*   The capital of the Baja, La Paz is an easygoing resort town famous for its pearl divers. The fishing is excellent, along with every other watersport, from jet skiing to scuba.

ELSEWHERE IN MEXICO

■ *Taxco*   Famous for the silver shops and silver factories that line its streets, Taxco is known as the most picturesque city in Mexico.

■ *Guadalajara*   Mexico's second largest city has over 3 million inhabitants and is the home of the largest U.S. retirement community. Close to it is Lake Chapala, the country's largest lake.

■ *Cuernavaca*   Called the "city of eternal springtime," Cuernavaca is famous for its flowers and its year-round pleasant climate. Here too there is a large community of Americans who have retirement homes.

OTHER LATIN AMERICAN COUNTRIES

PUERTO RICO

A tourist delight, with no passport or visa requirement for US citizens and just 3½ hours from New York, Puerto Rico is for those who want the benefits of civilization and English language in an exotic setting. Beaches, excellent hotels and casinos await the non-adventurous traveler who likes his margarita cold, the water warm, and the sand hot. When you are ready to leave the beach chair, see Old San Juan, the original city built by the Spaniards in the sixteenth century. One main attraction is El Morro, a fortress constructed to ward off attacks by English pirates. Also in Puerto Rico, visit El Yunque, a luxurious rain forest with exotic vegetation, waterfalls, and tropical birds.

DOMINICAN REPUBLIC

Santo Domingo is the capital and largest city (half a million inhabitants) of this pleasant and hot Caribbean island. The old cathedral is visited by tourists who come to see the tomb of Christopher Columbus. When here, also see:

■ *The Alcázar* The restored palace of Diego Columbus. It is richly furnished with paintings, furniture, and tapestries of the sixteenth century.

■ *Los Tres Ojos* (the three eyes)   Located on the outskirts of the capital, this is a marvelous natural phenomenon of three underground springs.

■ *Puerto Plata*   Noted for its white, sandy beaches on the northern coast of the island.

ARGENTINA

Arguably the most cosmopolitan city of South America, Buenos Aires offers varied and interesting architecture dating from the eighteenth century (the Cathedral, the Town Hall or Cabildo, and the churches of La Merced, Santa Catalina, and San Francisco) as well as nineteenth century buildings in the French Second Empire style. When one becomes tired of visiting the city's numerous museums, it is always a pleasure to sit in Palermo Park or to listen to opera at the Teatro Colón. Other important places include:

■ *Iguazú Falls*   Higher than Niagara and twice as wide, this is the world's mightiest waterfall where three countries, Argentina, Brazil, and Paraguay, meet.

■ *San Carlos de Bariloche*   A Latin Alpine town, 2,600 feet above sea level. Latin America's favorite mountain and lake resort (fishing, hunting, skiing).

■ *Ushuaia*   Southernmost town in the world. Fishing, rock climbing, cross-country skiing, snowmobiling, scuba diving, whale and dolphin watching.

BOLIVIA

■ *La Paz*   The highest capital city in the world (two and one half miles above sea level). Many open-air Indian markets, wonderful eighteenth-century architecture.

■ *Lake Titicaca*   With a surface of 3,500 square miles, it is the highest navigable lake in the world (13,000 feet above sea level). There are hydrofoil excursions to the Inca islands of the Sun and Moon.

■ *Potosí*   Once the largest city in the Americas. Renowned for its silver mines, which engendered the still-used expression, "It's worth a Potosí!" Visit La Casa de la

Moneda, a museum taking up an entire city block, containing colonial paintings and equipment used for producing silver ingots and coins.

CHILE

Plagued by earthquakes, Chile's main attractions are natural. The north includes the awesome Atacama Desert, rich in mineral deposits that color the land in various hues. The south is green, cool, hospitable, and offers magnificent lakes and mountains.

- *Santiago* Chile's capital and largest city with over four million people. Not far from Santiago are the slopes of Portillo, scene of the World Alpine Ski Championships.

- *Valparaíso* Chile's second largest city and chief seaport. Built on hills, with its cable cars and cobblestone streets, it resembles San Francisco. A paradise for seafood lovers.

- *Viña del Mar* Not far from Valparaiso, the "Pearl of the Pacific" has famous beaches, while the casino and racetrack draw thousands of tourists daily.

- *Torres del Paine National Park* An area of almost a half million acres in Chile's cold deep south, it shelters lakes, lagoons, waterfalls and glaciers, sculpted by the wind and snow during 12 million years. View wildlife such as guanacos, condors, Darwin rheas, ducks, geese, and more than 100 other different species of birds.

COLOMBIA

- *Bogotá* Capital city of over six million people. Plenty of museums and art galleries, numerous churches from the Colonial period. Don't miss the Baroque Cathedral, as well as the famous Salt Cathedral, located in the depths of the salt mine 31 miles north of the city. El Museo del Oro (The Gold Museum) is Bogota's most famous museum. It contains over 8,000 gold pieces (rings, bracelets, crowns, and so on) and a fabulous collection of emeralds, including the four largest emeralds in the world. (Colombia is the world's number one source of emeralds.)

■ *Cartagena* One hour by air from Bogota lies the Caribbean city of Cartagena. Surrounded by fortress-like walls (originally built to protect the inhabitants from pirates), the city looks as it did centuries ago. Its beautiful beaches make it a prime tourist destination.

ECUADOR

■ *Quito* Although it is located on the equator, Quito's climate is a humid springtime the year round because of its altitude. Its historic Old Town spans an area of over 800 acres. From Quito, you can take one-day trips to Indian settlements in the Amazon jungle.

■ *Galapagos Islands* Located 600 miles off the coast, the islands are the site where Darwin made scientific observations leading to his theory of evolution. The Galapagos are home for a mixture of creatures found nowhere else on earth. A visit always becomes an unforgettable experience. However, for ecological reasons many restrictions apply. Make sure to contact the Equadorian consulate before you travel.

PERU

■ *Lima* Founded by the conquistadores as a Spanish colonial city, Lima is now a huge metropolis of over seven million people, with stylish and sophisticated suburbs as well as old neighborhoods that still reflect its colonial past.

■ *Cuzco* The imperial city of the Incas, once the largest and most important city in the New World, is today a city whose present population is almost totally native American, living today much as it did hundreds of years ago.

■ *Machu Picchu* The incredible lost city of the Incas, a beautiful jewel in a beautiful setting, suspended in the mist like a ghost from the past.

URUGUAY

■ *Montevideo* A pleasant city with great views of Montevideo Bay. Don't miss the Rambla, a riverfront drive, which runs along the waterfront for 12 miles, linking all the beaches along the city's coast.

■ *Punta del Este* World famous international beach resort, the site of movies, festivals, and international conferences.

VENEZUELA

■ *Caracas* A modern metropolis of over three million people. At 3,000 feet above sea level, Caracas has one of the world's best climates. Take a cable car ride down to the Caribbean beaches below. Macuto Beach is one of the most popular ones.

■ *Colonia Tovar* Forty miles from Caracas is a "Black Forest" village founded by Bavarian immigrants—a mountain resort popular for its German food and culture.

■ *Margarita Island* A Caribbean resort and major tourist destination because of its lovely beaches and picturesque towns. A duty-free port, it has many shops catering to the thousands of visitors who arrive from Caracas by plane or hydrofoil.

COSTA RICA

A small democratic country, rich in natural beauty, offering an incredible variety of landscapes and comfortable climates. It is a country for nature lovers, who will marvel at the diverse and abundant flora and fauna, the abrupt and active volcanoes, and the sunny and exotic beaches of the Pacific Ocean and the Caribbean Sea. You may start with its beautiful capital city, San Jose, visit its popular beaches, and then move on to other unforgettable places.

■ *Lake Coter Region* Visit the Ecoadventure Lodge and the impressive Cloud Forest.

■ *Arenal Lake* Hiking, horseback riding, water skiing, windsurfing, fishing, hot springs of Tabacon, and the Arenal Volcano.

■ *Tortuguero National Park* Costa Rica's rich tropical rain forest where you can see over 800 species of birds (more than all of the U.S. and Canada combined), including brilliantly colored parrots, toucans and macaws, monkeys, iguanas, and many other species.

■ *Monteverde Cloud Forest Reserve*   Mountain trail walking tours.

BELIZE

There are few places on earth that can match the diversity found in Belize. Its lowland rain forests, mangrove swamps, and coral reefs offer an astonishing variety of flora and fauna. A place for physically active tourists.

GUATEMALA

■ *Lake Atitlán*   Its lake shore villages offer scenery and entertainment. Several handicraft markets sell belts, ponchos, blankets, and other sought-after items.

■ *Tikal*   Nestled in the jungle, the capital of the Mayan Empire with its many pyramids, temples and palaces, is one of the major archaeological sites of the Americas.

■ *Chichicastenango*   One of the largest native American open-air markets in the world.

PANAMA

■ *Panama City*   A cosmopolitan urban metropolis of over one half million people located on the Pacific Ocean. Plenty of nightlife with many discos, nightclubs, and plush gambling casinos.

Because of low import duties you can purchase many goods (cameras, laptops, camcorders, watches, jewelry, perfumes, etc.) at bargain prices.

■ *Panama Canal Tour*   Still an awesome feat of engineering, the Canal should be seen because of its visual, technological, and political significance.

■ *San Blas Islands*   An archipelago off Panama's Caribbean coast. Day trips to visit the villages of the San Blas's Native Americans.

PLANNING A TRIP

AIR SERVICES

Within Spain, two domestic airlines—Iberia and Avianco—fly to more than 36 cities. Unfortunately, to reach city A from B, you often have to go via Madrid and transfer. Barajas is ten miles from Madrid, but most airports are located within a few miles of a given city. A special ticket called "Visit Spain" gives unlimited air travel within Spain on Iberia for 45 days (you must fly Iberia to and from Spain; check for current price).

Flights within Mexico are easily arranged, particularly to other major tourist cities, such as Acapulco or the Yucatán. For trips among other Central and South American cities, check the Internet or consult your travel agent.

When is there a flight to ____?	**¿Cuándo hay un vuelo a ____?**	*KWAHN-doh AH-ee oon BWEHL-oh ah*
I would like a ____ ticket.	**Quisiera un billete ____.**	*kee-see-YEHR-ah oon bee-YEH-tay*
■ round trip	**de ida y vuelta**	*day EE-dah ee BWEHL-tah*
■ one way	**de ida**	*day EE-dah*
■ tourist class	**en clase turista**	*ehn KLAH-say toor-EES-tah*
■ first class	**en primera clase**	*ehn pree-MEHR-ah KLAH-say*
I would like a seat ____.	**Quisiera un asiento ____.**	*kee-see-YEHR-ah oon ah-SYEHN-toh*
■ next to the window	**de ventanilla**	*day behn-tah-NEE-yah*
■ on the aisle	**de pasillo**	*day pah-SEE-yoh*

What is the fare?	**¿Cuál es la tarifa?** *kwahl ehs lah tah-REE-fah*
Does that include all taxes?	**¿Incluye ésta todos los impuestos?** *een-KLOO-yeh EHS-tah TOH-dohs lohs eem-PWEHS-tohs*
Can I use the ticket for frequent flyer miles?	**¿Puedo usar el billete para recibir bonos de vuelo (kilometraje)?** *PWAY-doh oo-SAHR ehl bee-YET-eh pah-rah reh-see-BEER BO-nohs day BWEH-loh (kee-loh-meh-TRAH-heh)*
Are meals served?	**¿Se sirven comidas?** *say seer-behn koh-MEE-dahs*
When does the plane leave (arrive)?	**¿A qué hora sale (llega) el avión?** *ah kay oh-ra SAH-lay (YEH-gah) ehl ah-BYOHN*
When must I be at the airport?	**¿Cuándo debo estar en el aeropuerto?** *KWAHN-doh deh-boh ehs-TAHR en ehl ah-ehr-oh-PWEHR-toh*
What is my flight number?	**¿Cuál es el número del vuelo?** *kwahl ehs ehl NOO-mehr-oh dehl BWEH-loh*
What gate do we leave from?	**¿De qué puerta se sale?** *day kay PWEHR-tah say sah-lay*
I want to confirm (cancel) my reservation for flight ____.	**Quiero confirmar (cancelar) mi reservación para el vuelo ____.** *kee-YEHR-oh kohn-feer-MAHR (kahn-say-LAHR) mee reh-sehr-bah-SYOHN pah-rah ehl BWEH-loh*
I'd like to check my bags.	**Quisiera facturar mis maletas.** *kee-SYEHR-ah fahk-too-RAHR mees mah-LEH-tahs*
Must I pay for the second suitcase?	**¿Debo pagar por la segunda maleta?** *DEH-boh pah-GAHR pohr lah seh-GOON-dah mah-LEH-tah*

I have only carry-on baggage.	**Tengo solo equipaje de mano.** *TEN-goh so-loh ay-kee-PAH-hay day MAH-noh*

TRAIN SERVICE

In Spain, RENFE offers a kilometric ticket that can save you up to 20% of your fare; round-trip fares on some routes save 25%. A *Tarjeta Dorada* (Gold Card) can save up to 50% on rail trips—available only to those 65 years or older.

The Eurailpass is good in Spain, as well as 15 other countries. Tickets for unlimited train travel are available for 15 or 21 days or 1, 2, or 3 months. Note that the tickets should be purchased in your country of origin before you travel to Spain.

The following is a brief description of the varieties of Spanish trains.

AVE	The AVE (Alta Velocidad Española) is a high speed train that connects Madrid with Seville, Valencia, Malaga, and Barcelona at speeds of over 186 mph. The AVE has three classes of seating: first (*club*), business (*preferente*), and tourist (*turista*). This train, obviously, is more expensive than regular trains, but it is very punctual, has a buffet/bar and/or a restaurant with waiter service, air conditioning, reclining seats, video screens, and it will get you from Madrid to Barcelona in 2 hours and 35 minutes. A new rail passage across the Pyrenees mountains provides a cross-border, high-speed rail link connecting Paris, Barcelona, and Madrid. Many of these AVE lines originate at Madrid's Atocha Station.
Talgo	A luxury diesel express with reclining seats and air conditioning. It operates between Madrid and major cities—Barcelona, Bilbao, Cadiz, Malaga, Seville, Valencia, Zaragoza.

Electrotren	A luxury train, but it is slower than Talgo, makes more stops, and covers more of the country. It is cheaper than Talgo.
TER	A luxury diesel express train, slower than Talgo and makes more stops.
TAF	A second-class diesel train.
Expreso	A long-distance night train, with only a few major stops.
Rápido	A fast train (slower than the Expreso).
Omnibuses or ferrobuses	Local trains.

Railways in Latin America vary enormously in quality and mileage. Some countries are building up their infrastructure and modernizing their trains whereas others have virtually abandoned this form of mass transit in favor of intercity bus lines. Consult the Internet about the railroads of the country you plan to visit and make sure to read the comments of those who have used them!

A first (second) class ticket to _____ please.	**Un billete de primera (segunda) clase a _____ por favor.** *oon bee-YEH-teh day pree-MEHR-ah (say-GOON-dah) KLAH-say ah pohr fah-BOHR*
Give me a half price ticket	**Deme un medio billete** *DEH-meh oon MEH-dee-oh bee-YEH-teh*
Give me a round trip ticket	**Deme un billete de ida y vuelta** *DEH-meh oon bee-YEH-teh day EE-dah ee BWEHL-tah*
Give me a one way ticket	**Deme un billete de ida** *DEH-meh oon bee-YEH-teh day EE-dah*

When does the train arrive (leave)?	**¿Cuándo llega (sale) el tren?** *kwahn-doh YEH-gah (SAH-lay) ehl trehn*
From (at) what platform does it leave (arrive)?	**¿De (A) qué andén sale (llega)?** *day (ah) kay ahn-DEHN SAH-lay (YEH-gah)*
Does this train stop at ____?	**¿Para este tren en ____?** *PAH-rah ehs-tay trehn ehn*
Is the train late?	**¿Tiene retraso el tren?** *tee-YEH-nay ray-TRAH-soh ehl trehn*
How long does it stop?	**¿Cuánto tiempo para?** *kwahn-toh tee-EHM-poh PAH-rah*
Is there time to get a bite?	**¿Hay tiempo para tomar un bocado?** *ahy tee-EHM-poh PAH-rah toh-MAHR oon boh-KAH-doh*
Do we have to stand in line?	**¿Tenemos que hacer cola?** *tehn-EH-mohs kay ah-SEHR KOH-lah*
Are there discounts for students (seniors, groups, the handicapped)?	**¿Hay descuentos para estudiantes (ancianos, grupos, los minusválidos)?** *AH-ee des-KWEHN-tohs pah-rah ehs-too-dee-YAHN-tehs (ahn-see-YAH-nohs GROO-pohs lohs mee-noos-BAH-lee-dohs)*
How can I obtain a refund?	**¿Cómo puedo obtener un reembolso?** *KOH-moh PWAY-doh ob-ten-EHR oon ray-ehm-BOHL-so*
Are there special (weekly, monthly, group, tourist) passes?	**¿Hay pases especiales (para una semana, para un mes, para turistas)?** *AH-ee PAH-sehs ehs-peh-see-YAHL-ehs (pah-rah oo-nah seh-MAH-nah oon mehs pah-rah toor-EES-tahs)*

ON THE TRAIN

Is there a dining car (sleeping car)?	**¿Hay coche-comedor (cochecama)?** *ahy KOH-chay koh-may-DOHR (KOH-chay KAH-mah)*
Is it ____?	**¿Es ____?** *ehs*
■ a through train	**un tren directo** *oon trehn dee-REHK-toh*
■ a local	**un tren local (ómnibus, ordinario)** *oon trehn loh-KAHL (OHM-nee-boos ohr-dee-NAH-ree-oh)*
■ an express	**un expreso (rápido)** *oon eks-PREHS-oh (RAH-pee-doh)*
Do I have to change trains?	**¿Tengo que trasbordar?** *TEHN-goh kay trahs-bohr-DAHR*
Is this seat taken?	**¿Está ocupado este asiento?** *ehs-TAH oh-koo-PAH-doh EHS-tay ah-SYEHN-toh*
Where are we now?	**¿Dónde estamos ahora?** *DOHN-day ehs-TAH-mohs ah-OHR-ah*
Will we arrive on time (late)?	**¿Llegaremos a tiempo (tarde)?** *yeh-gahr-EH-mohs ah tee-EHM-poh (tahr-day)*
Can I check my bag through to ____?	**¿Puedo facturar mi maleta hasta ____?** *PWEH-doh fahk-toor-AHR mee mah-LEH-tah AHS-tah*
Excuse me, but you are in my seat.	**Perdón, creo que está ocupando mi asiento.** *pehr-DOHN KRAY-oh key ehs-TAH oh-koo-PAHN-doh mee ah-SYEHN-toh*

SHIPBOARD TRAVEL

If you want to visit any surrounding islands, then you'll want to arrange to take a boat there.

Where is the dock?	**¿Dónde está el muelle?** *DOHN-day ehs-TAH ehl MWEH-yeh*
When does the next boat leave for ___?	**¿Cuándo sale el próximo barco para ___?** *KWAHN-doh SAH-lay ehl PROHKS-ee-moh BAHR-koh PAH-rah*
How long does the crossing take?	**¿Cuánto dura la travesía?** *KWAHN-toh DOO-rah lah trah-beh-SEE-ah*
Do we stop at any other ports?	**¿Hacemos escala en algunos puertos?** *ah-SAY-mohs ehs-KAH-lah ehn ahl-GOO-nohs PWEHR-tohs*
How long will we remain in the port?	**¿Cuánto tiempo permaneceremos en el puerto?** *KWAHN-toh tee-EHM-poh pehr-mah-neh-sehr-EH-mohs ehn ehl PWEHR-toh*

When do we land?	**¿Cuándo desembarcamos?** *KWAHN-doh dehs-ehm-bahr-KAH-mohs*
At what time do we have to be back on board?	**¿A qué hora debemos volver a bordo?** *ah kay OHR-ah deh-BAY-mohs bohl-BEHR ah BOHR-doh*
I'd like a ____ ticket.	**Quisiera un pasaje ____.** *kee-SYEHR-ah oon pah-SAH-hay*
■ first class	**de primera clase** *day pree-MEHR-ah KLAH-say*
■ tourist class	**de clase turista** *day KLAH-say toor-EES-tah*
■ cabin	**para un camarote** *PAH-rah oon kah-mah-ROH-tay*
I don't feel well.	**No me siento bien.** *noh may SYEHN-toh byehn*
Can you give me something for sea sickness?	**¿Puede usted darme algo contra el mareo?** *PWEH-day oos-TEHD DAHR-may AHL-goh KOHN-trah ehl mah-RAY-oh*

Travel Tips Luggage is sometimes lost or arrives long after you do. To avoid problems, some people travel light and carry on everything. At the very least, take one complete change of clothing, basic grooming items, and any regular medication aboard with you. Because airlines will not replace valuable jewelry when paying for lost luggage, it should be carried on your person. Safer yet, select one set of basic, simple jewelry that can be worn everywhere—even in the shower—and wear it during your whole trip. Remember, carry-on bags must be small enough to fit in overhead bins or to slide under your seat.

DRIVING A CAR

Driving is an easy way to travel in Spain. Roads are generally good, though there are just a few superhighways (**autopistas**). More common are national and country roads, which are usually two- or three-lane asphalt roads. Roads are well marked with international highway symbols. Mileage is designated in kilometers. A mile is five eighths of a kilometer; see chart on page 90. Gas prices are the same at stations all over the country. In smaller towns, gas stations are few and far between, so it is wise to "gas up" when you can. Note that seat belts are mandatory. If stopped by the police, you will be fined for not wearing a belt.

The western United States and the western Latin American countries (except Colombia) are connected by the Panamerican Highway (**Carretera panamericana**). It is possible to go south from Alaska to Canada to Washington State and all the way to Panama, get your car on a ferry, disembark in Ecuador, and continue south until you reach the southern Chilean city of Puerto Montt. From Santiago, in Chile, you can start a journey to the east, cross into Argentina through the Andes Mountains (**Cordillera de los Andes**) and from Argentina you can reach Uruguay, Paraguay, Brazil, and Bolivia. Quite a trip!

However, geography and finances are factors that make it impossible to draw a general picture. Driving conditions in Latin America, including availability of good hotels and motels, gas stations, and so on change from country to country, so it is best to check with the tourist information office of the country you plan to visit before you start your trip.

CAR RENTALS

In Spain rentals can be arranged before departure through a travel agent or upon arrival at a rental office in the major airports and in or near the railroad station in a larger city or town. You'll find Hertz, Avis, Atesa (Budget), Europcar, and Godfrey Davis, among other car rental agencies. The usual rate is by the day or week, with a charge per kilometer. Requirements: you must be 18 years old or older and hold a valid U.S. or international driver's license. Many rental companies also require you to have held your driver's license for a minimum of one or two years. A credit card is the preferred method of payment.

In Latin America the satisfaction derived from car rental depends on the country. Contact the tourist information offices and check the Internet.

Where can I rent ____?	**¿Dónde puedo alquilar ____?** *dohn-day PWEH-doh ahl-kee-LAHR*
■ a car	**un coche** *oon KOH-chay*
■ a four-wheel-drive vehicle	**un vehículo con tracción en las cuatro ruedas** *oon-beh-EE-koo-loh kohn trahk-SYOHN en lahs KWAH-troh roo-WAY-dahs*
■ a minivan	**un mínivan** *oon MEE-nee-bahn*
I want a ____.	**Quiero ____.** *kee-EH-roh*
■ small car	**un coche pequeño** *oon KOH-chay peh-KAYN-yoh*
■ large car	**un coche grande** *oon KOH-chay GRAHN-day*
■ sports car	**un coche deportivo** *oon KOH-chay day-pohr-TEE-boh*
I prefer automatic transmission (power steering, power windows, power mirrors).	**Prefiero el cambio automático (dirección asistida, ventanillas eléctricas, espejos eléctricos).** *preh-fee-EHR-oh ehl KAHM-bee-oh AH-oo-toh-MAH-tee-koh dee-rehk-SYOHN ah-sees-TEE-dah ben-tah-NEE-yahs eh-LEK-tree-kahs ehs-PEH-hohs eh-LEK-tree-kohs*
How much does it cost ____?	**¿Cuánto cuesta ____?** *KWAHN-toh KWEHS-tah*
■ per day	**por día** *pohr DEE-ah*

◼ per week	**por semana** *pohr seh-MAHN-ah*
◼ per kilometer	**por kilómetro** *pohr kee-LOH-meht-roh*
◼ with unlimited mileage	**con kilometraje ilimitado** *kohn kee-loh-may-TRAH-hay ee-lee-mee-TAH-doh*
How much is the insurance?	**¿Cuánto es el seguro?** *KWAHN-toh ehs ehl seh-GOOR-oh*
Is the gas included?	**¿Está incluída la gasolina?** *ehs-TAH een-kloo-EE-dah lah gahs-oh LEEN-ah*
Do you accept credit cards?	**¿Acepta usted tarjetas de crédito?** *ah-sehp-tah oos-TEHD tahr-HAY-tahs day KREH-dee-toh*
Here's my driver's license.	**Aquí tiene mi licencia de conducir.** *ah-KEE tee-EH-nay mee lee-SEN-see-ah day kohn-doo-SEER*
Do I have to leave a deposit?	**¿Tengo que dejar un depósito?** *ten-goh kay day-hahr oon day-POHS-ee-toh*
I want to rent the car here and leave it in ____.	**Quiero alquilar el coche aquí y dejarlo en ____.** *kee-YEHR-oh ahl-kee-LAHR ehl KOH-chay ah-KEE ee day-HAHR-loh ehn*
What kind of gasoline does it take?	**¿Qué tipo de gasolina necesita?** *kay TEE-poh day gah-so-LEE-nah neh-seh-SEE-tah*

PARKING

In a town or city, park only in designated places, usually marked by a sign with a big "E" or "P" (for parking). If you park in a no-parking zone, you run the very real risk of having your car towed away.

Is this a legal parking place?	**¿Es ésto un lugar para estacionar?** *ehs EHS-toh oon loo-GAHR pah-rah ehs-tah-syohn-AHR*
What is the parking fee?	**¿Cuánto cuesta estacionar aquí?** *KWAHN-toh KWEHS-tah ehs-tah-syohn-AHR ah-KEE*
Where can I find a place to park?	**¿Dónde puedo encontrar un sitio de estacionamiento?** *DOHN-day PWEH-doh ehn-kohn-TRAHR oon SEE-tee-oh day ehs-tah-syohn-ah-mee-YEHN-toh*

ON THE ROAD

In Spain turnpikes are called **autopistas** and are marked as "A" roads on the map. **Autopistas de peaje** are toll roads.

National highways are called **carreteras nacionales** and are marked with a red "N" on the map. Regional highways are reasonably good and are numbered with the prefix "C." Speed limits are:

autopistas	120 km/h (74½ m.p.h.)
double-lane highways	100 km/h (62 m.p.h.)
other roads	90 km/h (56 m.p.h.)
populated areas	50 km/h (31 m.p.h.)

And pay attention to speed limits. They are enforced. Radar control is commonplace, and if you exceed the limit, you may receive a ticket by mail after you have returned home. Driving in a city can be confusing. Many streets are one-way and are very narrow, twisting, and crowded.

Latin American roads cover the full range, from excellent to terrible, often within the same country, so it is not possible to present a coherent picture. Speed limits vary, as does their enforcement.

Excuse me, can you tell me ____?	**Por favor, ¿puede usted decirme ____?** *pohr fah-BOHR pweh-day oos-TEHD day-SEER-may*
Which way is it to ____?	**¿Por dónde se va a ____?** *pohr DOHN-day say bah ah*
I think we're lost.	**Creo que estamos perdidos.** *KRAY-oh kay ehs-TAH-mohs pehr-DEE-dohs*
Is this the way to ____?	**¿Es éste el camino a ____?** *ehs EHS-tay ehl kah-MEE-noh ah*
Is it a good road?	**¿Es buena la carretera?** *ehs BWAY-nah la kahr-ray-TEHR-ah*
Where does this highway go to?	**¿Adónde va esta carretera?** *ah-DOHN-day bah ehs-tah kah-ray-TEHR-ah*
Is this the shortest way?	**¿Es éste el camino más corto?** *ehs EHS-tay ehl kah-MEE-noh mahs KOHR-toh*

Are there any detours?	**¿Hay desviaciones?** *AH-ee des-bee-ah-SYOHN-ays*
Do I go straight?	**¿Sigo derecho?** *see-goh deh-RAY-choh*
Do I turn to the right (to the left)?	**¿Doblo a la derecha (a la izquierda)?** *DOH-bloh ah lah deh-RAY-chah (ah lah ees-kee-YEHR-dah)*
How far away is ____?	**¿A qué distancia está ____?** *ah kay dees-TAHN-see-ah ehs-tah*
Do you have a road map?	**¿Tiene usted un mapa de carreteras?** *tee-yehn-ay oos-TEHD oon MAH-pah day kahr-ray-TEHR-ahs*
Can you show it to me on the map?	**¿Puede indicármelo en el mapa?** *PWEH-day een-dee-KAHR-may-loh ehn ehl MAH-pah*
Can I park here?	**¿Puedo estacionar aquí?** *PWEH-doh ehs-tah-see-oh-NAHR ah-KEE*

AT THE SERVICE STATION

Gasoline (petrol) is sold by the liter, and for the traveler accustomed to gallons, it may seem confusing, especially if you want to calculate your mileage per gallon (kilometer per liter). Here are some tips on making those conversions.

LIQUID MEASURES (Approximate)			
LITERS	GALLONS	LITERS	GALLONS
1	0.26	50	13.0
5	1.3	60	15.6
10	2.6	70	18.2
20	5.2	80	20.8
30	7.8	90	23.4
40	10.4	100	26.0

DISTANCE MEASURES (Approximate)			
KILOMETERS	MILES	KILOMETERS	MILES
1	0.62	30	18.6
5	3.1	35	21.7
10	6.2	40	24.8
15	9.3	45	27.9
20	12.4	50	31.1
25	15.5	100	62.1

Where is there a gas (petrol) station?	**¿Dónde hay una estación de gasolina?** *DOHN-day AH-ee oo-nah ehs-tah-SYOHN day gahs-oh-LEE-nah*
Fill it up with ____.	**Llénelo con ____.** *YAY-nay-loh kohn*
■ diesel	**diesel** *dee-EH-sel*
■ regular (90 octane)	**normal** *nohr-MAHL*
■ super (96 octane)	**super** *SOO-pehr*
■ extra (98 octane)	**extra** *EHS-trah*
Give me ____ liters.	**Déme ____ litros.** *DAY-may LEE-trohs*

TIRE PRESSURE			
LB/SQ. IN.	KG/SQ. CM.	LB/SQ. IN.	KG/SQ. CM.
18	1.3	30	2.1
20	1.4	31	2.2
21	1.5	33	2.3
23	1.6	34	2.4
24	1.7	36	2.5
26	1.8	37	2.6
27	1.9	38	2.7
28	2.0	40	2.8

Please check _____.

¿Quiere inspeccionar ____? *kee-YEHR-ay eens-pehk-syohn-ahr*

■ the battery

la batería *lah bah-tehr-EE-ah*

■ the oil

el aceite *ehl ah-SAY-tay*

■ the spark plugs

las bujías *lahs boo-HEE-ahs*

■ the tires

las llantas, los neumáticos *lahs YAHN-tahs lohs new-MAH-tee-kohs*

■ the tire pressure

la presión de las llantas *lah preh-SYOHN day lahs YAHN-tahs*

■ the antifreeze

el agua del radiador *ehl AH-gwah dehl rah-dee-ah-DOHR*

Change the oil.

Cambie el aceite. *KAHM-bee-ay ehl ah-SAY-tay*

Charge the battery.

Cargue la batería. *KAHR-gay lah bah-tehr-EE-ah*

Change the tire.

Cambie esta llanta. *KAHM-bee-ay ehs-tah YAHN-tah*

Wash the car.

Lave el coche. *LAH-bay ehl KOH-chay*

Guarded railroad crossing

Yield

Stop

Right of way

Dangerous intersection
ahead

Gasoline (petrol) ahead

Parking

No vehicles allowed

Dangerous curve

Pedestrian crossing

Oncoming traffic
has right of way

No bicycles allowed

No parking allowed

No entry

No left turn

No U-turn

No passing

Border crossing

Traffic signal ahead

Speed limit

Traffic circle (roundabout) ahead

Minimum speed limit (kilometers)

All traffic turns left

End of no passing zone

One-way street

Detour

Danger ahead

Entrance to expressway

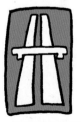

Expressway ends

ACCIDENTS AND REPAIRS

My car has broken down.	**Mi coche se ha averiado.** *mee KOH-chay say ah ah-behr-ee-AH-doh*
I need a mechanic (tow truck).	**Necesito on mecánico (remolcador).** *neh-seh-SEE-toh oon meh-KAHN-ee-koh (ray-mohl-kah-DOHR)*
It overheats.	**Se calienta demasiado.** *say kahl-YEN-tah day-mahs-ee-AH-doh*
It doesn't start.	**No arranca.** *noh ah-RAHN-kah*
I have a flat tire.	**Se me ha pinchado una rueda.** *say may ah peen-CHAH-doh oon-ah RWEH-dah*
The radiator is leaking.	**El radiador tiene un agujero.** *ehl rah-de-ah-dohr tee-YEHN-ay oon ah-goo-HEHR-oh*
The battery is dead.	**Tengo la batería descargada.** *ten-goh lah bah-tehr-EE-ah des-kahr-GAH-dah*
The keys are locked inside the car.	**Las puertas están cerradas con las llaves adentro.** *lahs PWEHR-tahs ehs-TAHN sehr-AH-dahs kohn lahs YAH-bays ah-DEN troh*
Is there a garage (repair shop) near here?	**¿Hay un garage (taller) por aquí?** *AH-ee oon gah-RAH-hay (tah-YEHR) pohr ah-KEE*
Can you _____?	**¿Puede usted _____?** *PWEH-day oos-TEHD*
■ give me a push	**empujarme** *ehm-poo-HAHR-may*
■ help me	**ayudarme** *ah-yoo-DAHR-may*

I don't have any tools.	**No tengo herramientas.** *oh ten-goh ehr-ah-MYEHN-tahs*
Can you lend me ____?	**¿Puede usted prestarme ____?** *PWEH-day oos-TEHD prehs-TAHR-may*
■ a flashlight	**una linterna** *oo-nah leen-TEHR-nah*
■ a hammer	**un martillo** *oon mahr-TEE-yoh*
■ a jack	**un gato** *oon GAH-toh*
■ a monkey wench	**una llave inglesa** *oo-nah YAH-beh een-GLAY-sah*
■ pliers	**alicates** *ah-lee-KAH-tays*
■ a screwdriver	**un destornillador** *oon des-tohrn-EE-yah-DOHR*
I need ____.	**Necesito ____.** *neh-seh-see-toh*
■ a bolt	**un perno** *oon PEHR-noh*
■ a bulb	**una bombilla** *oo-nah bohm-BEE-yah*
■ a filter	**un filtro** *oon FEEL-troh*
■ a nut	**una tuerca** *oo-nah TWEHR-kah*
Can you fix the car?	**¿Puede usted arreglar el coche?** *PWEH-day oos-TEHD ah-ray-GLAHR ehl KOH-chay*
Can you repair it temporarily?	**¿Puede repararlo temporalmente?** *PWEH-day ray-pahr-AHR-loh tem-pohr-AHL-men-tay*
Do you have the part?	**¿Tiene la pieza?** *tee-EHN-ay lah pee-ay-sah*

I think there's something wrong with ____.	**Creo que pasa algo con ____.** *KRAY-oh kay PAH-sah AHL-goh kohn*
■ the directional signal	**el indicador de dirección** *ehl een-dee-kah-DOHR day dee-rek-SYOHN*
■ the electrical system	**el sistema eléctrico** *ehl sees-TAY-mah eh-LEK-tree-koh*
■ the fan	**el ventilador** *ehl ben-tee-lah-DOHR*
■ the fan belt	**la correa de ventilador** *lah koh-ray-ah day ben-tee-lah-DOHR*
■ the fuel pump	**la bomba de gasolina** *lah BOHM-bah day gahs-oh-LEE-nah*
■ the gearshift	**el cambio de velocidad** *ehl KAHM-bee-oh day beh-loh-see-DAHD*
■ the headlight	**el faro delantero** *ehl fah-ROH deh-lahn-TEHR-oh*
■ the horn	**la bocina** *lah boh-SEEN-ah*
■ the ignition	**el encendido** *ehl ehn-sehn-DEE-doh*
■ the radio	**la radio** *lah RAH-dee-oh*
■ the starter	**el arranque** *ehl ah-RAHN-kay*
■ the steering wheel	**el volante** *ehl boh-LAHN-tay*
■ the taillight	**el faro trasero** *ehl fah-ROH trah-SEHR-oh*
■ the transmission	**la transmisión** *lah trahns-mee-SYOHN*
■ the water pump	**la bomba de agua** *lah BOHM-bah day AH-gwah*
■ the windshield (windscreen) wiper	**el limpiaparabrisas** *ehl LEEM-pee-ah-pah-rah-BREE-sahs*

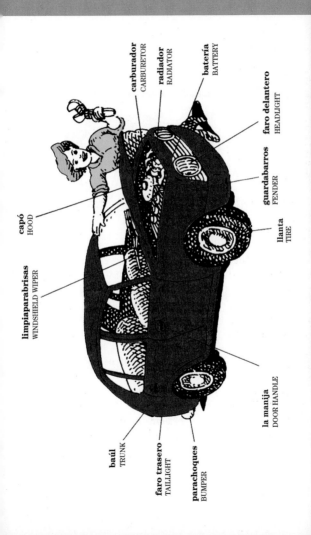

carburador
CARBURETOR

radiador
RADIATOR

batería
BATTERY

faro delantero
HEADLIGHT

guardabarros
FENDER

llanta
TIRE

capó
HOOD

limpiaparabrisas
WINDSHIELD WIPER

la manija
DOOR HANDLE

baúl
TRUNK

faro trasero
TAILLIGHT

parachoques
BUMPER

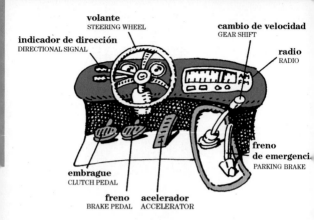

volante
STEERING WHEEL

cambio de velocidad
GEAR SHIFT

indicador de dirección
DIRECTIONAL SIGNAL

radio
RADIO

**freno
de emergencia**
PARKING BRAKE

embrague
CLUTCH PEDAL

freno
BRAKE PEDAL

acelerador
ACCELERATOR

Can you look at (check out) ____?	**¿Quiere mirar (revisar) ____?** *kee-YEHR-ay meer-AHR (reh-bee-SAHR)*

■ the brakes — **los frenos** *lohs FRAY-nohs*

■ the bumper — **el parachoques** *ehl pah-rah-CHOH-kays*

■ the exhaust system — **el escape** *ehl ehs-KAH-pay*

■ the fender — **el guardabarros** *ehl gwahr-dah-BAH-rohs*

■ the gas tank — **el tanque** *ehl TAHN-kay*

■ the hood — **el capó** *ehl kah-POH*

■ the trunk (boot) — **el baúl** *ehl bah-OOL*

What's the matter? — **¿Qué pasa?** *kay PAH-sah*

Would it be possible to fix it today? — **¿Sería posible arreglarlo hoy?** *sehr-EE-ah poh-SEE-blay ah-ray-GLAHR-loh oy*

How long will it take?

¿Cuánto tiempo tardará? *KWAHN-toh tee-EHM-poh tahr-dahr-AH*

Thank you very much. How much do I owe you?

Muchas gracias. ¿Cuánto le debo? *moo-chas GRAH-see-yahs KWAHN-toh lay DEH-boh*

Do you take credit cards?

¿Acepta tarjetas de crédito? *ah-SEHP-tah tahr-HEH-tahs deh KREH-dee-toh*

ENTERTAINMENT AND DIVERSIONS

MOVIES, THEATER, CONCERTS, OPERA, BALLET

To find out what's doing in Madrid, consult the daily newspaper *ABC*, under the heading **"Espectáculos"**; *En Madrid*, a monthly English-Spanish leaflet available at the Madrid Tourist Office; or *Guía del Ocio* (Leisure Guide), a weekly listing of entertainment, hours, and admission fees.

The latest movies are at theaters along the Gran Vía in Madrid. The movies are dubbed into Spanish. Admission is usually 2 euros or less. Ushers should be tipped about 20 cents.

There are 23 theaters in Madrid. **Teatro Zarzuela** is the most fun for tourists who are not well-versed in Spanish. Zarzuela consists of nineteenth-century light operas or operettas, with lots of music, dance, and pretty costumes. Classical Spanish theater can be seen at **Teatro Español** and **María Guerrero Theater**. Theater prices range from 3 to 20 euros. Everything runs late in Spain. Matinees are at 7 or 7:30 P.M., evening performances are at 10:30 P.M.

Symphonic concerts can be heard at the beautiful ninteenth century **Teatro Real**, the Madrid Cultural Center auditorium, **Fundación Juan March**, or Sundays in the Plaza del Maestro Villa in Retiro Park. Pop, rock, and jazz music can be heard in many discos, certain movie theaters, college auditoriums, and at various bars and pubs. Check the above-mentioned listings to determine where and when.

Theater and concert schedules and procedures vary throughout the rest of the Spanish-speaking world, so we advise you to check the Internet or ask your hotel concierge in order to find out what is going on and where to get tickets.

Let's go to the ____.	**Vamos al ____.** *BAH-mohs ahl*
movies (cinema)	**cine** *SEE-nay*
theater	**teatro** *tay-AH-troh*
What are they showing today?	**¿Qué ponen hoy?** *kay POH-nehn oy*
Is it a ____?	**¿Es ____?** *ehs*
mystery	**un misterio** *oon mee-STEHR-ee-oh*
comedy	**una comedia** *oo-nah koh-MEH-dee-ah*
drama	**un drama** *oon DRAH-mah*
musical	**una obra musical** *oo-nah OH-brah moo-see-KAHL*
romance	**una obra romántica** *oo-nah OH-brah roh-MAHN-tee-kah*
war film	**una película de guerra** *oo-nah pehl-EE-koo-lah day GHEHR-ah*
science fiction film	**una película de ciencia ficción** *oo-nah pehl-EE-koo-lah day see-EHN-see-ah feek-SYOHN*
Is it in English?	**¿Es hablada en inglés?** *ehs ah-BLAH-dah ehn een-GLAYSS*
Has it been dubbed?	**¿Ha sido doblada?** *ah SEE-doh doh-BLAH-dah*
Where is the box office?	**¿Dónde está la taquilla?** *DOHN-day ehs-TAH lah tah-KEE-yah*
What time does the (first) show begin?	**¿A qué hora empieza la (primera) función?** *ah kay OHR-ah ehm-PYEH-sah lah (pree-MEHR-ah) foon-SYOHN*

BUYING TICKETS

I need two ____ tickets.	**Necesito dos entradas ____.** *neh-seh-SEE-toh dohs ehn-TRAH-dahs*
■ orchestra	**de platea** *day plah-TAY-ah*
■ balcony	**de galería** *day gahl-ehr-EE-ah*
■ mezzanine	**de anfiteatro** *day ahn-fee-tay-AH-troh*
We would like to attend ____.	**Quisiéramos asistir a ____.** *kee-SYEHR-ah-mohs ah-sees-TEER ah*
■ a ballet	**un ballet** *oon bah-LEH*
■ a concert	**un concierto** *oon kohn-SYEHR-toh*

■ an opera	**una ópera** *oo-nah OH-pehr-ah*
What are they playing (singing)?	**¿Qué están interpretando?** *kay ehs-TAHN een-tehr-pray-TAHN-doh*
Who is the conductor?	**¿Quién es el director?** *kee-YEHN ehs ehl dee-rehk-TOHR*
I prefer ____.	**Prefiero ____.** *preh-fee-YEHR-oh*
■ classical music	**la música clásica** *lah MOO-see-kah KLAH-see-kah*

■ popular music **la música popular** *lah MOO-see-kah poh-poo-LAHR*

■ folk dance **el ballet folklórico** *ehl bah-LEH fohl-KLOHR-ee-koh*

■ ballet **el ballet** *ehl bah-LEH*

Are there any seats for tonight's performance? **¿Hay localidades para la representación de esta noche?** *AH-ee loh-kahl-ee-DAHD-ays pah-rah lah rep-reh-sen-tah-SYOHN day ehs-tah NOH-chay*

Should I get the tickets in advance? **¿Debo sacar las entradas de antemano?** *deh-boh sah-KAHR lahs ehn-TRAH-dahs day ahn-tay-MAH-noh*

Do I have to dress formally? **¿Tengo que ir de etiqueta?** *TEN-goh kay eer day eh-tee-KEH-tah*

How much are the front row seats? **¿Cuánto vaten los asientos delanteros?** *KWAHN-toh bah-lehn lohs ahs-YEHN-tohs day-lahn-TEHR-ohs*

What are the least expensive seats? **¿Cuáles son los asientos más baratos?** *KWAHL-ays sohn lohs ahs-YEHN-tohs mahs bah-RAH-tohs*

May I buy a program? **¿Puedo comprar un programa?** *PWEH-doh kohm-PRAHR oon pro-GRAHM-ah*

What opera (ballet) are they performing? **¿Qué ópera (ballet) ponen?** *kay OH-pehr-ah (bah-LEH) POH-nen*

Who's singing (tenor, soprano, baritone, contralto)? **¿Quién canta (tenor, soprano, barítono, contralto)?** *kee-YEHN KAHN-tah (ten-OHR soh-PRAH-noh bah-REE-toh-noh kohn-TRAHL-toh)*

NIGHTCLUBS, DANCING

Every large Spanish city has **discotecas** and nightclubs and big Las Vegas-type shows at some of the larger, new hotels. There are even a few satirical reviews in cafe settings. Madrid is now as wide-open after dark as any European capital, more so than some. You will find **flamenco** performed in small clubs, such as Café de Chintas, off the Gran Vía.

Hours at discos are approximately 7 P.M. to 3 A.M. Nightclub shows are at 11 P.M. or midnight or 1 A.M. **Tablao flamenco** places are open from 10 P.M. to 3 A.M., with shows at 12 and 1:30 or so. It is customary, but not required, to dine at the nightclub or flamenco place before the show, in which case you would arrive about 10 or 11 P.M., then stay for the midnight show.

Nightlife is similar in all large cities, and the nightclubs of Latin America are no exception. If you want local color, consult with the concierge of your hotel and you may end up enjoying some unique entertainment. Folk music and dances vary widely from the north to the south of the Americas, and you may enjoy the African and indigenous influence on Central American artistic expressions as much as the European impact on Argentinean and Chilean music.

Let's go to a nightclub	**Vamos a un cabaret.** *BAH-mohs ah oon kah-bah-REH*
Is a reservation necessary?	**¿Hace falta una reserva?** *ah-say FAHL-tah oo-nah reh-SEHR-bah*
Is it customary to dine there as well?	**¿Se puede comer allá también?** *say PWEH-day koh-MEHR ah-YAH tahm-BYEHN*
Is there a good discotheque here?	**¿Hay aquí una buena discoteca?** *AH-ee ah-KEE oo-nah BWEH-nah dees-koh-TAY-kah*

Is there dancing at the hotel?	**¿Hay un baile en el hotel?** *AH-ee oon BAH-ee-lay ehn ehl oh-TEL*
We'd like a table near the dance floor.	**Quisiéramos una mesa cerca de la pista.** *kee-SYEHR-ah-mohs oo-nah MAY-sah SEHR-kah day lah PEES-tah*
Is there a minimum (cover charge)?	**¿Hay un mínimo?** *AH-ee oon MEE-nee-moh*
Where is the check-room?	**¿Dónde está el guardarropa?** *DOHN-day eh-STAH ehl gwahr-dah-ROH-pah*
At what time does the floor show go on?	**¿A qué hora empieza el espectáculo?** *ah kay OH-rah ehm-pee-EH-sah ehl ehs-peh-TAH-kool-oh*

SPECTATOR SPORTS

THE BULLFIGHT

The bullfight season in Spain runs from March to October. Sunday is the day, 5 or 7 P.M. the time. In Madrid there are two **plaza de toros**—the larger is Plaza de Toros Monumental de las Ventas, the smaller is Plaza de Toros de Vista Alegre. Ticket prices vary depending on sun (**al sol**) or shade (**a la sombra**) locations. You can purchase tickets through your hotel concierge, at the **plaza de toros,** or at the official city box office at 3 Calle de la Victoria.

If you have not seen a bullfight before, be aware that it is a dangerous mixture of art and sport involving blood and death. Opinions, even among the Spaniards, are divided. Some tend to describe the **corrida** as "vital," "vigorous," and "dramatic," others lean toward "cruel" and "painful," and often refuse to go or take their children to see it.

| **el matador** | kills the bull with his **espada** (sword) |

el banderillero	thrusts three sets of long darts (**banderillas**) into the bull's neck to enfuriate him
el picador	bullfighter mounted on a horse who weakens the bull with his lance (**pica**)
la cuadrilla	a team of helpers for the torero, who confuse and tire the bull with their capes (**capas**)
el monosabio	assistant who does various jobs in the **redondel** (bullring)
Is there a bullfight this afternoon? (every Sunday)?	**¿Hay una corrida de toros esta tarde (todos los domingos)?** *AH-ee oo-nah koh-REE-dah day TOH-rohs ehs-tah TAHR-day (toh-dohs lohs doh-MEEN-gohs)*
Where is the bullring?	**¿Dónde está la Plaza de Toros?** *DOHN-day ehs-TAH lah PLAH-sah day TOHR-ohs*
I'd like a seat in the shade (in the sun).	**Quisiera un sitio a la sombra (al sol).** *kees-YEH-rah oon SEE-tee-oh ah lah SOHM-brah (ahl sohl)*
Bravo!	**¡Olé!** *oh-LAY*

SOCCER

Soccer—called **fútbol**—is the most popular sport in Spain, Latin America, and the world. In season, between September to June, you're sure to find a game somewhere any Sunday at 5 P.M. Madrid has two teams: *Atlético de Madrid* plays in the Vicente Calderón Stadium and *Real Madrid* plays in Santiago Bernabeu Stadium. Tickets are available through your hotel concierge or at the stadium.

I'd like to watch a soccer match.	**Quisiera ver un partido de fútbol.** *kee-SYEHR-ah behr oon pahr-TEE-doh day FOOT-bohl*

Where's the stadium?	**¿Dónde está el estadio?** *DOHN-day ehs-TAH ehl ehs-TAH-dee-oh*
When does the first half begin?	**¿Cuándo empieza el primer tiempo?** *KWAHN-doh ehm-pee-EH-sah ehl pree-MEHR tee-EM-poh*
What teams are going to play?	**¿Qué equipos van a jugar?** *kay eh-KEE-pohs bahn ah hoo-GAHR*
What is the score?	**¿Cuál es la anotación?** *kwahl ehs lah ah-noh-tah-SYOHN*

JAI ALAI

Pelota *(jai alai)* is a very fast Basque game played in a court called a **frontón.** There are two teams of two players each. The players each have a **cesta** (curved basket) to throw and catch the ball with. During the match, spectators may place bets on the teams. Hours are 5:30 P.M. daily, in Spain.

I'd like to see a jai alai match.	**Me gustaría ver un partido de pelota.** *may goos-tahr-EE-ah behr oon par-TEE-doh day pel-OH-tah*
Where can I get tickets?	**¿Dónde puedo conseguir billetes?** *DOHN-day pweh-doh kohn-seh-GEER bee-YEH-tays*
Where is the jai alai court?	**¿Dónde está el frontón?** *DOHN-day ehs-TAH ehl frohn-TOHN*
Who are the players?	**¿Quiénes son los jugadores?** *kee-YEHN-ehs sohn lohs hoo-gah-DOHR-ays*
Where do I place my bet?	**¿Dónde hago la apuesta?** *DOHN-day ah-goh lah ah-PWEH-stah*

HORSE RACING

There is no horse racing in Spain in the summer. In season, it is available at El Hipódromo de la Zarzuela on La Carretera de la Coruña.

Is there a racetrack here?	**¿Hay un hipódromo aquí?** *AH-ee oon ee-POH-droh-moh ah-KEE*
I want to see the races.	**Quiero ver las carreras de caballos.** *kee-EHR-oh behr lahs kahr-EHR-ahs day kah-BAH-yohs*

ACTIVE SPORTS

I like to ____.	**Me gusta ____.** *may GOOS-tah*
▥ play baseball	**jugar béisbol** *hoo-GAHR BAYS-bohl*
▥ play basketball	**jugar básquetbol** *hoo-GAHR BAHS-ket-bohl*
▥ ride a bicycle	**andar en bicicleta** *ahn-DAHR en bee-see-KLEH-tah*
▥ go boating	**navegar** *nah-bay-GAHR*
▥ go canoeing	**remar en canoa** *ray-MAHR en kah-no-ah*
▥ fish	**pescar** *pehs-KAHR*
▥ play football	**jugar fútbol americano** *hoo-GAHR FOOT-bohl ah-mehr-ee-KAH-no*
▥ play golf	**jugar golf** *hoo-GAHR gohlf*
▥ play hockey	**jugar hockey** *hoo-GAHR HOH-kee*
▥ go horseback riding	**andar a caballo** *ahn-DAHR ah kah-BAH-yo*
▥ hunt	**cazar** *kah-SAHR*
▥ ice skate	**patinar sobre hielo** *pah-tee-NAHR soh-breh YEH-loh*
▥ jog	**hacer footing** *ah-SEHR FOO-teen*

■ go mountain climbing	**el alpinismo**	*ehl ahl-pee-NEES-moh*
■ parasail	**volar en parapente**	*bo-LAHR en pahr-ah-PEN-teh*
■ play ping-pong	**jugar pimpón**	*hoo-GAHR peem-POHN*
■ roller skate	**patinar**	*pah-tee-NAHR*
■ go sailing	**navegar a vela**	*nah-beh-GAHR ah BEH-lah*
■ scuba dive	**bucear con escafandra**	*boo-say-AHR kohn es-kah-FAHN-drah*
■ skate	**patinar**	*pah-tee-NAHR*
■ ski	**esquiar**	*es-kee-AHR*
■ play soccer	**jugar fútbol**	*hoo-GAHR FOOT-bohl*
■ go surfing	**ir surfing**	*eer SOOR-feen*
■ swim	**nadar**	*nah-DAHR*
■ play tennis	**jugar tenis**	*hoo-GAHR TEN-ees*
■ do track and field	**hacer atletismo**	*ah-SEHR aht-let-EES-moh*
■ play volleyball	**jugar voleibol**	*hoo-GAHR bol-eh-BOHL*
■ waterski	**el esquí acuático**	*ehl es-KEE ah-KWAH-tee-koh*

PLAYING FIELDS

Shall we go to the ____?	**¿Vamos ____?**	*BAH-mohs*
■ beach	**a la playa**	*ah lah-PLAH-yah*
■ court	**al patio**	*ahl PAH-tee-yoh*
■ field	**a la cancha**	*ah lah KAHN-chah*
■ golf course	**al campo de golf**	*ahl KAHM-poh day gohlf*
■ gymnasium	**al gimnasio**	*ahl heem-NAH-see-yoh*

▦ jai alai court	**a la cancha de jai alai** *ah lah KAHN-chah day HA-ee ah-LAH-ee*
▦ mountain	**a la montaña** *ah lah mohn-TAHN-yah*
▦ ocean	**al océano** *ahl oh-SAY-ah-no*
▦ park	**al parque** *ahl PAHR-keh*
▦ path	**al camino** *ahl kah-MEE-no*
▦ pool	**a la piscina** *ah lah pee-SEE-nah*
▦ rink	**a la pista de patinaje** *ah lah PEES-tah day pah-tee-NAH-hay*
▦ sea	**al mar** *ahl MAHR*
▦ stadium	**al estadio** *ahl es-TAH-dee-yo*
▦ track	**a la pista** *ah lah PEES-tah*

SPORTS EQUIPMENT

I need a ____.	**Necesito ____.** *Neh-seh-SEE-toh*
▦ ball	**una pelota** *oo-nah pel-OH-tah*
▦ bat	**un bate** *oon BAH-tay*
▦ bicycle	**una bicicleta** *oo-nah bee-see-KLAY-tah*
▦ boat	**un bote** *oon BOTT-tay*
▦ canoe	**una canoa** *oo-nah kah-NO-ah*
▦ diving suit	**un traje de buceo** *oon trah-hay day boo-SAY-oh*
▦ fishing rod	**una caña de pescar** *oo-nah KAHN-yah day pes-KAHR*
▦ flippers	**aletas** *ah-LET-ahs*
▦ golf clubs	**palos de golf** *pah-lohs day GOHLF*
▦ hockey stick	**un palo de hockey** *oon pah-loh day HOH-kee*
▦ ice skates	**patines de hielo** *pah-teen-ays day YEHL-oh*

▦ in-line skates	**patines en línea** *pah-teen-ays ehn LEE-nay-ah*
▦ jogging shoes	**zapatillas de footing** *sah-pah-TEE-yahs day FOO-teen*
▦ jogging suit	**un traje de footing** *oon TRAH-hay day FOO-teen*
▦ kneepads	**rodilleras** *roh-dee-YEHR-ahs*
▦ mitts	**mitones** *mee-TOH-nays*
▦ net	**una red** *oo-nah red*
▦ roller skates	**patines** *pah-TEEN-ays*
▦ skateboard	**tabla de patinar** *tah-blah day pah-tee-NAHR*
▦ ski bindings	**fijaciones de esquís** *fee-hah-SYOH-nays day es-KEES*
▦ ski boots	**botas de esquí** *boh-TAHS day es-KEE*
▦ ski poles	**bastones de esquí** *bahs-TOH-nays day es-KEE*
▦ skis	**esquís** *es-KEES*
▦ surfboard	**acuaplano** *ah-kwah-PLAH-no*
▦ swimsuit	**traje de baño** *trah-hay day BAHN-yoh*
▦ waterskis	**esquí acuático** *es-KEE ah-KWAH-tee-koh*
▦ weights	**pesas** *PEH-sahs*
Where is a safe place to run?	**¿Dónde hay un sitio seguro para correr?** *DOHN-day AH-ee oon SEE-tee-oh seh-GOOR-oh pah-rah kohr-EHR*
Where is there a health club (spa)?	**¿Dónde hay un gimnasio (balneario)?** *DOHN-day AH-ee oon heem-NAH-see-oh (bahl-nay-AHR-ee-oh)*

Where can I rent a (mountain, racing, touring) bike, in-line skates, a skateboard?

¿Dónde puedo alquilar una bicicleta (de montaña, de carrera, de turismo), patines en línea, una tabla de patinar? *DOHN-day PWEH-doh ahl-kee-LAHR oo-nah bee-see-KLAY-tah (day mohn-TAH-nyah day kahr-REH-rah day toor-EES-moh) pah-TEE-nehs en LEE-neh-ah oo-nah TAH-blah day pah-tee-NAHR*

TENNIS

Do you play tennis?

¿Sabe usted jugar al tenis? *SAH-bay oos-TEHD hoo-GAHR ahl TEN-ees*

I (don't) play very well.

(No) juego muy bien. *(noh) hoo-AY-goh mwee bee-EHN*

Do you play singles (doubles)?

¿Juega usted solo (en pareja)? *HWAY-gah oos-TEHD SOH-loh (ehn pahr-AY-hah)*

Do you know where there is a court?

¿Sabe usted dónde hay una cancha? *SAH-bay oos-TEHD DOHN-day AH-ee oo-nah KAHN-chah*

Is it a private club? I'm not a member.

¿Es un club privado? No soy socio. *ehs oon kloob pree-BAH-do noh soy SOH-see-oh*

Can I rent a racquet?

¿Se puede alquilar una raqueta? *say PWEH-day ahl-kee-LAHR oo-nah rah-KAY-tah*

How much do they charge per hour (per day)?

¿Cuánto cobran por hora (por día)? *KWAHN-toh KOH-brahn pohr OH-rah (pohr DEE-ah)?*

I serve (You serve) first.

Yo saco (Usted saca) primero. *yoh SAH-koh (oos-TEHD SAH-kah) pree-MEHR-oh*

You play very well.	**Usted juega muy bien.** *oos-TEHD hoo-EH-gah mwee bee-EHN*
You've won.	**Usted ha ganado.** *oos-TEHD oh gah-NAH-doh*

AT THE BEACH/POOL

Let's go to the beach (to the pool).	**Vamos a la playa (piscina).** *BAH-mohs ah lah PLAH-ee-ah (pee-SEEN-ah)*
Which bus will take us to the beach?	**¿Qué autobús nos lleva a la playa?** *kay AH-oo-toh-BOOS nohs yeh-bah oh lah PLAH-ee-ah*
Is there an indoor pool (outdoor) in the hotel?	**¿Hay una piscina cubierta (al aire libre) en el hotel?** *AH-ee oo-nah pee-SEE-nah ehn ehl oh-TEL*
I (don't) know how to swim well.	**(No) sé nadar bien.** *(noh) say nah-DAHR bee-EHN*
Is it safe to swim here?	**¿Se puede nadar aquí sin peligro?** *say PWEH-day nah-DAHR ah-KEE seen peh-LEE-groh*
Is it dangerous for children?	**¿Hay peligro para los niños?** *AH-ee pel-EE-groh pah-rah lohs NEEN-yohs*
Is there a lifeguard?	**¿Hay salvavidas?** *AH-ee sahl-bah-BEE-dahs*
Help! I'm drowning!	**¡Auxilio! ¡Socorro! ¡Me ahogo!** *owk-SEEL-yo so-COHR-oh may ah-OH-go*

Where can I get ____?	¿Dónde puedo conseguir ____? *DOHN-day PWEH-doh kohn-seh-GHEER*
▓ an air mattress	un colchón flotante *oon kohl-CHOHN floh-tahn-tay*
▓ a bathing suit	un traje de baño *oon trah-hay day BAHN-yoh*
▓ a beach ball	una pelota de playa *oo-nah pel-OH-tah day PLAH-ee-ah*
▓ a beach chair	un sillón de playa *oon see-YOHN day PLAH-ee-ah*
▓ a beach towel	una toalla de playa *oo-nah toh-AH-yah day PLAH-ee-yah*
▓ a beach umbrella	una sombrilla playera *oo-nah sohm-BREE-yah plah-YEHR-ah*
▓ diving equipment	equipo de buceo *eh-KEE-poh day boo-SAY-oh*
▓ sunglasses	gafas de sol *GAH-fahs day sohl*
▓ suntan lotion	loción para broncear *loh-SYOHN pah-rah brohn-SAY-ahr*

ON THE SLOPES

The main ski areas in Spain are the Pyrenees, the Guadarrama mountains, the Sierra Nevada, and the Cantabrian mountains. **Pistas** (ski runs) are marked with colored arrows according to their difficulty.

Green	very easy slopes
Blue	easy slopes
Red	difficult slopes for experienced skiers
Black	very difficult slopes for professionals

In South America, skiing choices are very limited. Most skiers head for the Andes, for resorts in Argentina and Chile.

| Which ski area do you recommend? | **¿Qué sitio de esquiar recomienda usted?** *kay SEE-tee-oh day ehs-kee-AHR ray-koh-MYEHN-dah oos-TEHD* |

| I am a novice (intermediate, expert) skier. | **Soy principiante (intermedio, experto).** *soy preen-seep-YAHN-tay (een-tehr-MEHD-ee-oh ehs-PEHR-toh)* |

| Is there enough snow at this time of year? | **¿Hay bastante nieve durante esta temporada?** *AH-ee bahs-TAHN-tay nee-EHB-ay door-ahn-tay ehs-tah temp-ohr-AH-dah* |

| How would I get to that place? | **¿Por dónde se va a ese sitio?** *pohr DOHN-day say bah ah eh-say SEE-tee-oh* |

Can I rent ____ there?	**¿Puedo alquilar ____?** *PWEH-doh ahl-kee-lahr*
▓ equipment	**equipo** *eh-KEEP-oh*
▓ poles	**palos** *PAH-lohs*
▓ skis	**esquís** *ehs-KEES*
▓ ski boots	**botas de esquiar** *BOH-tahs day ehs-kee-AHR*

Do they have ski lifts?	**¿Tienen funicular?** *TYEHN-eh foo-nee-koo-LAHR*
How much does the lift cost?	**¿Cuánto cobran?** *KWAHN-toh KOH-brahn*
Do they give lessons?	**¿Dan lecciones?** *dahn lek-SYOHN-ays*
Where can I stay?	**¿Dónde puedo alojarme?** *DOHN-day PWEH-doh ah-loh-HAHR-may*

ON THE LINKS

Is there a golf course?	**¿Hay un campo de golf?** *AH-ee oon KAHM-poh day gohlf*
Can one rent clubs?	**¿Se puede alquilar los palos?** *say PWEH-day ahl-kee-LAHR lohs PAH-lohs*

CAMPING

There are over 700 campgrounds in Spain. About 500 are located along the coast. Many of them have excellent facilities such as swimming pools, sport areas, restaurants, and supermarkets. The Spanish National Tourist Office furnishes a list of approved campsites.

Campsites (**campamentos**) are classified as follows.

de lujo	luxury
primera clase	first class
segunda clase	second class
tercera clase	third class

In parts of Latin America, a tourist must have a permit to camp, and camping only in designated sites is recommended.

Is there a camping area near here?	**¿Hay un camping cerca de aquí?** *AH-ee oon KAHM-peeng sehr-kah day ah-KEE*
Do we pick our own site?	**¿Escogemos nuestro propio sitio?** *ehs-koh-HAY-mohs NWEHS-troh PROH-pee-oh SEE-tee-oh*
We only have a tent.	**Tenemos solo una tienda.** *ten-AY-mohs SOH-loh oo-nah TYEHN-dah*
Can we camp for one night only?	**¿Se puede acampar por una noche sola?** *say PWEH-day ah-kahm-pahr pohr oo-nah noh-chay SOH-lah*
Can we park our trailer (our caravan)?	**¿Podemos estacionar nuestro coche-vivienda (nuestra caravana)?** *poh-DAY-mos ehs-stah-syohn-AHR nwehs-troh KOH-chay bee-bee-EHN-dah (NWEHS-trah kahr-ah-BAHN-ah)*
Is (are) there ____?	**¿Hay ____?** *AH-ee*
▓ camp guards	**guardias de campamento** *GWAHR-dee-yahs day kahm-pah-MEN-toh*
▓ a children's playground	**un parque infantil** *oon PAHR-kay een-fahn-TEEL*
▓ cooking facilites	**instalaciones para cocinar** *een-stah-lah-SYOHN-ays pah-rah koh-see-NAHR*

▓ drinking water	**agua potable** *AH-gwah poh-TAH-blay*
▓ electricity	**electricidad** *eh-lek-tree-see-DAHD*
▓ fireplaces	**hogueras** *oh-GEHR-ahs*
▓ flush toilets	**servicios** *sehr-BEE-see-ohs*
▓ a grocery store	**una tienda de comestibles** *oo-nah tee-EHN-dah day koh-mes-TEE-blays*
▓ picnic tables	**mesas de camping** *may-sahs day KAHM-peeng*
▓ showers	**duchas** *DOO-chahs*

How much do they charge per person (per car)?	**¿Cuánto cobran por persona (por coche)?** *KWAHN-toh KOH-brahn pohr pehr-SOHN-ah (pohr koh-chay)*
We intend staying ____ days (weeks).	**Pensamos quedamos ____ días (semanas).** *pen-SAH-mohs kay-DAHR-nohs DEE-ahs (seh-MAHN-ahs)*

IN THE COUNTRYSIDE

Are there tours to the countryside?	**¿Hay excursiones al campo?** *AH-ee ehs-koor-SYOHN-ays ahl KAHM-poh*
I would like to take a hike.	**Me gustaría hacer una caminata.** *meh goos-tah-REE-ah ah-SEHR OO-nah kah-mee-NAH-tah*
Look at ____.	**Mire ____.** *MEER-ay*
▓ the barn	**el granero** *ehl grah-NEHR-oh*
▓ the birds	**los pájaros** *lohs PAH-hahr-ohs*
▓ the bridge	**el puente** *ehl PWEHN-tay*
▓ the cottages	**las casitas** *lahs kah-SEE-tahs*
▓ the farm	**la granja** *lah GRAHN-hah*

the fields	**los campos**	*lohs KAHM-pohs*
the flowers	**las flores**	*lahs FLOHR-ays*
the forest	**el bosque**	*ehl BOHS-kay*
the hill	**la colina**	*lah koh-LEE-nah*
the lake	**el lago**	*ehl LAH-goh*
the mountains	**las montañas**	*lahs mohn-TAHN-yahs*
the ocean	**el mar**	*ehl mahr*
the plants	**las plantas**	*lahs PLAHN-tahs*
the pond	**el estanque**	*ehl ehs-TAHN-kay*
the river	**el rio**	*ehl REE-oh*
the stream	**el arroyo**	*ehl ah-ROY-yoh*
the trees	**los árboles**	*lohs AHR-boh-lays*
the valley	**el valle**	*ehl BAH-yeh*
the village	**el pueblo**	*ehl PWEHB-loh*
the waterfall	**la catarata**	*lah kah-tahr-AH-tah*

Where does this path lead to?

¿Adónde lleva el sendero? *ah-DOHN-day YEH-bah ehl sen-DEHR-oh*

How long does it take to get to _____?

¿Cuánto tiempo toma para llegar a _____? *KWAHN-toh TYEHM-poh TOH-mah pah-rah yehg-AHR ah*

I am lost.

Estoy perdido(a). *es-TOY pehr-DEE-doh(dah)*

Can you show me the road to _____?

¿Puede usted mostrarme el camino a _____? *PWEH-day oos-TED mohs-TRAHR-may ehl kah-MEE-no ah*

FOOD AND DRINK

The Spanish-speaking world is a vast one, so any information on its food is, of necessity, very general. There are many similarities between the foods and eating habits of Spain and those of Latin America, since Latin American culture was largely shaped by Spanish invaders. Likewise, foods were brought back from the New World and rapidly incorporated into the cooking in Spain. But Latin American cooking is also greatly influenced by the preferences of its ancient peoples—the Incas, Aztecs, and Mayans. To sort all this out most clearly for you, we have divided the information in this chapter into two portions when appropriate: one for references to Spain, and the other for information on Latin America. Of the latter, most tips pertain to Mexico, with only minor variations for the remainder of Latin America.

IN SPAIN

Spanish restaurants are officially ranked from 5-fork (luxury) to 1-fork (4th class). The ratings—which you will see designated by forks on a sign outside each establishment—are based on the number of dishes served in specific categories, not on the quality of the establishment.

Dining hours in Spain, except for breakfast, are late: the midday meal, **comida**, is served from 1:30 to 4 P.M., dinner, **cena**, from 8:30 P.M. to midnight. Outside Madrid, the hours are a little earlier. Restaurants post their menus outside their doors, so you may study the menu and make your decision before entering.

Madrid, as Spain's capital, has restaurants specializing in the cuisine of all its regions. You will find restaurants with Basque, Catalan, Galician, Asturian, Andalusian, and other specialties. Madrid, as the center of Castile, naturally has a wide number of Castilian restaurants, where roast pork and roast lamb are the premier specialties.

Some pointers about dining out in Spain: Spaniards customarily do their drinking and have their aperitifs in a bar or **tasca**, usually standing and socializing, before going into a restaurant to sit down and dine. Drinking at the table usually consists of having wine with the meal. Many Spaniards have their large meal in midday, a light supper at night. At midday there are usually three courses consumed: appetizer or fish course, entree, and dessert. To call a waiter in Spain, it is customary to say **"Camarero"** (waiter), **"Oiga"** (listen), or **"Por favor"** (please). *Do not clap your hands or call* **"Chico"** (boy).

As in most countries, there is a variety of places in which you can obtain something to eat. Here we list a few of the common ones.

café	small place that serves alcoholic and nonalcoholic drinks, plus simple snacks; very casual
cafetería	not a self-service restaurant, as the name implies in English, but a cafe-type place specializing in informal food such as sandwiches, snacks, sweets, aperitifs, coffee, and tea

bar (tasca, taberna)	similar to a pub or bar in the U.S., in which drinks and small snacks (**tapas** or **pinchos**) are served
fonda (hostería, venta, posada)	small, informal inn that usually specializes in regional dishes
merendero (chiringuito)	outdoor stall (usually at the beaches or piers) selling seafood, soft drinks, and ice cream
restaurante	traditional restaurant, varying in the extensiveness of their menu, usually offering a blending of regional specialties and more broad-based dishes, often also offers a tourist menu

IN LATIN AMERICA

In Mexico, people often eat several times a day. Breakfast (**desayuno**) is early, usually between 8 and 10 and often at a street vendor's stand or in the market. Lunch (**almuerzo**) is anywhere from 1 to 4 P.M. and can be a hearty meal. But sometime between breakfast and lunch, many people sneak in a snack (**antojo**), often a taco. Dinner (**cena**) is usually begun around 8 P.M., but can be served until midnight. Most other Latin American countries follow this basic timing as well, although dinner often starts a bit earlier.

In Mexico City, you'll find some restaurants that specialize in foods from other parts of Mexico as well. And in other regions of Mexico, you'll find a differing array of specialties from those areas. Mexican food is intriguing, with many fruits and vegetables that will be novel to British or American tourists. Much of the food is based on a variety of chilies, so the food often is firey-hot, especially if you are not accustomed to such spices.

The cuisine in other countries of Latin America changes according to racial and cultural influences. Corn-based dishes and generous use of native fruits and vegetables are typical of northern countries, reflecting the stronger native American influence, whereas the south of the continent relies mostly on wheat and its dishes reveal a strong European background. Geography, of course, also plays a major role. You will find few fish dishes in landlocked Bolivia, and few tropical fruits in Chile.

Overall, go with the flow. Avoid strong personal preferences and sample the regional specialties. Argentina's beef and meat dishes (and portions!) are world-renowned, Chilean fish and shellfish are excellent, and Chile's wines are on the par with the best France has to offer (except the price). In Venezuela you must go to a *cervecería*, a relaxing mix of beer, snacks, guitars and songs. In Peru don't miss the better restaurants and their creative mix of native and international flavors.

For information on specific dishes, check South and Central American Foods, on page 156.

In general, the following categories of food establishments exist.

bar	serves drinks and **botanas** (snacks)
cantina (northern countries)	men's bar, usually also serving snacks; this is a place for the neighborhood men to gather
hacienda	a ranch-style restaurant, usually with a garden and dining out-of-doors; gracious, usually with regional specialties
hostería (fonda, posada, café)	a casual restaurant, usually with regional specialties
restaurante	varying from the most casual, neighborhood place to a fancy establishment catering to tourists

The international fast-food chains have a strong presence in every country. You will find a Pizza-Hut and a McDonald's even in remote villages, as well as Nestlé's chocolates, M&M candies and, of course, Coca-Cola.

EATING OUT

Do you know a good restaurant?	**¿Conoce usted un buen restaurante?** *koh-NOH-say oos-TEHD oon bwehn rehs-tah-oo-RAHN-tay*
Is it very expensive?	**¿Es muy caro?** *ehs mwee KAH-roh*
Do you know a restaurant that serves native dishes?	**¿Conoce usted un restaurante típico?** *koh-NOH-say oos-TEHD oon rehs-tah-oo-RAHN-tay TEE-pee-koh*
Waiter!	**¡Camarero!** *kah-mah-REHR-oh*
Miss!	**¡Señorita!** *sen-yohr-EE-tah*
A table for two, ____ please.	**Una mesa para dos, por favor.** *oo-nah MAY-sah pah-rah dohs pohr fa-BOHR*
▓ in the corner	**en el rincón** *ehn ehl reen-KOHN*
▓ near the window	**cerca de la ventana** *sehr-kah day lah ben-TAHN-ah*
▓ on the terrace	**en la terraza** *ehn lah teh-RAH-sah*
I would like to make a reservation ____.	**Quisiera hacer una reserva ____.** *kee-see-EHR-ah ah-SEHR oo-nah ray-SEHR-bah*
▓ for tonight	**para esta noche** *pah-rah ehs-tah NOH-chay*
▓ for tomorrow evening	**para mañana por la noche** *pah-rah mahn-YAH-nah pohr lah NOH-chay*
▓ for two (four) persons	**para dos (cuatro) personas** *pah-rah dohs (KWAH-troh) pehr-SOHN-ahs*
▓ for 9 P.M.	**para las nueve** *pah-rah las NWEH-bay*
▓ for 9:30	**para las nueve y media** *pah-rah lahs NWEH-bay ee MEHD-yah*

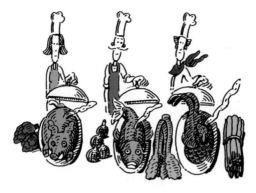

We'd like to have lunch now.	**Queremos almorzar ahora.** *kehr-AY-mohs ahl-mohr-SAHR oh-OHR-ah*
How long would we have to wait?	**¿Cuánto será necesario esperar?** *KWAHN-toh seh-RAH neh-seh-SAH-ree-oh ehs-peh-RAHR*
The menu, please.	**La carta, por favor.** *lah KAHR-tah pohr fa-BOHR*
I'd like the set menu.	**Quisiera el menú del día.** *kee-see-YEHR-ah ehl men-OO del DEE-ah*

Many restaurants have a special fixed-price meal called the **Plato Combinado**, **Menú Turístico**, or **Menú del Día**. There is a smaller selection to choose from, but the price is much less than choosing á la carte and the wine, tax, and tip are usually included. The usual tip is 10 to 15 percent of the bill. However, if the service is included in the bill—**servicio incluido**—it is customary to leave some change as well.

| What's today's special? | **¿Cuál es el plato del día de hoy?** *KWAHL ehs ehl PLAH-toh del DEE-ah day oy* |

What do you recommend?	**¿Qué recomienda usted?** *KAY reh-koh-mee-EHN-dah oos-TEHD*
What's the house specialty?	**¿Cuál es la especialidad de la casa?** *KWAHL ehs lah ehs-peh-see-ah-lee-DAHD day lah KAH-sah*
Do you have a children's menu?	**¿Tiene un menú para niños?** *tee-YEHN-ay oon men-OO pah-rah NEEN-yohs*
To begin with, please bring us ____.	**Para empezar, tráiganos ____ por favor.** *pahr-rah ehm-peh-SAHR TRAH-ee-gah-nohs pohr fa-BOHR*
▓ an aperitif	**un aperitivo** *oon ah-pehr-ee-TEE-boh*
▓ some white (red) wine	**un vino blanco (tinto)** *oon BEE-noh BLAHN-koh (TEEN-toh)*
▓ some ice water	**agua helada** *AH-gwah eh-LAH-dah*
▓ a bottle of mineral water, with (without) gas	**una botella de agua mineral, con (sin) gas** *oo-nah boh-TEH-yah day AH-gwah mee-nehr-AHL kohn (seen) gahs*
▓ a beer	**una cerveza** *oo-nah sehr-BEH-sah*
I'd like (to order now).	**Me gustaría (ordenar ahora).** *may goos-tahr-EE-ah (ohr-den-AHR-ah ah-OHR-ah)*

See the listings that follow for indvidual dishes, and also the regional specialties noted on pages 151–159.

Do you have a house wine?	**¿Tiene un vino de la casa?** *tee-YEHN-ay oon BEE-noh day lah KAH-SAH*
Is it dry (mellow, sweet)?	**¿Es seco (suave, dulce)?** *ehs SAY-koh (SWAH-bay DOOL-say)*

Please also bring us ____.	**Tráiganos también** ____. *TRAH-ee-gah-nohs tahm-BYEHN*
a roll	**un panecillo** *oon pah-neh-SEE-yoh*
bread	**pan** *pahn*
bread and butter	**pan y mantequilla** *pahn ee mahn-tay-KEE-yah*
tortillas (Mexico)	**tortillas** *tahr-TEE-yahs*
Waiter, we need ____.	**Camarero, necesitamos** ____. *kah-mah-REH-roh neh-seh-see-TAH-mohs*
a knife	**un cuchillo** *oon koo-CHEE-yoh*
a fork	**un tenedor** *oon ten-eh-DOHR*
a spoon	**una cuchara** *oo-nah koo-CHAHR-ah*
a teaspoon	**una cucharita** *oo-nah koo-chahr-EE-tah*
a soup spoon	**una cuchara de sopa** *oo-nah koo-CHAH-rah day SOH-pah*
a glass	**un vaso** *oon BAH-soh*
a cup	**una taza** *oo-nah TAH-sah*
a saucer	**un platillo** *oon plah-TEE-yoh*
a plate	**un plato** *oon PLAH-toh*
a napkin	**una servilleta** *oo-nah sehr-bee-YEH-tah*

APPETIZERS (STARTERS)

Tapas (bar snacks) are very popular in Spain. For a listing of typical tapas, see page 147, given with information on food specialties. The following are items you are likely to see on a restaurant menu.

alcachofas	artichokes
almejas	clams
anguilas ahumadas	smoked eels
calamares	squid
caracoles	snails
champiñones	mushrooms
chorizo	spicy sausage, usually pork
cigalas	crayfish
gambas (Spain only)	shrimp
huevos	eggs
jamón serrano (Spain only)	cured ham
melón	melon
moluscos	mussels
ostras (ostiones)	oysters
quisquillas (Spain only)	small shrimp
sardinas	sardines

And in Latin America, there would be some of the following:

camarones	shrimp
guacamole	puréed avocado spread
tostadas	tortilla chips with various pepper and cheese toppings

SOUPS

Soups are wonderful, whether you are enjoying them in Spain or Latin America.

gazpacho	a highly variable purée of fresh, uncooked vegetables, including cucumbers, peppers, onions, and tomatoes; served cold
potaje madrileño	a thick soup of puréed chick peas, cod, and spinach
sopa de ajo	garlic soup
sopa de cebolla	onion soup
sopa de fideos	noodle soup
sopa de mariscos	seafood soup
sopa de gambas	shrimp soup
sopa de albóndigas	soup with meatballs
sopa de pescado	fish soup
sopa de verduras	soup made from puréed greens and vegetables

In Latin America, particularly Mexico, you are also likely to find:

cazuela	a spicy soup-stew, simmered for a long time in an earthenware pot; can be fish, vegetables, or meat
pozole	a hearty pork and hominy stew
sopa de aguacate	creamed avocado soup
sopa de huitlacoche	black corn soup made from the fungus that grows on corn cobs

MEAT

The main course of a meal in Spain is likely to be meat if you are inland and seafood if you are along the coast.

carne de	*KAHR-nay day*	meat of
▇ buey	*bway*	beef
▇ cabrito	*kah-BREE-toh*	goat (kid)
▇ carnero	*kahr-NEHR-oh*	mutton
▇ cerdo	*SEHR-doh*	pork
▇ cordero	*kohr-DEHR-oh*	lamb
▇ ternera	*tehr-NEHR-ah*	veal
▇ vaca, res	*BAH-kah rehs*	beef

Some common cuts of meat, plus other terms you'll find on a menu.

albóndigas	*ahl-BOHN-dee-gahs*	meatballs
bistec	*bees-TEHK*	beef steak
carne picada	*kahr-nay pee-KAH-dah*	ground (minced) meat
chuletas	*choo-LEH-tahs*	chops
churrasco	*choo-RAHS-koh*	charcoal-grilled steak
cocido	*koh-SEE-doh*	stew
costilla	*kohs-TEE-yah*	cutlet
corazón	*koh-rah-SOHN*	heart
criadillas	*kree-ah-DEE-yahs*	sweetbreads

filete	*fee-LEH-tay*	filet
hígado	*EE-gah-doh*	liver
jamón	*ha-MOHN*	ham
lechón	*leh-CHOHN*	suckling pig
lengua	*LEN-gwah*	tongue
morcilla	*mohr-SEE-yah*	blood sausage
rabo de buey	*RAH-boh day BWAY*	oxtails
riñones	*reen-YOH-nays*	kidneys
salchichas	*sahl-CHEE-chahs*	sausages
sesos	*SAY-sohs*	brains
solomillo	*soh-loh-MEE-yoh*	pork tenderloin steak
tocino	*toh-SEE-noh*	bacon
tripas	*TREE-pahs*	tripe

FISH AND SEAFOOD

You won't always recognize the types of fish available, since the waters around Spain or the Latin American countries are generally warmer, with more tropical varieties. Here is a general guide, with our advice that you sample what's offered and discover new types that you like.

almejas	*ahl-MAY-has*	clams
anchoas	*ahn-CHOH-ahs*	anchovies
anguilas	*ahn-GHEE-lahs*	eels
arenque, ahumado	*ah-REHN-kay ah-oo-MAH-doh*	smoked herring

atún	*ah-TOON*	tuna
bacalao	*bah-kah-LAH-oh*	codfish
besugo	*beh-SOO-goh*	sea bream
boquerones	*boh-keh-ROH-nehs*	whitebait
caballa	*kah-BAH-yah*	mackerel
calamares	*kahl-ah-MAHR-ayss*	squid
camarones	*kah-mah-ROH-nayss*	shrimp
cangrejos	*kahn-GRAY-hohs*	crabs
caracoles	*kahr-ah-KOH-layss*	snails
cigalas	*see-GAH-lahs*	large crayfish
congrio	*KOHN-gree-oh*	conger eel
gambas	*GAHM-bahs*	large shrimp
lampreas	*lahm-PRAY-ahs*	lamprey
langosta	*lahn-GOH-stah*	spiny lobster
langostino	*lahn-gohs-TEE-noh*	small crayfish
lenguado	*len-GWAH-doh*	flounder, sole
mejillones	*meh-hee-YOH-nayss*	mussels
mújol	*MOO-hohl*	mullet
merluza	*mehr-LOOS-ah*	bass, hake
pescadilla	*pehs-kah-DEE-yah*	whiting
pulpo	*POOL-poh*	octopus
quesquillas	*kehs-KEE-yahs*	shrimp
rape	*RAH-pay*	monkfish, anglerfish
salmón	*sahl-MOHN*	salmon

sardinas	*sahr-DEE-nahs*	sardines
trucha	*TROO-chah*	trout

And some terms for fowl and game:

capón	*kah-POHN*	capon
codorniz	*koh-dohr-NEES*	quail
conejo	*kohn-AY-hoh*	rabbit
faisán	*fah-ee-SAHN*	pheasant
ganso	*GAHN-soh*	goose
pato	*PAH-toh*	duck
pavo	*PAH-boh*	turkey
perdiz	*pehr-DEES*	partridge
pichón	*pee-CHOHN*	squab
pollo	*POH-yoh*	chicken
venado	*beh-NAH-doh*	venison

Is the meat ____?	**¿Es carne ____?** *ehs KAHR-nay*
▦ baked	**al horno** *ahl OHR-noh*
▦ boiled	**guisada** *ghee-SAH-dah*
▦ braised (stewed)	**estofada** *ehs-toh-FAH-dah*
▦ broiled	**a la parrilla** *ah lah pahr-EE-yah*
▦ roasted	**asada** *ah-SAH-dah*
▦ poached	**escalfada** *ehs KAHL-fah-dah*

I like the meat ____.	**Me gustaría la carne ____.** *may goos-tah-REE-ah lah KAHR-nay*
▦ well done	**bien hecha** *bee-EHN EH-chah*
▦ medium	**término medio** *TEHR-mee-noh MED-yoh*

| rare | **poco hecha** *POH-koh EH-chah* |
| tender | **tierna** *tee-EHR-nah* |

RICE DISHES

Rice forms the foundation of several dishes in Spain, especially **paella.** This specialty varies with the region, but always features saffron-flavored rice. You are likely to see it on a menu in any of these forms.

a la campesina	with ham, chicken, sausage, and small game birds
a la catalana	with sausages, pork, squid, chilies, and peas, or with chicken, snails, beans, and artichokes
alicantina	with rabbit, mussels, and shrimp
bruta	with pork, chicken, and whitefish
de mariscos	with crayfish, anglerfish, and other seafood
valenciana	with chicken, seafood, peas, and tomatoes—the most well-known version

TORTILLA-BASED DISHES

In Mexico particularly, the **tortilla** forms the basis for many dishes; this flat cornmeal cake is roughly the equivalent of bread there, and it is served along with some dishes as well as a main dish, rolled and stuffed, layered with other ingredients and sauced, and fried until crisp. Here are some of the items you'll see on menus featuring tortilla dishes.

chalupas	tortillas that have been curled at the edges and filled with cheese or a ground pork filling, served with a green chili sauce
chilaquiles	layers of tortillas, alternated with beans, meat, chicken, and cheese, then baked
enchiladas	soft corn tortillas rolled around meat and topped with sauce and melted cheese
flautas	sort of a tortilla sandwich that is then rolled and deep-fried
quesadillas	tortillas that are stuffed with cheese and deep-fried
tacos	crisp toasted tortillas stuffed with a variety of fillings (chopped beef, refried beans, turkey, chicken) topped with shredded lettuce, cheese, and sauce

SALADS

In Spain, salads are often part of the appetizer and consist of a zesty mixture of seafood or vegetables. In Latin America, the salad is frequently served along with the main course. (Tourists should be wary of ordering salads of raw vegetables or greens, since these items may have been washed in water that has not been treated for bacteria.) Here are some useful terms for ordering salads.

aceitunas	*ah-say-TOO-nahs*	olives
lechuga	*leh-CHOO-gah*	lettuce
pepino	*pep-EE-noh*	cucumber
tomate	*toh-MAH-tay*	tomato

EGG DISHES

In Spain, eggs are not usually eaten as a breakfast food, and when served usually are in an omelet **(tortilla)** with other ingredients such as ham, potatoes, peppers, shrimp, or mushrooms. Eggs are also served baked with a tomato sauce, or boiled with fish, or scrambled with vegetables.

eggs	**huevos**	*WEH-bohs*
omelet	**tortilla**	*tohr-TEE-yah*

In Latin America, if you want an omelet you can ask for a **tortilla** but in Mexico you are more likely to get a cornmeal cake. When in Mexico, ask for a **tortilla de huevo**. As for other egg preparations, you will be better off with an English (American) breakfast.

fried eggs	**huevos fritos**	*WEH-bohs FREE-tohs*
hard-boiled eggs	**huevos duros**	*WEH-bohs DOOR-ohs*
scrambled eggs	**huevos revueltos**	*WEH-bohs ray-BWEHL-tohs*
soft-boiled eggs	**huevos pasados por agua**	*WEH-bohs pah-SAH-dohs pohr AH-gwah*

On a menu, you are likely to see:

huevos con chorizo	eggs with a spicy sausage
huevos rancheros	fried eggs on a tortilla, served with spicy ranchero sauce (chopped green peppers, tomatoes and onions) and guacomole or sliced avocado.

VEGETABLES

alcachofas	*ahl-kah-CHOH-fahs*	artichokes
apio	*AH-pee-oh*	celery
berenjena	*behr-ehn-HAY-nah*	eggplant (aubergine)
calabacín	*kah-lah-bah-SEEN*	zucchini
cebollas	*seh-BOH-yahs*	onions
col	*kohl*	cabbage
coliflor	*kohl-ee-FLOHR*	cauliflower
espinacas	*eh-spee-NAH-kahs*	spinach
espárragos	*ehs-PAHR-ah-gohs*	asparagus
champiñones	*chahm-peen-YOH-nays*	mushrooms
garbanzos	*gahr-BAHN-sohs*	chickpeas
guisantes	*ghee-SAHN-tays*	peas
judías	*hoo-DEE-ahs*	green beans
papas, patatas	*PAH-pahs pah-TAH-tahs*	potatoes
▧ **papas fritas**	*PAH-pahs FREE-tahs*	french fries
pimiento	*pee-MYEHN-toh*	pepper
puerros	*PWEHR-ohs*	leeks
maíz	*mah-EES*	corn
tomate	*toh-MAH-tay*	tomato
zanahorias	*sah-nah-OHR-ee-ahs*	carrots

In parts of Latin America you are likely also to see the following on a menu:

chile	*CHEE-lay*	chili peppers, of any variety (see pages 139–140)
frijoles	*free-HOH-lays*	beans, usually kidney or pinto
huitlacoche	*WEET-lah-koh-chay*	corn fungus
nopalito	*noh-pah-LEE-toh*	prickly pear cactus
yuca	*YOO-kah*	root vegetable, from yucca plant

SEASONINGS AND CONDIMENTS

Seasonings in Spain tend to be lively but not fiery hot. Personal preferences sometimes intercede, however, and you might want something additional for your meal. Here's how to ask for what you want.

butter	**la mantequilla** *lah mahn-teh-KEE-yah*
horseradish	**el rábano picante** *ehl RAH-bah-noh pee-KAHN-tay*
lemon	**el limón** *ehl lee-MOHN*
margarine	**la margarina** *lah mahr-gahr-EE-nah*
mayonnaise	**la mayonesa** *lah mah-ee-oh-NAY-sah*
mustard	**la mostaza** *lah mohs-TAH-sah*
oil	**el aceite** *ehl ah-SAY-tay*

pepper (black)	**la pimienta** *lah pee-mee-EHN-tah*
pepper (red) (Spain only)	**el pimiento** *ehl pee-mee-EHN-toh*
pepper (red) (Latin America)	**el ají** *ehl ah-HEE*
salt	**la sal** *lah sahl*
sugar	**el azúcar** *ehl ah-SOO-kahr*
saccharine	**la sacarina** *lah sah-kah-REE-nah*
vinegar	**el vinagre** *ehl bee-NAH-gray*
Worchestershire sauce	**la salsa inglesa** *lah SAHL-sah een-GLAY-sah*

In Latin America, foods tend to be more heavily spiced, especially in Mexico. Here are some terms you might encounter on menus, describing the dish in terms of its major flavoring.

achiote	*ah-chee-OH-tay*	annatto
albahaca	*ahl-bah-AH-kah*	basil
azafrán	*ah-sah-FRAHN*	saffron
cilantro	*see-LAHN-troh*	coriander
orégano	*oh-REH-ga-noh*	oregano
romero	*roh-MEHR-oh*	rosemary

Descriptions of the different types of chilies could fill an entire book. Here we will mention a few of the major ones likely to be seen on menus.

| **ancho** | mild to hot, with mild most common |
| **chipotle** | medium hot to hot, with a smokey flavor |

jalapeño	hot, with a meaty flavor
pasilla	mild to medium hot, with a rich sweet flavor
pequín	hot
pimiento	sweet bell pepper
poblano	mild to hot, with a rich flavor
serrano	hot to very hot, with a bright flavor

And in sauces, you'll find:

salsa cruda	an uncooked tomato sauce, often served as a dip or table seasoning
salsa de tomatillo	delicate sauce made from Mexican green tomatoes (a husk tomato unlike the regular red tomato)
salsa de perejil	parsley sauce
ají de queso	cheese sauce
adobo	sauce made with ancho and pasilla chilies, sesame seeds, nuts, and spices
mole	a sauce of varying ingredients, made from chilies, sesame seeds, cocoa, and spices
pipián	sauce made from pumpkin seeds, chilies, coriander, and bread crumbs
verde	sauce of green chilies and green tomatoes

Oftentime, the Mexicans drink **atole**, a cornmeal drink that resembles a milk shake, with spicy foods. It is commonly served in a large pitcher for all at the table to drink.

DESSERTS—SWEETS

Desserts are not extensive in Spanish-speaking countries, but here are a few items that you may be offered.

arroz con leche	*ah-ROHS kohn LEH-chay*	rice pudding
crema catalana or **flan**	*krem-ah kah-tah-LAN-nah* or *flahn*	caramel custard
galletas	*gah-YEH-tahs*	cookies (biscuits)
helado	*ay-LAH-doh*	ice cream
■ **de chocolate**	*day cho-koh-LAH-tay*	chocolate
■ **de pistacho**	*day pees-TAH-choh*	pistachio
■ **de vainilla**	*day bah-ee-NEE-yah*	vanilla
■ **de nueces**	*day NWEH-says*	walnut
■ **de fresa**	*day FRAY-sah*	strawberry
mazapán	*mah-sah-PAHN*	marzipan
merengue	*meh-REHN-gay*	meringue
natilla	*nah-TEE-yah*	cream pudding
pastel	*pahs-TEHL*	pastry
tarta	*TAHR-tah*	tart, usually fruit

FRUITS AND NUTS

What kind of fruit do you have?	**¿Qué frutas tiene?**	*kay FROO-tahs tee-YEHN-ay*
albaricoque	*ahl-bahr-ee-KOH-kay*	apricot

banana, plátano	*bah-NAH-nah* *PLAH-ta-noh*	banana, plantain (green banana)
cereza	*sehr-AY-sah*	cherry
ciruela	*seer-WEH-lah*	plum
coco	*KOH-koh*	coconut
dátil	*DAH-teel*	date
frambuesa	*frahm-BWEH-sah*	raspberry
fresa	*FRAY-sah*	strawberry
guayaba	*gwah-ee-AH-bah*	guava
higo	*EE-goh*	fig
jícama	*HEE-kah-mah*	jicama
lima	*LEE-mah*	lime
limón	*lee-MOHN*	lemon
mandarina	*mahn-dahr-EE-nah*	tangerine
mango	*MAHN-goh*	mango
manzana	*mahn-SAH-nah*	apple
melocotón	*mel-oh-koh-TOHN*	peach
melón	*meh-LOHN*	melon
naranja	*nah-RAHN-hah*	orange
pera	*PEH-rah*	pear
piña	*PEEN-yah*	pineapple
pomelo	*poh-MEH-loh*	grapefruit
sandía	*sahn-DEE-ah*	watermelon
tuna	*TOO-nah*	prickly pear
uva	*OO-bah*	grape

For some common varities of nuts:

almendras	*ahl-MEN-drahs*	almonds
castañas	*kahs-TAHN-yahs*	chestnuts
avellanas	*ah-bay-YAHN-ahs*	hazelnuts (filberts)
nueces	*NWEH-sayss*	walnuts

SPECIAL CIRCUMSTANCES

Many travelers have special dietary requirements, so here are a few phrases that might help you get what you need or avoid what does you wrong.

I am on a diet. **Estoy en dieta.** *es-TOY en DYEH-tah*

I am a vegetarian. **Soy vegetariano(a).** *soy beh-heh-tahr-ee-YAH-no(nah)*

I am allergic to peanuts. **Tengo alergia al maní.** (Latin America) **Tengo alergia a los cacahuates.** (Mexico, Spain) *TEHN-goh ah-LEHR-hee-ah ahl mah-NEE TEHN-goh ah-LEHR-hee-ah ah lohs kah-kah-HWAH-tehs*

I want a dish ____. **Quiero un plato ____.** *KYEHR-oh oon PLAH-toh*

■ low in fat **con poca grasa** *kohn POH-kah GRAH-sah*

■ low in sodium **con poco contenido de sodio** *kohn POH-koh kohn-ten-EE-doh day SO-dee-oh*

■ nondairy **sin productos lácteos** *seen pro-DOOK-tohs LAHK-tay-ohs*

■ salt-free **sin sal** *seen sahl*

■ sugar-free **sin azúcar** *seen ah-SOO-kahr*

■ without artificial coloring **sin colorantes artificiales** *seen koh-lohr-AHN-tays ahr-tee-fee-SYAHL-ays*

■ without
preservatives
sin preservativos *seen pray-sehr-bah-TEE-bohs*

■ without garlic
sin ajo *seen AH-ho*

I don't want
anything
fried (salted).
No quiero nada frito (salado).
*noh kee-YEHR-oh nah-dah FREE-toh
(sah LAH-doh)*

Do you have
anything that is not
spicy?
¿Tiene algo que no sea picante?
tee-YEHN-ay AHL-goh kay noh SAY-ah pee-KAHN-tay

Do you have any
dishes without meat?
¿Tiene platos sin carne? *tee-YEHN-ay PLAH-tohs seen KAHR-nay*

BEVERAGES

See pages 148–149 for information on Spanish wines and
liquors. As for other beverages, we give you the following
phrases to help you ask for exactly what you wish.

Waiter, please
bring me ____.
**Camarero, tráiganos por favor
____.** *kah-mah-REHR-oh, TRAH-ee-gah-nohs pohr fah-BOHR*

coffee
café *kah-FAY*

■ black coffee
café solo *kah-FAY SOH-loh*

■ with cream
café con crema *kah-FAY kohn
KRAY-mah*

■ with milk
un cortado *oon kohr-TAH-doh*

■ espresso
un exprés (un expreso) *oon ehs-PRESS (oon ehs-PRESS-oh)*

■ half coffee/half
milk (drunk in
morning)
café con leche *kah-FAY kohn
LEH-chay*

■ iced coffee	**café helado** *kah FAY eh-LAH-doh*
tea	**té** *tay*
■ with milk	**con leche** *kohn LEH-chay*
■ with lemon	**con limón** *kohn lee-MOHN*
■ with sugar	**con azúcar** *kohn ah-SOO-kahr*
■ iced tea	**té helado** *tay eh-LAH-doh*
chocolate (hot)	**chocolate** *choh-koh-LAH-tay*
water	**agua** *AH-gwah*
■ cold	**agua fría** *AH-gwah FREE-ah*
■ ice	**agua helada** *AH-gwah ay-LAH-dah*
■ mineral, with gas (without gas)	**agua mineral, con gas (sin gas)** *AH-gwah mee-nehr-AHL kohn gahs (seen gahs)*
cider	**una sidra** *oo-nah SEE-drah*
juice	**un jugo** *oon HOO-goh*
lemonade	**una limonada** *oo-nah lee-moh-NAH-dah*
milk	**leche** *LEH-chay*
■ malted milk	**una leche malteada** *oo-nah LEH-chay mahl-tay-AH-dah*
■ milk shake	**un batido de leche** *oon bah-TEE-doh day LEH-chay*
orangeade	**una naranjada** *oo-nah nahr-ahn-HAH-dah*
punch	**un ponche** *oon POHN-chay*
soda	**una gaseosa** *oo-nah gah-say-OH-sah*
tonic water	**un agua tónica** *oon AH-gwah TOH-nee-kah*

You might also wish to try an old Spanish favorite, **horchata de churas**, an ice-cold drink made from ground earth almonds. It is a thin, milk-like substance that is mildly sweet and very refreshing on a hot day. Usually it is scooped up from large vats that are kept chilled, and served in a tall glass.

The check, please.	**La cuenta, par favor.** *lah KWEHN-tah pohr fah-BOHR*
Separate checks.	**Cuentas saparadas.** *KWEHN-tahs sep-ahr-AH-dahs*
Is the service (tip) included?	**¿Está incluida la propina?** *ehs-TAH een-kloo-EE-dah lah proh-PEE-nah*
I haven't ordered this.	**No he pedido ésto.** *noh ay ped-EE-doh EHS-toh*
I don't think the bill is right.	**Me parece que hay un error en la cuenta.** *may pah-RAY-say kay AH-ee oon ehr-OHR ehn lah KWEHN-tah*
This is for you.	**Esto es para usted.** *EHS-toh ehs pah-rah oos-TEHD*
We're in a hurry.	**Tenemos prisa.** *ten-EH-mohs PREE-sah*

DRINKS AND SNACKS

In Spain, bars and cocktail lounges sometimes also call themselves pubs. **Cervecerías** are tascas or pubs that specialize in German beer in the barrel, as well as wine. Some pubs are more like piano bars, others are like classical-music coffee houses.

Spanish beer, a German-style brew, is both national (San Miguel and Aguila brands) and local (such as Alhambra in Granada, Vitoria in Malaga, Cruz Campo in Seville) in nature. Regular, light, and dark **(negra)** are the types, usually served ice cold.

Sidra, or cider, is available still or sparkling. The most famous sparkling sidra is produced in the north in Asturias and is called **sidra champaña**.

TAPAS (BAR SNACKS)

One of the delights of Spain is its **tapas**, light snacks that are varied samplings of Spanish cuisine. These hors d'oeuvres might include some of the following items.

aceitunas	olives
alcachofas a la vinagreta	artichokes with vinaigrette dressing
almejas en salsa de ajo	clams in a garlic sauce
anguilas	fried baby eels

calamares a la romana	batter-fried squid strips
caracoles en salsa	snails in a tomato sauce
chorizo al diablo	sausage, especially spicy
entremeses variados	platter of assorted snacks
gambas a la plancha	grilled shrimp
huevos rellenos	stuffed hard-boiled eggs
palitos de queso	cheese straws
pan con jamón	toast slices with ham
pinchitos	kebabs
salchichón	salami

SPANISH WINES

Wine is as much the "drink of the country" in Spain as in France and Italy. Premier table wines are the Bordeaux and Burgundy types produced in the Rioja area along the Ebro River in the north. Sherry, Spain's most famous white wine, is produced in the south. There are five sherry types: fino, manzanilla, amontillado, oloroso, and cream. Fino and manzanilla are the driest and are favorite aperitifs. The others are served with dessert or as after-dinner drinks.

Spanish brandy and numerous liqueurs are produced in Spain and are inexpensive.

WINE	REGION	DESCRIPTION	ORDER WITH
Chacoli	Basque	A light, refreshing petillant white	Seafood, poultry
Espumoso	Catalonia	Superb, champagne-like white	Celebrations, desserts
Málaga	Malaga	Heavy, sweet muscatel	Desserts, after-dinner
Panades	Catalonia	Fine, robust reds, some with great character —also some pleasant whites	Meats, game Seafood, poultry
Priorato	Tarragona	Astringent whites, table reds	Seafood Meats
Ribeiro	Galicia	Light, refreshing, crackling whites	Seafood, cheese
Rioja	Old Castile, Navarra	Long-lived, deep rich reds of great character —also Riesling-type whites	Meats, game, spicy foods Seafood, cheese
Sherry	Andalucia	*fino* (very dry) *manzanilla* (dry) *amontillado* (slightly sweet) *oloroso* (sweet and nutty) *cream* (sweet, syrupy nectar)	aperitif aperitif Dessert, cheese Dessert or after-dinner After-dinner

I would like ___.	**Quisiera ___.** *kee-SYEHR-ah*
■ a glass of wine	**un vaso de vino** *oon BAH-soh day BEE-noh*
■ a bottle of wine	**una botella de vino** *oo-nah boh-TEH-yah day BEE-noh*
Is it ___?	**¿Es ___?** *ehs*
■ red	**tinto** *TEEN-toh*
■ white	**blanco** *BLAHN-koh*
■ rosé	**rosado** *oh-SAH-doh*
light	**ligero** *lee-GEH-roh*
sparkling	**espumoso** *ehs-poo-MOH-soh*
dry	**seco** *SAY-koh*
sweet	**dulce** *DOOL-say*

Sangría is a refreshing fruit punch made from red wine, brandy, fruit, sugar, and soda water. It is usually enjoyed on picnics and in the afternoon, but not at dinner.

LATIN AMERICAN DRINKS

From the Caribbean come a variety of colorful drinks, most of which use rum combined with tropical fruits such as pineapple, coconut, passion fruit, and papaya. Many of these drinks are also available in other Latin American countries, including Mexico. First we list a few of these, then give you descriptions of some of the less familiar Mexican drinks that are particular to that country.

In Mexico **tequila** is a very popular drink, drunk neat (straight) with salt and lime and often also jalapeño peppers. It is distilled from the juice of the agave (maguey) plant (a cactus-like succulent) and comes in both clear and amber; the amber has been aged and has a more mellow flavor.

cuba libre	rum, lime juice, and Coca Cola
margarita	tequila, lime juice, and salt
piña colada	coconut cream, pineapple juice, and rum
ponche	fruit juice and rum or tequila
pulque	the fermented juice of the agave (maguey) plant, often with flavorings added such as herbs, pineapple, celery; available in special pulque bars
tequila sunrise	orange juice, grenadine, tequila

SOUTH AMERICAN WINES

Wine grapes only grow well in moderate climates, so the countries with any wines at all are Argentina, Chile, Uruguay, and parts of Brazil. Chile's wine is one of the world's best, and prices are still rather modest. Ask for it wherever you are. Argentina produces the most wine (quite a bit, as compared with North America), and most of it is quite good. Elsewhere, you will be able to enjoy European wines and California wines in the larger hotels and restaurants that cater to tourists.

FOOD SPECIALTIES OF SPAIN

There are no hard-and-fast rules for Spanish cooking. Seasonings and ingredients will vary from region to region, depending on what's available and what the background is of the people. In Basque country, the helpings are large and the food is heavy with seafood: fried cod, fried eels, squid, and sea bream. Along the Cantabrian coast are excellent cheeses and exquisite sardines. **Sopa montañesa** (a regional soup) is famous, as are **caracoles a la santona** (snails) and **tortilla a la montañesa**, the regional omelet. In Asturias, have a good plate of **fabada**, the beans and blood sausage stew. Tripe is also good. In Galicia, the **pote gallego** (hot pot) is tasty, as is **merluza a la gallega** (hake). Santiago clams, spider crabs, and rock barnacle (**centollas** and **percebes**), are succulent.

Along the eastern coast, in Catalonia, you'll sample **escudella i carn d'olla**, a vegetable and meat stew, or **butifarra con judías**, pork sausage with beans. **Habas estofadas** is stewed broad beans. Toward Valencia the land of **paella**, the famous saffron-tinted rice that is mixed with a variety of seafood and meats. If you travel to the Balearic Islands, sample **sopas mallorqinas** (soups), sausages, sardine omelet, or Ibiza-style lobster.

Castilian cuisine is famous for a chickpea and blood sausage stew (**cocido a la madrileña**). In Segovia and Sepulveda you should eat the lamb and suckling pig. **Chorizo** and smoked ham (**jamón serrano**) are world famous. In Toledo, enjoy the **huevos a caballo**, stewed partridge, and marzipan.

Andalusian food is famous for **gazpacho**, a cold, spicy soup of raw tomatoes, peppers, cucumber, and other ingredients depending on the cook. Also here try the mixed fried fishes.

Some other specialties include the following.

bacalao a la vizcaína	salt cod stewed with olive oil, peppers, tomatoes and onions
calmares en su tinta	baby squid cooked in its own ink
callos a la andaluza	tripe stew, with sausages, vegetables and seasonings
camarones en salsa verde	shrimps in a green sauce

capón relleno a la catalana	roasted capon stuffed with meat and nuts
carnero verde	stewed lamb with herbs and pignolis
cocido madrileño	mixed meat stew with chickpeas and vegetables
criadillas fritas	fried prairie oysters
empanadas	deep-fried pies filled with meat and vegetables
fabada asturiana	spicy mixture of white beans, pork, and sausages
gallina en pepitoria	chicken (fish with nuts, rice, garlic, and herbs)
huevos a la flamenca	baked eggs with green vegetables, pimento, tomato, chorizo and ham (a popular first course or light supper)
langosta a la barcelonesa	spiny lobster sauteed with chicken and tomatoes, garnished with almonds
lenguado a la andaluza	stuffed flounder or sole with a vegetable sauce
liebre estofada	hare and green beans, cooked in a tart liquid
marmitako	Basque tuna stew
pato a la sevillana	duck with olives
pescado a la sal	a white fish, packed in salt and roasted
pisto manchego	vegetable stew of tomatoes, peppers, onions, eggplant, and zucchini
rabo de toro	oxtail stewed in wine sauce
riñones al jerez	kidneys in sherry wine

| **sesos en caldereta** | calves brains, simmered in wine |
| **zarzuela** | fish stew; varies greatly depending on region but usually similar to a bouillabaisse |

SOME MEXICAN SPECIALTIES

The Mexican restaurants that proliferate throughout the U.S. are not truly representative of Mexican cooking. What is most familiar to non-Mexicans are the tortilla-based dishes described on page 134 and other dishes such as tamales (corn meal mixture stuffed with meat and steamed in a corn husk) but Mexicans view these as snacks. True Mexican cooking is as varied as the country itself, with much seafood along the coasts and other unusual dishes inland. Almost all Mexican cooking, however, is united in its use of chiles—those marvelously varied flavoring agents that range from very sweet to fiery hot. Also serving to unify Mexican cuisine are corn, beans, and rice, plus the herbs coriander and cumin and the spices cinnamon and cloves. As mentioned earlier, tortillas are the bread of this culture. Most often they are made from cornmeal, but in some parts of the country they are made from wheat flour instead.

In the vicinity of Mexico City, the food is fairly sophisticated, with a variety of ingredients appearing in dishes made with chicken, seafood, and various types of meat. Perhaps most famous is the **mole poblano**, in which turkey is served with a dark brown sauce that contains a variety of spices, ground poblano chiles, and a hint of chocolate.

Along the Mexican coast around Acapulco, as well as along the Gulf Coast, the dishes are mostly made with fresh ingredients, including seafood and fruit. In the Yucatán, the dishes reflect very strongly the ancient Mayan culture, and include **pollo pibil**, a chicken dish that is colored with annato, rolled in banana leaves, and steamed in a pit.

Wherever you are, ask for the local specialties. You are apt to sample one of the following.

amarillito	chicken or pork stew with green tomatoes, pumpkin, and chilies
carne asada	marinated pieces of beef that have been grilled
ceviche acapulqueño	raw fish or shellfish marinated in lime juice
chile relleno	stuffed chile (usually with cheese), that is coated with a light batter and fried
cochinita pibil	a suckling pig stuffed with fruits, chilies, and spices, then wrapped and baked in a pit
coloradito	chicken stew made with ancho chilies, tomatoes, and red peppers
frijoles refritos	kidney or pinto beans that have been cooked then mashed and reheated, often with chilies
guajolote relleno	turkey stuffed with fruit, nuts, and chilies and braised in wine
gorditas	bits of meat and cheese, fried and served with guacamole
guacamole	a purée of avocado, onion, garlic, and chilies, used as a condiment and a sauce for a variety of dishes
huachinango a la veracruzana	red snapper marinated in lime juice and baked with tomatoes, olives, capers, and chilies
jaibas en chilpachole	crabs cooked in a tomato sauce, flavored with the Mexican spice epazote
mancha manteles	a stew of chicken or pork, with a mixture of vegetables and in a sauce of nuts, green tomatoes, and chilies

muk-bil pollo	chicken pie with a cornmeal topping
papazul	rolled tortillas in a pumpkin sauce
panuchos	chicken dish baked with black beans and eggs
puchero	a stew made from a variety of meats, vegetables, fruits; served as a soup, then a main course
sopa de lima	a chicken soup laced with lime

SOUTH AND CENTRAL AMERICAN FOODS

This is a large area to cover, and any attempt to describe all the dishes is likely to be a bit foolish. Nevertheless, whereas Spain and Mexico have established readily identifiable cuisines, most countries in South and Central America also have some special dishes.

Peru and Ecuador, and parts of Bolivia and Chile, have a heritage of Incan culture and so the food is a combination of Indian and Spanish. Here are some specialties of this region.

anticuchos	skewered chunks of marinated beef heart, served with a hot sauce
caldillo de congrio	conger eel in a stew
humitas	cornmeal bits flavored with onion, peppers, and spices
llapingachos	potato-cheese croquettes
papas a la huancaína	potatoes in a spicy cheese sauce
pupusas (El Salvador)	cornmeal tortillas, stuffed with mashed kidney beans and crumbled fried bacon, cheese or pork

Argentina, Uruguay, and Paraguay are countries that favor beef, so some of their notable dishes include **carbonada**, a stew of meat with vegetables served in a pumpkin shell. **Carne con cuero** is roasted beef (done in the skin), and **matambre** is a large steak stuffed with spinach, eggs, and carrots, then braised. The **parrillada** is a type of English mixed grill, but just about every part of the animal is served (sweetbreads, kidney, liver). It usually comes with *chimichurri*, a piquant sauce made with garlic, parsley and olive oil. **Yerba mate** is a tea drunk in this region made by steeping leaves from a holly bush.

Colombia and Venezuela are noted for their **arepas**, which are cornmeal buns filled with meat, chicken or cheese. **Buñuelos** are balls of fried cornmeal, dusted with powdered sugar. **Empanadas** are also popular here, and these pies are usually stuffed with meat, onions, and raisins. **Hallacas** is a seasoned mixture of meat stuffed into cornmeal dough and wrapped in banana leaves—sort of a tamale. For fish, the Colombians have **vindo de pescado**, a fish stew that is cooked on an outdoor grill.

Bolivia is well known for its roast suckling pig, as well as **picante de pollo**, a fried chicken that is rather spicy. **Lomo montado** is a steak topped with a fried egg.

The Central American countries reflect the tastes and dishes of the Spanish, but incorporate many tropical fruits in their food. Look for **gallo en sidra** (chicken in cider), tripe and vegetable stews, and a whole range of meat stews-soups.

FOODS OF THE CARIBBEAN

There are some Spanish influences in Caribbean cooking, but you'll also find that West Africans have contributed to this food as have the French. If we concentrate on those islands where Spanish is spoken, the following items are likely to be found on menus.

asopao	a chicken and rice soup-stew with ham, peas, and peppers
chicharrones	deep-fried pork cracklings
frituras de bacalao (bacalaítos)	fish cakes that are fried in hot oil
mondongo	thick stew of beef tripe, potatoes, tomatoes, pumpkin, chickpeas, and tropical vegetables
moros y cristianos	black beans and rice
pasteles	a mixture of plantain and seasonings, steamed in a banana leaf
picadillo	mixture of chopped pork and beef with peppers, olives, raisins, and tomatoes
plátanos fritos	sliced, fried green bananas (plantains)
relleno de papa	potato dough stuffed with a mixture of meat, olives, and tomatoes
ropa vieja	literally "old clothes," this is shredded beef cooked with tomatoes and peppers
sancocho	a hearty Dominican stew with beef, pork, chicken, potatoes, tomatoes, and tropical vegetables (plantains, yams, pumpkin, yucca, yautía)

sandwich cubano   a half-loaf of crisp Italian or French bread filled with fresh pork, ham, cheese, and pickle, served oven-warmed

tostones   fried green plantain slices

yuca con mojo   stewed yucca root (cassava), in a garlic sauce

Travel Tips Save receipts on foreign purchases for declaring at customs on re-entry to the U.S. Some countries return a sales or value-added tax to foreign visitors. Take receipts to a special office at the store or to a tax rebate window at the airport of departure. Americans who buy costly objects abroad may be surprised to get a bill from their state tax collector. Most states with a sales tax levy "use" tariff on all items bought outside the home state, including those purchased abroad. Most tax agencies in these states will send a form for declaring and paying the assessment.

MEETING PEOPLE

Here are some greetings, introductions, and invitations, plus some phrases you might need if dating. Remember to shake hands when meeting people; a Spanish person may feel offended if you do not.

The Spanish, like ourselves, don't ask questions that are too personal at the beginning of an acquaintance. *Never* tell how much money you make, nor ask how much money the other person makes, unless you are lifelong friends.

Spanish people often invite recent acquaintances to their homes. In such cases, remember that modesty and diplomacy are your best assets.

SMALL TALK

My name is ___.	**Me llamo ___.**	*may YAH-mo*
Do you live here?	**¿Vive usted aquí?**	*BEE-bay oos-TEHD ah-KEE*
Where are you from?	**¿De dónde es usted?**	*day DOHN-day ehs oos-TEHD*
I am ___.	**Soy ___.**	*soy*
▓ from the United States	**de Estados Unidos**	*day ehs-TAH-dohs oo-NEE-dohs*
▓ from Canada	**de Canadá**	*de cah-nah-DAH*
▓ from England	**de Inglaterra**	*day een-glah-TEHR-ah*
I like Spain (South America) very much.	**Me gusta mucho España (Sud América).**	*may GOOS-tah MOO-choh ehs-PAHN-yah (sood ah-MEHR-ee-kah)*
How long will you be staying?	**¿Cuánto tiempo va a quedarse?**	*KWAHN-toh tee-EHM-poh bah ah kay-DAHR-say*

I'll stay for a few days (a week).	**Me quedaré unos días (una semana).** *may kay-dahr-AY oo-nohs DEE-ahs (oo-nah sehm-AHN-ah)*
What hotel are you at?	**¿En qué hotel está?** *ehn kay oh-TEL ehs-TAH*
I think it's ____.	**Creo que es ____.** *KREH-oh kay ehs*
■ (very) beautiful	**(muy) bonito(a)** *(mwee) bohn-EE-toh(ah)*
■ interesting	**interesante** *een-tehr-ehs-AHN-tay*
■ magnificent	**magnífico(a)** *mahg-NEEF-ee-koh(kah)*
■ wonderful	**maravilloso(a)** *mahr-ah-bee-YOH-soh(sah)*
■ boring	**aburrido(a)** *ah-boo-REE-doh(ah)*
■ ugly	**feo(a)** *FEH-oh(ah)*
■ too expensive	**demasiado caro(a)** *day-mah-SYAH-doh KAR-oh(ah)*
■ inexpensive	**barato(a)** *bah-RAH-toh(ah)*

INTRODUCTIONS

May I introduce my ____?	**Le presento a mi ____.** *lay pray-SENT-oh ah mee*
■ brother (sister)	**hermano(a)** *ehr-MAH-noh(nah)*
■ father (dad) [mother (mom)]	**padre (papá) [madre (mamá)]** *PAH-dray (pah-PAH) MAH-dray (mah-MAH)*
■ friend	**amigo(a)** *ah-MEE-goh(gah)*
■ husband (wife)	**marido (esposa)** *mahr-EE-doh (ehs-POH-sah)*
■ sweetheart	**novio(a)** *NOH-bee-oh(ah)*
■ son (daughter)	**hijo(a)** *EE-hoh(hah)*
How do you do?	**Mucho gusto (en conocerle).**

(Glad to meet you.)	*MOO-choh GOOS-toh (ehn koh-noh-SEHR-lay)*
The pleasure is mine.	**El gusto es mío.** *ehl GOOS-toh ehs MEE-oh*
I am a ____.	**Soy ____.** *soy*
■ teacher	**maestro(a)** *mah-EHS-troh(trah)*
■ doctor	**médico** *MED-ee-koh*
■ lawyer	**abogado** *ah-boh-GAH-doh*
■ businessperson	**persona de negocios** *pehr-SOHN-ah day neh-GOH-see-ohs*
■ student	**estudiante** *ehs-too-DYAHN-tay*
■ accountant	**contador** *kohn-tah-DOHR*
■ dentist	**dentista** *den-TEES-tah*
■ jeweler	**joyero** *hoy-EHR-oh*
■ nurse	**enfermera** *en-fehr-MEHR-ah*
■ manager	**gerente** *hehr-EN-teh*
■ salesman	**vendedor** *ben-deh-DOHR*
■ I'm retired	**estoy jubilado(a)** *es-toy hoo-bee-LAH-doh(ah)*
Let's take a picture.	**Saquemos una foto.** *sah-KEH-mohs oo-nah FOH-toh*
Stand here (there).	**Párese aquí (allá).** *PAH-ray-say ah-KEE (ah-YAH)*
Smile. That's it.	**Sonría. ¡Así es!** *sohn-REE-ah ah-SEE ehs*

DATING AND SOCIALIZING

Would you like to dance?	**¿Quiere usted bailar?** *kee-YEHR-ay oos-TEHD bah-ee-LAHR*

Yes, of course.	**Sí, con mucho gusto.** *see kohn MOO-choh GOOS-toh*
Would you like a drink?	**¿Quiere tomar algo?** *kee-YEHR-ay toh-MAHR AHL-goh*
May I take you home?	**¿Me permite llevarle a casa?** *may pehr-MEE-tay yeh-BAHR-lay ah KAH-sah*
May I call you?	**¿Puedo llamarle?** *PWEH-doh yah-MAHR-lay*
Are you doing anything tomorrow?	**¿Está libre mañana?** *eh-STAH LEE-bray mahn-YAH-nah*
Are you free this evening?	**¿Está usted libre esta tarde?** *eh-STAH oos-TEHD LEE-bray ehs-tah TAHR-day*
Would you like to go with me to ____?	**¿Quiere acompañarme a ____?** *kee-YEHR-ay ah-kohm-pahn-YAHR-may ah*
I'll wait for you in front of the hotel.	**Le espero delante del hotel.** *lay ehs-PEHR-oh del-AHN-tay del oh-TEL*
I'll pick you up at your house (hotel).	**Le recogeré en su casa (hotel).** *lay ray-koh-hehr-AY ehn soo KAH-sah (oh-TEL)*
What is your telephone number?	**¿Cuál es su número de teléfono?** *kwahl ehs soo NOO-mehr-oh day tel-EH-foh-noh*
Here's my telephone number (address).	**Aquí tiene mi número de teléfono (mi dirección).** *ah-KEE tee-EH-nay mee NOO-mehr-oh day tel-EH-foh-noh (mee dee-rehk-SYOHN)*
What is your e-mail address?	**¿Cuál es su correo electrónico?** *kwahl ehs soo kohr-REH-oh eh-lehk-TROH-nee-koh*

Will you write to me?	**¿Me escribirá?** *may ehs-kree-beer-AH*
I'm single (married).	**Soy soltero(a) casado(a).** *soy sohl-TEHR-oh(ah) kah-SAH-doh(ah)*
Is your husband (wife) here?	**¿Está aquí so esposo (esposa)?** *eh-STAH ah-KEE soo ehs-POH-soh (ehs-POH-sah)*
I'm here with my family.	**Estoy aquí con mi familia.** *ehs-TOY ah-KEE kohn mee fah-MEEL-yah*
Do you have any children?	**¿Tiene usted hijos?** *tee-EH-nay oos-TEHD EE-hohs*
How many?	**¿Cuántos?** *KWAHN-tohs*

SAYING GOOD-BYE

Nice to have met you.	**Ha sido un verdadero gusto.** *ah SEED-oh oon behr-dah-DEHR-oh GOOS-toh*
The pleasure was mine.	**El gusto ha sido mío.** *ehl GOOS-toh ah SEE-doh MEE-oh*
Regards to ____.	**Saludos a ____ de mi parte.** *sah-LOO-dohs ah day mee PAHR-tay*
Thanks for a wonderful evening.	**Gracias por su invitación. Ha sido una noche extraordinaria.** *GRAH-see-ahs pohr soo een-bee-tah-SYOHN. Ah see-doh oo-nah NOH-chay ehs-trah-ohr-dee-NAHR-ee-ah*
I must go home now.	**Tengo que marchame ahora.** *TEN-goh kay mahr-CHAR-may ah-OH-rah*
You must come to visit us.	**Debe venir a visitarnos.** *DEH-bay ben-EER ah bee-see-TAHR-nohs*

SHOPPING

Madrid is a city where you can still have clothes, suits, shoes, boots, and other things custom-made. Prices are not cheap, but for fine workmanship, the price is still considerably lower than in many other countries. Ready-to-wear shoes are also a good value—in style, workmanship, and price.

Handicrafts, such as pottery, leather work, weaving, and embroideries, are still found in many regions of Spain. Official government handicraft stores, called **Artespania**, are located in cities throughout Spain. There are three in Madrid alone. There are regional specialties, such as pottery, in Talavera (near Toledo) and Manises (near Valencia); damascene ware and steel knives and swords in Toledo; weaving and rug-making in Granada; fans, dolls, combs, and mantillas in Seville; leatherwork in Cordoba and Majorca and Menorca; olive wood products, pottery, embroideries, glassware, and artificial pearls in Majorca; and trendy, boutique sports clothes and jewelry in Ibiza.

Antiques are also widely available in Spain, ranging from **santos** (small wooden sculptures of saints) and rare books to painted cabinets, portable desks, and glass paintings. Many fine antique shops in Madrid are located along Calle de Prado, Carrera de San Jerónimo, and in El Rastro. There is a stamp-and-coin market held every Sunday morning from 10 A.M. to 2 P.M. on the Plaza Mayor in Madrid.

Modern art is also a good buy, especially in Madrid and Barcelona, where you will find works by internationally known Spanish artists such as Miró, Tapies, Sempere, and others. Kreister II, Galería Vijande, and Galería Egam are among the many reputable galleries in Madrid. In Barcelona there are many galleries along Rambla de Cataluña.

Madrid has three major department stores with branches in many other cities. They are Galerías Preciados, with three Madrid locations; El Corte Inglés, with four Madrid locations; and Celso García, with two Madrid stores.

Prices are fixed in department stores and most shops. In flea markets, antique shops, and some art galleries and custom workshops, you can attempt to "negotiate" prices if you wish.

In Mexico your money will bring you great values for crafts and handmade goods. In particular, Mexico has to offer some fine embroidery, silver items, and paper goods. You'll also find small, detailed figurines made from straw, wood carvings, pottery, and leather goods. Since it is such a large country, with so many different specialties, we can only suggest that you look about where you are, go to local markets, and see what you like. In the markets you will have to bargain for what you want; in shops, the prices are often fixed or there is only a small margin for bargaining.

The remainder of Latin America is too vast an area to be able to offer tips on specialty items. We suggest you read some tourist guides before leaving on your trip. In Latin American countries, shops are generally open from about 9 A.M. to 1 P.M., then open again about 3 P.M. and remain open until early evening, about 7. On Sunday, most shops are closed, but some markets are open and bustling.

GOING SHOPPING

Where can I find _____?	**¿Dónde se puede encontrar ____?** *DOHN-day say pweh-day ehn-kohn-TRAHR*
■ a bakery	**una panadería** *oo-nah pah-nah-dehr-EE-ah*
■ a bookstore	**una librería** *oo-nah leeb-rehr-EE-ah*
■ a butcher shop	**una carnicería** *oo-nah kahr-nee-sehr-EE-ah*
■ a camera shop	**una tienda de fotografía** *oo-nah tee-EHN-dah day foh-toh-grah-FEE-ah*
■ a candy store	**una confitería** *oo-nah kohn-fee-tehr-EE-ah*
■ a clothing store	**una tienda de ropa** *oo-nah tee-YEHN-dah day ROH-pah*

■ a delicatessen	**una tienda de ultramarinos** *oo-nah tee-YEHN-dah day ool-trah-mah-REE-nohs*
■ a department store	**una tienda de departamentos** *oo-nah tee-YEHN-dah day deh-pahr-tah-MEHN-tohs*
■ a pharmacy (chemist)	**una farmacia** *oo-nah fahr-MAH-see-ah*
■ a florist	**una florería** *oo-nah flohr-ehr-EE-ah*
■ a gift (souvenir) shop	**una tienda de regalos (recuerdos)** *oo-nah tee-YEHN-dah day ray-GAHL-ohs (ray-kwehr-dohs)*
■ a grocery store	**una tienda de comestibles** *oo-nah tee-YEHN-dah day koh-mehs-TEE-blays*
■ a hardware store (ironmonger)	**una ferretería** *oo-nah feh-reh-teh-REE-ah*
■ a jewelry store	**una joyería** *oo-nah hoy-ehr-EE-ah*
■ a liquor store	**una licorería** *oo-nah lee-kohr-ehr-EE-ah*
■ a newsstand	**un puesto de periódicos** *oon PWEHS-toh day peh-ree-OH-dee-kohs*
■ a shoe store	**una zapatería** *oo-nah sah-pah-tehr-EE-ah*
■ a shopping mall	**una galería comercial** *oo-nah gah-leh-REE-ah koh-mehr-see-AHL*
■ a supermarket	**un supermercado** *oon SOO-pehr-mehr-KAH-doh*
■ a tobacco shop	**un estanco** *oon ehs-TAHN-koh*
■ a toy store	**una juguetería** *oo-nah hoo-get-ehr-EE-ah*

BEING HELPED

Young man. Can you wait on me?

Joven. ¿Puede usted atenderme? *HOH-ben PWEH-day oos-TEHD ah-ten-DEHR-may*

Miss. Can you help me?

Señorita. ¿Me podría ayudar? *sehn-yohr-EE-tah may poh-DREE-ah ah-yoo-DAHR*

Do you take _____ cards?

¿Acepta tarjetas de _____? *ah-SEP-tah tahr-HAY-tahs day*

■ credit

crédito *KRED-ee-toh*

■ debit

débito *DEH-bee-toh*

■ which ones?

¿cuáles? *KWAH-lehs*

Can I pay with a traveler's check?

¿Puedo pagar con un cheque de viajero? *PWEH-doh pah-GAHR kohn oon CHEH-kay day bee-ah-HEHR-oh*

BOOKS

Is there a store that sells English-language books?

¿Hay una tienda que venda libros en inglés? *AH-ee oo-nah TYEHN-dah kay VEHN-dah LEE-brohs ehn een-GLAYS*

What is the best (biggest) bookstore here?

¿Cuál es la mejor librería (la librería más grande) de aquí? *kwahl ehs lah meh-HOHR lee-brehr-EE-ah (lah lee-brehr-EE-ah mahs grahn-day) day ah-KEE*

I'm looking for a copy of _____.

Busco un ejemplar de _____. *boos-koh oon eh-hem-PLAHR day*

I don't know the title (author).

No sé el título (autor). *noh say ehl TEE-too-loh (AH-oo-TOHR)*

I'm just looking.	**Estoy sólo mirando.** *ehs-TOY SOH-loh meer-AHN-doh*
Do you have books (novels) in English?	**¿Tiene usted libros (novelas) en inglés?** *tee-EHN-eh oos-TEHD LEE-brohs (noh-BEL-ahs) ehn een-GLAYSS*
I want a ____.	**Quiero ____.** *kee-EHR-oh*
■ guidebook	**una guía** *oon-ah GHEE-ah*
■ map of this city	**un plano de esta ciudad** *oon PLAH-noh day ehs-tah see-oo-DAHD*
■ a newspaper	**un periódico** *oon peh-ree-OH-dee-koh*
■ pocket dictionary	**un diccionario de bolsillo** *oon deek-syohn-AHR-ee-oh day bohl-SEE-yoh*
■ Spanish-English dictionary	**un diccionario español-inglés** *oon deek-syohn-AHR-ee-oh ehs-pahn-YOHL-een-GLAYSS*
Will you wrap them, please?	**¿Quiere envolverlos, por favor?** *kee-YEHR-ay ehn-bohl-BEHR-lohs pohr fah-BOHR*

CLOTHING

Would you please show me ____?	**¿Quiere enseñarme ____, por favor?** *kee-YEHR-ay ehn-sehn-YAHR-may pohr fah-BOHR*
■ a bathing suit	**un traje de baño** *oon TRAH-hay day BAHN-yo*
■ a belt	**un cinturón** *oon seen-toor-OHN*
■ a blouse	**una blusa** *oon-ah BLOO-sah*
■ boots	**botas** *BOH-tahs*
■ a bra	**un sostén** *oon soh-STEHN*

■ a dress **un vestido** *oon bes-TEE-doh*

■ an evening gown **un traje de noche** *oon TRAH-hay day NOH-chay*

■ leather (suede) gloves **guantes de cuero (de gamuza)** *GWAHN-tays day KWEHR-oh (day gah-MOOS-ah)*

■ a hat **un sombrero** *oon sohm-BREHR-oh*

■ a jacket **una chaqueta** *oon-nah chah-KAY-tah*

■ a pair of jeans **un par de vaqueros, un par de jeans** *oon pahr day bah-KEHR-ohs oon pahr day jeens*

■ a jogging suit **un traje de footing** *oon trah-hay day FOO-teen*

■ an overcoat **un abrigo** *oon ah-BREE-goh*

■ pajamas **piyamas** *pee-YAH-mahs*

■ panties **bragas** *BRAH-gahs*

■ pants **pantalones** *pahn-tah-LOHN-ays*

■ pantyhose **pantimedias** *pahn-tee-MEHD-ee-ahs*

■ a raincoat **un impermeable** *oon eem-pehr-may-AH-blay*

■ a robe **una bata** *oon-nah BAH-tah*

■ sandals **sandalias** *sahn-DAHL-ee-ahs*

■ a scarf **una bufanda** *oo-nah boo-FAHN-dah*

■ a shirt **una camisa** *oo-nah kah-MEES-ah*

■ (a pair of) shoes **(un par de) zapatos** *(oon pahr day) sah-PAH-tohs*

■ shorts (briefs) **calzoncillos** *kahl-sohn-SEE-yohs*

■ stockings **medias** *MED-ee-ahs*

■ a t-shirt **una camiseta** *oo-nah kah-mee-SEH-tah*

Do you have something ____?	**¿Tiene algo ____?**	*tee-EH-nay AHL-goh*
■ else	**más**	*mahs*
■ larger	**más grande**	*mahs grahn-day*
■ less expensive	**menos caro**	*may-nohs KAHR-oh*
■ longer	**más largo**	*mahs LAHR-goh*
■ of better quality	**de más alta calidad**	*day mahs AHL-tah kahl-ee-DAHD*
■ shorter	**más corto**	*mahs KOHR-toh*
■ smaller	**más pequeño**	*mahs peh-KAYN-yoh*

COLORS AND FABRICS

I (don't) like the color.	**(No) me gusta este color.**	*(noh) may GOOS-tah ehs-tay koh-LOHR*
Do you have it in ____?	**¿Tiene algo en ____?**	*tee-EHN-ay ahl-goh ehn*
■ black	**negro**	*NEH-groh*
■ blue	**azul**	*ah-SOOL*
■ brown	**marrón, pardo**	*mah-ROHN PAHR-doh*
■ gray	**gris**	*grees*
■ green	**verde**	*BEHR-day*
■ orange	**anaranjado**	*ah-nah-rahn-HAH-do*
■ pink	**rosado**	*roh-SAH-doh*
■ red	**rojo**	*ROH-hoh*
■ white	**blanco**	*BLAHN-koh*
■ yellow	**amarillo**	*ah-mah-REE-yoh*
I want something in ____.	**Quiero algo en ____.**	*kee-YEHR-oh AHL-goh ehn*
■ chiffon	**gasa**	*GAH-sah*
■ corduroy	**pana**	*PAH-nah*
■ cotton	**algodón**	*ahl-goh-DOHN*

■ denim	**dril de algodón, tela tejana** *dreel day ahl-goh-DOHN TEH-la tay-HAH-nah*
■ felt	**fieltro** *fee-EHL-troh*
■ flannel	**franela** *frah-NEHL-ah*
■ gabardine	**gabardina** *gah-bahr-DEEN-ah*
■ lace	**encaje** *ehn-KAH-hay*
■ leather	**cuero** *KWEHR-oh*
■ linen	**hilo** *EE-loh*
■ nylon	**nilón** *nee-LOHN*
■ satin	**raso** *RAH-soh*
■ silk	**seda** *SAY-dah*
■ suede	**gamuza** *gah-MOO-sah*
■ taffeta	**tafetán** *tah-fay-TAHN*
■ terrycloth	**tela de toalla** *TEHL-ah day toh-AH-yah*
■ velvet	**terciopelo** *tehr-see-oh-PEHL-oh*
■ wool	**lana** *LAH-nah*
■ worsted	**estambre** *ehs-TAHM-bray*
■ synthetic (polyester)	**sintético** *seen-TET-ee-koh*

I prefer ____.	**Prefiero ____.** *preh-FYEHR-oh*
■ permanent press	**algo inarrugable** *AHL-goh een-ah-roo-GAH-blay*
■ wash and wear	**algo que no se necesita planchar** *AHL-goh kay noh seh neh-seh-SEE-tah plahn-CHAHR*

Show me something ____.	**Muéstreme algo ____.** *MWEHS-ray-may AHL-goh*
■ in a solid color	**de color liso** *day koh-LOHR LEE-soh*
■ with stripes	**de rayas** *day RAH-ee-ahs*
■ with polka dots	**de lunares** *day loo-NAHR-ays*
■ in plaid	**de cuadros** *day KWAH-drohs*

Please take my measurements.	**¿Quiere tomarme la medida?** *kee-YEHR-ay toh-MAHR-may lah meh-DEE-dah*

I take size (My size is) ____.	**Llevo el tamaño (Mi talla es)** *YEH-boh ehl tah-MAHN-yoh (mee TAH-yah ehs)*
■ small	**pequeño(a)** *peh-KAYN-yoh(yah)*
■ medium	**mediano(a)** *meh-dee-AH-noh(yah)*
■ large	**grande** *GRAHN-day*

Can I try it on?	**¿Puedo probármelo?** *PWEHD-oh proh-BAHR-may-loh*
Can you alter it?	**¿Puede arreglarlo?** *PWEH-day ah-ray-GLAHR-loh*
Can I return the article?	**¿Puedo devolver el artículo?** *PWEH-doh day-bohl-BEHR ehl ahr-TEE-koo-loh*
Do you have something handmade?	**¿Tiene algo hecho a mano?** *tee-YEH-nay AHL-goh AY-choh ah MAH-noh*

CLOTHING MEASUREMENTS

MEN							
SHOES							
American	7	8	9	10	11	12	
British	6	7	8	9	10	11	
Continental	39	41	43	44	45	46	
SUITS, COATS							
American	34	36	38	40	42	44	46	48
British	44	46	48	50	54	56	58	60
Continental	44	46	48	50	52	56	58	60
SHIRTS							
American	14	$14\frac{1}{2}$	15	$15\frac{1}{2}$	16	$16\frac{1}{2}$	17	$17\frac{1}{2}$
British	14	$14\frac{1}{2}$	15	$15\frac{1}{2}$	16	$16\frac{1}{2}$	17	$17\frac{1}{2}$
Continental	36	37	38	39	40	41	42	43

WOMEN						
SHOES						
American	4	5	6	7	8	9
British	3	4	5	6	7	8
Continental	35	36	37	38	39	40
DRESSES, SUITS						
American	8	10	12	14	16	18
British	10	12	14	16	18	20
Continental	36	38	40	42	44	46
BLOUSES, SWEATERS						
American	32	34	36	38	40	42
British	34	36	38	40	42	44
Continental	40	42	44	46	48	50

The zipper doesn't work.	**No funciona la cremallera.** *noh foon-SYOHN-ah lah kray-mah-YEH-rah*
It doesn't fit me.	**No me queda bien.** *noh may KAY-dah BYEHN*
It fits very well.	**Me queda muy bien.** *may KAY-dah mwee BYEHN*
I'll take it.	**Me lo llevo.** *may loh YEH-boh*
Will you wrap it?	**¿Quiere envolverlo?** *kee-YEHR-ay ehn-bohl-BEHR-loh*
I'd like to see the pair of shoes (boots) in the window.	**Quisiera ver el par de zapatos (botas) de la vitrina.** *kee-see-YEH-rah behr ehl pahr day sah-PAH-tohs (BOH-tahs) day lah bee-TREE-nah*
They're too narrow (wide).	**Son demasiado estrechos (anchos).** *sohn day-mahs-ee-AH-doh ehs-TRAY-chohs (AHN-chohs)*
I'll take them.	**Me los llevo.** *may lohs YEH-boh*
I also need shoe-laces.	**También necesito cordones de zapato.** *tahm-BYEHN neh-say-SEE-toh kohr-DOHN-ays day sah-PAH-toh*
That's all I want for now.	**Eso es todo por ahora.** *eh-soh ehs TOH-doh pohr ah-OHR-ah*

ELECTRICAL APPLIANCES

Electric current in the U.S. is 110V AC, whereas in Spain it is 220V AC. Unless your electric shaver or charger for laptop/phone is able to handle both currents, you will need to purchase an adapter. When making a purchase, please be aware that *some* Spanish products are engineered to work with either system while others will require an adapter. When making a purchase, be careful to check the warranty to ensure that the product is covered internationally.

FOODS AND HOUSEHOLD ITEMS

Always keep in mind the restrictions you will face at customs when you return to your own country. Fresh foods often are not permitted.

When you go to a food market or shop, bring your own bag along with you to tote home your groceries. A collapsible net bag is very useful.

I'd like ____.   **Quisiera ____.** *kee-SYEHR-ah*

■ a bar of soap   **una pastilla de jabón** *oo-nah pahs-TEE-yah day hah-BOHN*

■ a bottle of juice   **una botella de jugo** *oo-nah boh-TEH-yah day HOO-goh*

■ a box of cereal   **una caja de cereal** *oo-nah KAH-hah day sehr-ay-AHL*

■ a half-kilo of cherries   **medio kilo de cerezas** *MED-ee-oh KEE-loh day sehr-AY-sahs*

■ a liter of milk   **un litro de leche** *oon LEE-troh day LEH-chay*

■ a package of candies   **un paquete de dulces** *oon pah-KEH-tay day dool-sayss*

■ 100 grams of cheese   **cien gramos de queso** *see-EHN GRAH-mohs day KAY-soh*

■ a roll of toilet paper   **un rollo de papel higiénico** *oon ROH-yoh day pah-pel ee-hee-EHN-ee-koh*

What is this (that)?	**¿Qué es esto (eso)?** *kay ehs EHS-toh (EHS-oh)*
Is it fresh?	**¿Está fresco?** *ehs-TAH FRES-koh*
I'd like a kilo (about 2 pounds) of oranges.*	**Quisiera un kilo de naranjas.** *kee-SYEHR-ah oon KEE-loh day nah-RAHN-hahs*

■ 200 grams (about ½ pound) of cookies (cakes)

doscientos gramos de galletas (pasteles) *dohs-SYEHN-tohs GRAH-mohs day gah-YEH-tahs (pahs-TEH-lehs)*

■ 100 grams (about ¼ pound) of ham

cien gramos de jamón *SYEHN GRAH-mohs day hah-MOHN*

* Note: Common measurements for purchasing foods are a kilo, or fractions thereof, and 100, 200, and 500 grams. See also the pages on numbers, 13–17.

METRIC WEIGHTS AND MEASURES			
Solid Measures (approximate measurements only)			
OUNCES	GRAMS (GRAMOS)	GRAMS	OUNCES
¼	7	10	⅓
½	14	100	3½
¾	21	300	10½
1	28	500	18
POUNDS	KILOGRAMS (KILOS)	KILOGRAMS	POUNDS
1	½	1	2¼
5	2¼	3	6½
10	4½	5	11
20	9	10	22
50	23	50	110
100	45	100	220

METRIC WEIGHTS AND MEASURES			
Liquid Measures (approximate measurements only)			
OUNCES	MILLILITERS **(MILILITROS)**	MILLILITERS	OUNCES
1	30	10	$\frac{1}{3}$
6	175	50	$1\frac{1}{2}$
12	350	100	$3\frac{1}{2}$
16	475	150	5
GALLONS	LITERS **(LITROS)**	LITERS	GALLONS
1	$3\frac{3}{4}$	1	$\frac{1}{4}$ (1 quart)
5	19	5	$1\frac{1}{3}$
10	38	10	$2\frac{1}{2}$

JEWELRY

I'd like to see ____.   **Quisiera ver ____.** *kee-SYEHR-ah behr*

- a bracelet   **un brazalete** *oon brah-sah-LAY-tay*
- a brooch   **un broche** *oon BROH-chay*
- a chain   **una cadena** *oon-nah kah-DAY-nah*
- a charm   **un dije** *oon DEE-hay*
- some earrings   **unos aretes** (in Spain, **pendientes**) *oo-nohs ah-REH-tays (pen-DYEHN-tays)*
- a necklace   **un collar** *oon koh-YAHR*
- a pin   **un alfiler** *oon ahl-fee-LEHR*

a ring	**un anillo (una sortija)** *oon ahn-EE-yoh (oo-nah sohr-TEE-hah)*
a rosary	**un rosario** *oon roh-SAHR-ee-oh*
a (wrist) watch	**un reloj (de pulsera)** *oon ray-LOH (day pool-SEHR-ah)*
Is this ____?	**¿Es esto ____?** *ehs EHS-toh*
gold	**oro** *OH-roh*
platinum	**platino** *plah-TEE-noh*
silver	**plata** *PLAH-tah*
stainless steel	**acero inoxidable** *ah-SEHR-oh een-ohks-ee-DAH-blay*
Is it solid or gold-plated?	**¿Es macizo o dorado?** *ehs mah-SEE-soh oh dohr-AH-doh*
How many carats is it?	**¿De cuántos quilates es?** *day KWAHN-tohs kee-LAH-tays ehs*
What is that stone?	**¿Qué es esa piedra?** *kay ehs EHS-ah pee-YEHD-drah*
I want ____.	**Quiero ____.** *kee-YEHR-oh*
an amethyst	**una amatista** *oo-nah ah-mah-TEES-tah*
an aquamarine	**una aguamarina** *oo-nah ah-gwah-mah-REE-nah*
a diamond	**un diamante** *oon dee-ah-MAHN-tay*
an emerald	**una esmeralda** *oon-nah ehs-mehr-AHL-dah*
ivory	**marfil** *mahr-FEEL*
jade	**jade** *HAH-day*
onyx	**ónix** *OH-neeks*
pearls	**perlas** *PEHR-lahs*
a ruby	**un rubí** *oon roo-BEE*

■ a sapphire	**un zafiro** *oon sah-FEER-oh*
■ a topaz	**un topacio** *oon toh-PAH-see-oh*
■ turquoise	**turquesa** *toor-KAY-sah*
How much is it?	**¿Cuánto vale?** *KWAHN-toh BAH-lay*
Can you fix this watch for me?	**¿Me puede arreglar este reloj?** *may PWEH-day ah-ray-GLAHR EHS-tay ray-LOH*
It's stopped.	**Está parado.** *ehs-TAH pah-RAH-doh*
It's running slow (fast).	**Se atrasa (Se adelanta).** *say ah-TRAH-sah (say ah-deh-LAHN-tah)*
When will it be ready?	**¿Cuándo estará listo?** *KWAHN-doh ehs-tah-RAH LEES-toh*
I need ____.	**Necesito ____.** *neh-say-SEE-toh*
■ a crystal	**un cristal** *oon kree-STAHL*
■ a battery	**una pila** *oo-nah PEE-lah*

NEWSPAPERS AND MAGAZINES

Do you carry English newspapers (magazines)?	**¿Tiene usted periódicos (revistas) en inglés?** *tee-YEHN-ay oos-TEHD peh-ree-OH-dee-kohs (ray-BEES-tahs) en een-GLAYSS*
I'd like to buy some postcards.	**Quisiera comprar postales.** *kee-SYEHR-ah kohm-PRAHR pohs-TAHL-ays*
Do you have stamps?	**¿Tiene sellos?** *tee-YEHN-ay SEH-yohs*
How much is that?	**¿Cuánto es?** *KWAHN-toh ehs*

PHOTOGRAPHY, VIDEO, AND AUDIO EQUIPMENT

Where is there a camera shop? | **¿Dónde hay una tienda de fotografía?** *DOHN-day AH-ee oo-nah tee-EHN-dah deh foh-toh-grah-FEE-ah*

Do you sell cameras? | **¿Vende usted cámaras?** *VEHN-deh oos-TEHD KAH-mah-rahs*

I would like a(n) ____ camera. | **Quiero una cámara ____.** *kee-EH-roh oo-nah KAH-mah-rah*

 disposable | **desechable** *deh-seh-CHAH-bleh*

inexpensive | **no muy cara** *noh MOO-ee KAH-rah*

14-megapixel | **de catorce megapíxeles** *deh kah-TOHR-seh meh-gah-PEEK-seh-lehs*

3-inch screen | **con pantalla de tres pulgadas** *kohn pahn-TAH-yah deh trehs pool-GAH-dahs*

point-and-shoot | **automática** *ow-toh-MAH-tee-kah*

reflex | **réflex** *REH-flehks*

waterproof | **impermeable** *eem-pehr-meh-AH-bleh*

I need a camera with ____. | **Necesito una cámara con ____.** *neh-seh-SEE-toh oo-nah KAH-mah-rah kohn*

movie mode | **modalidad de cine** *moh-dah-lee-DAHD deh SEE-neh*

manual controls | **controles manuales** *kohn-TROH-lehs mahn-WAH-lehs*

■ interchangeable
lenses

lentes intercambiables *LEHN-tehs
een-tehr-kahm-bee-AH-blehs*

■ an adjustable
screen

una pantalla ajustable *oo-nah
pahn-TAH-yah ah-hoos-TAH-bleh*

I need a _____.

Necesito _____. *Neh-seh-SEE-toh*

■ memory card

una tarjeta de memoria *oo-nah
tahr-HEH-tah deh meh-MOH-ree-ah*

■ a battery

una pila *oo-nah PEE-lah*

■ a case

un estuche *oon ehs-TOO-cheh*

■ a tripod

un trípode *oon TREE-poh-deh*

■ a filter

un filtro *oon FEEL-troh*

■ a Canon zoom
lens

un lente zoom para Canon *oon
LEHN-teh PAH-rah KAH-nohn*

How much does
it cost?

¿Cuánto cuesta? *KWAHN-toh
KWEHS-tah*

Here's the card.

Aquí está la tarjeta. *Ah-KEE ehs-
TAH lah tahr-HEH-tah*

Please make three
prints from each
frame.

**Por favor, haga tres copias de cada
cuadro.** *pohr fah-BOHR AH-gah
trehs KOH-pee-ahs deh KAH-dah
KWAH-droh*

When can I pick
up the pictures?

¿Cuándo puedo recoger las fotos?
*KWAHN-doh PWEH-doh reh-koh-
HEHR lahs FOH-tohs*

Be aware that Europe uses broadcasting and recording
systems that are often incompatible with those of
the U.S.

Is there a
multimedia store
around here?

**¿Hay una tienda de productos
electrónicos por aquí?** *AH-ee oo-
nah tee-EHN-dah deh ahr-TEE-koo-
lohs eh-lehk-TROH-nee-kohs pohr
ah-KEE*

I'm looking for iPod (iPad) accessories.	**Busco accesorios para el iPod (iPad).** *BOOS-koh ahk-seh-SOH-ree-ohs PAH-rah ehl ee-pohd (ee-pahd)*
I would like ____.	**Quisiera ____.** *kee-see-EH-rah*
▨ a base	**una base** *oo-nah BAH-seh*
▨ cables	**cables** *KAHB-lehs*
▨ earpieces	**auriculares** *ow-ree-koo-LAH-rehs*
▨ a jack	**un enchufe hembra** *oon ehn-CHOO-feh EHM-brah*
▨ a case	**un estuche** *oon ehs-TOO-cheh*
▨ a memory card	**una tarjeta de memoria** *oo-nah tahr-HEH-tah deh meh-MOH-ree-ah*
I want a video recorder.	**Quiero una filmadora de vídeo.** *kee-EH-roh oo-nah feel-mah-DOH-rah deh vee-DEH-oh*
Will the warranty be honored in the United States?	**¿Será válida la garantía en los Estados Unidos?** *seh-RAH VAH-lee-dah lah gah-rahn-TEE-ah ehn lohs ehs-TAH-dohs oo-NEE-dohs*
Do you sell (rent) DVD movies?	**¿Venden (Arriendan) películas en DVD?** *VEHN-dehn (ahr-ree-EHN-dahn) peh-LEE-koo-lahs ehn deh-veh-DEH?*
Are these dubbed or with subtitles?	**¿Son éstas dobladas o con subtítulos?** *sohn EHS-tahs doh-BLAH-dahs oh kohn soob-TEE-too-lohs*

How much for renting one?	**¿Cuánto cuesta arrendar una?** *KWAHN-toh KWEHS-tah ahr-rehn-DAHR oo-nah*
How long can I keep it?	**¿Cuánto tiempo puedo tenerla?** *KWAHN-toh tee-EHM-poh PWEH-doh teh-NEHR-lah*
Where is the ____ section?	**¿Dónde está la sección de ____?** *DOHN-day ehs-TAH lah sek-SYOHN day*

- classical music **la música clásica** *lah MOO-see-kah KLAHS-ee-kah*
- folk music **la música folklórica** *lah MOO-see-kah fohl-KLOHR-ee-kah*
- latest hits **los últimos éxitos** *lahs OOL-tee-mohs EHK-see-tohs*
- rock 'n roll **el rocanrol** *ehl rohk-ahn-ROHL*
- opera **la ópera** *lah OH-pehr-ah*
- popular music **la música popular** *lah MOO-see-kah poh-poo-LAHR*
- Spanish music **la música española** *lah MOO-see-kah ehs-pahn-YOH-lah*

SOUVENIRS, HANDICRAFTS

I'd like ____.	**Quisiera ____.** *kee-SYEHR-ah*
a pretty gift	**un regalo bonito** *oon ray-GAH-loh boh-NEE-toh*
a small gift	**un regalito** *oon ray-gah-LEE-toh*
a souvenir	**un recuerdo** *oon ray-KWEHR-doh*
It's for ____.	**Es para ____.** *ehs pah-rah*

I don't want to spend more than ____ dollars.	**No quiero gastar más de ____ dólares.** *noh kee-YEHR-oh gahs-TAHR mahs day ___ DOH-lahr-ays*
Could you suggest something?	**¿Podría usted sugerir algo?** *poh-DREE-ah oos-TEHD soo-hehr-EER AHL-goh*
Would you show me your selection of ____?	**¿Quiere enseñarme su surtido de ____?** *kee-YEHR-ay ehn-sen-YAHR-may soo soor-TEE-doh day*

▪ blown glass **vidrio soplado** *BEE-dree-oh soh-PLAH-doh*

▪ carved objects **objetos de madera tallada** *ohb-HET-ohs day mah-DEHR-ah tah-YAH-dah*

▪ cut crystal **vidrio tallado** *BEE-dree-oh tah-YAH-doh*

▪ dolls **muñecas** *moon-YEH-kahs*

▪ earthenware (pottery) **loza** *LOH-sah*

▪ fans **abanicos** *ah-bah-NEE-kohs*

▪ jewelry **joyas** *HOY-ahs*

▪ lace **encaje** *ehn-KAH-hay*

▪ leather goods **objetos de cuero** *ohb-HET-ohs day KWEHR-oh*

▪ musical instruments **instrumentos musicales** *een-stroo-MEN-tohs moo-see-KAHL-ays*

▪ perfumes **perfumes** *pehr-FOO-mays*

▪ pictures **dibujos** *dee-BOO-hohs*

▪ posters **carteles** *kahr-TEHL-ays*

▪ religious articles **artículos religiosos** *ahr-TEE-koo-lohs ray-lee-hee-OH-sohs*

LITTLE TREASURES

Is this an antique?	**¿Es una antigüedad?** *ehs oo-nah ahn-tee-gway-DAHD*
Is it a reproduction?	**¿Es una reproducción?** *ehs oo-nah ray-proh-dook-SYOHN*
Is this handmade?	**¿Está hecho a mano?** *eh-STAH AY-choh ah MAH-noh*
What is the name of this type of work?	**¿Cómo se llama este tipo de trabajo?** *KOH-moh say YAH-mah EHS-tay TEE-poh day trah-BAH-ho*
What are the local specialties?	**¿Cuáles son las especialidades locales?** *KWAHL-ays sohn lahs ehs-pehs-yah-lee-DAHD-ays loh-KAHL-ays*
Is this washable?	**¿Es lavable?** *ehs lah-bah-blay*
Will it shrink?	**¿Se encoge?** *say ehn-KOH-hay*
Should it be washed by hand?	**¿Debe lavarse a mano?** *DEH-bay lah-BAHR-say ah MAH-noh*
Should it be washed in cold water?	**¿Debe lavarse en agua fría?** *DEH-bay lah-BAHR-say ehn AH-gwah FREE-ah*
Can it go in the dryer?	**¿Se puede meter en la secadora?** *say PWEHD-ay meh-TEHR ehn lah seh-kah-DOHR-ah*
Can this go in the dishwasher?	**¿Se puede meter esto en el lava-platos?** *say PWEH-day meh-TEHR ehs-toh ehn ehl lah-bah-PLAH-tohs*
Is it ovenproof?	**¿Está a prueba de horno?** *ehs-TAH ah PRWEH-bah day OR-noh*

Is this safe to use for cooking?	**¿Se puede usar sin peligro para cocinar?** *say PWEH-day oo-SAHR SEEN pe-LEE-groh pah-rah koh-see-NAHR*
What is the lead content?	**¿Qué contenido de plomo tiene?** *kay kohn-ten-EE-doh day PLOH-moh tee-YEHN-ay*
Did you make this yourself?	**¿Lo ha hecho usted?** *loh ah AY-choh oss-TEHD*

BARGAINING

In Latin American open markets you will be expected to bargain for everything you want to purchase. The key to successful bargaining is to end up with a price that is fair for both you and the merchant. Begin by asking the price, then make your own offer about half to two-thirds of the asking price. Usually the merchant will make another offer and you can listen and consider the object, perhaps finding a little problem with it—a tear, a scrape, some unevenness. A little discussion back and forth, and you'll soon have it at a fair price. If you do not understand numbers, then the seller will write the number down for you. At the conclusion, smile and thank the merchant, expressing your happiness with the result.

Please, madam, how much is this?	**Por favor, señora, ¿cuánto vale ésto?** *pohr fah-BOHR sehn-YOHR-ah KWAHN-toh BAH-lay EHS-toh*
Oh, no, that is more than I can spend.	**Ay, no, eso es más de lo que puedo gastar.** *AH-ee noh EHS-oh ehs MAHS day loh kay PWEH-doh gahs-TAHR*
How about ___?	**¿Y si le doy ___?** *EE see lay doy*
No, that is too high. Would you take ___?	**No, eso es demasiado. ¿Aceptaría ___?** *noh EHS-oh ehs day-mahs-ee-AH-doh ah-sep-tahr-ER-ah*

But there seems to be a scratch (tear) here.	**Me parece que hay un arañazo (un roto) aquí.** *may pahr-ay-say kay AH-ee oon ah-rahn-YAH-soh ah-KEE*
Yes, that's fine. I'll take it.	**Así está bien. Me lo llevo.** *ah-SEE ehs-TAH byehn may loh YEH-boh*
Thank you. Have a nice day.	**Gracias. Que lo pase bien.** *GRAH-see-ahs kay loh PAH-say byehn*

STATIONERY ITEMS

I want to buy ____.	**Quiero comprar ____.** *kee-YEHR-oh kohm-PRAHR*
▓ a ball-point pen	**un bolígrafo** *oon boh-LEE-grah-foh*
▓ a deck of cards	**una baraja** *oo-nah bahr-AH-hah*
▓ envelopes	**sobres** *SOH-brays*
▓ an eraser	**una goma de borrar** *oo-nah GOH-mah day bohr-AHR*
▓ glue	**pegamento** *peh-gah-MEHN-toh*
▓ a notebook	**un cuaderno** *oon kwah-DEHR-noh*
▓ pencils	**lápices** *LAH-pee-sayss*
▓ a pencil sharpener	**un sacapuntas** *oon sah-kah-POON-tahs*
▓ printing paper	**papel para impresora** *pah-PEL PAH-rah eem-preh-SOH-rah*
▓ a ruler	**una regla** *oo-nah REHG-lah*
▓ Scotch tape	**cinta adhesiva** *SEEN-tah ahd-ehs-EE-bah*
▓ some string	**cuerda** *KWEHR-dah*

| wrapping paper | **papel de envolver** *pah-PEL day ehn-bohl-BEHR* |
| a writing pad | **un bloc de papel** *oon blohk day pah-PEL* |

TOILETRIES

In Spain, a drugstore (chemist) doesn't carry toiletries. There you will have to go to a **perfumería**. In Latin America, however, you'll find cosmetics and other toiletries at drugstores and pharmacies as well.

Do you have ____?	**¿Tiene usted ____?** *tee-YEHN-ay oo-STEHD*
bobby pins	**horquillas** *ohr-KEE-yahs*
a brush	**un cepillo** *oon sep-EE-yoh*
cleansing cream	**crema limpiadora** *KRAY-mah leem-pee-ah-DOHR-ah*
a comb	**un peine** *oon PAY-nay*
condoms	**condones** *kohn-DOH-nehs*
deodorant	**un desodorante** *oon dehs-oh-dohr-AHN-tay*
(disposable) diapers	**pañales (desechables)** *pahn-YAH-lays (dehs-ay-CHAH-blays)*
emery boards	**limas de cartón** *LEE-mahs day kahr-TOHN*
eyeliner	**un lápiz de ojos** *oon LAH-pees day OH-hohs*
hairspray	**laca** *LAH-kah*
lipstick	**lápiz de labios** *LAH-pees day LAH-bee-ohs*

■ makeup	**maquillaje**	*mah-kee-YAH-hay*
■ mascara	**rimel**	*ree-MEHL*
■ a mirror	**un espejo**	*oon ehs-PAY-ho*
■ mouthwash	**un lavado bucal**	*oon lah-bah-doh boo-kahl*
■ nail clippers	**un cortauñas**	*oon kohr-tah-oon-yahs*
■ a nail file	**una lima de uñas**	*oo-nah lee-mah day OON-yahs*
■ nail polish	**esmalte de uñas**	*ehs-MAHL-tay day OON-yahs*
■ nail polish remover	**un quita-esmalte**	*oon kee-tah ehs-MAHL-tay*
■ a razor	**una navaja**	*oo-nah nah-BAH-hah*
■ razor blades	**hojas de afeitar**	*OH-hahs day ah-fay-TAHR*
■ sanitary napkins	**servilletas higiénicas**	*sehr-bee-YEH-tahs ee-HYEHN-ee-kahs*

▥ scissors	**tijeras**	*tee-HAIR-ahs*
▥ shampoo	**champú**	*chahm-POO*
▥ shaving lotion	**loción de afeitar**	*loh-SYOHN day ah-fay-TAHR*
▥ soap	**jabón**	*hah-BOHN*
▥ a sponge	**una esponja**	*oo-nah ehs-POHN-hah*
▥ talcum powder	**talco**	*TAHL-koh*
▥ tampons	**tapones**	*tah-POHN-ays*
▥ tissues	**pañuelos de papel**	*pahn-yoo-EH-lohs day pah-PEL*
▥ toilet paper	**papel higiénico**	*pah-PEL ee-hy-EHN-ee-koh*
▥ a toothbrush	**un cepillo de dientes**	*oon sep-EE-yoh day dee-YEHN-tays*
▥ toothpaste	**pasta de dientes**	*pah-stah day dee-YEHN-tays*
▥ tweezers	**pinzas**	*PEEN-sahs*

PERSONAL CARE AND SERVICES

If your hotel doesn't offer these services, ask the attendant at the desk to recommend someone nearby.

AT THE BARBER

Where is there a good barber shop?	**¿Dónde hay una buena barbería?** *DOHN-day AH-ee oo-nah BWEH-nah bahr-behr-EE-ah*
Do I have to wait long?	**¿Tengo que esperar mucho?** *ten-goh kay ehs-pehr-AHR MOO-choh*
Am I next?	**¿Me toca a mí?** *may TOH-kay ah mee*
I want a shave.	**Quiero que me afeiten.** *kee-YEHR-oh kay may ah-FAY-tehn*
I want a haircut (razorcut).	**Quiero un corte de pelo (a navaja)** *kee-YEHR-oh oon KOHR-tay day PEH-loh (ah nah-BAH-hah)*
Leave it long.	**Déjelo largo.** *DAY-hay-loh LAHR-goh*
I want it (very) short.	**Lo quiero (muy) corto.** *loh kee-YEHR-oh (mwee) KOHR-toh*
You can cut a little ____.	**Puede cortar on poquito ____.** *PWEH-day kohr-TAHR oon poh-KEE toh*
■ in back	**por detrás** *pohr day-TRAHS*
■ in front	**por delante** *pohr day-LAHN-tay*

▩ off the top	**de arriba** *day ah-REE-bah*
▩ on the sides	**a los lados** *ah lohs LAH-dohs*

Cut a little bit more here.

Córteme on poco más aquí. *KOHR-tay-may oon POH-koh mahs ah-KEE*

That's enough.

Eso es bastante. *EH-soh ehs bah-STAHN-tay*

I (don't) want ____.

(No) quiero ____. *(noh) kee-YEHR-oh*

▩ shampoo	**champú** *chahm-POO*
▩ tonic	**tónico** *TOHN-ee-koh*

Use the scissors only.

Use sólo las tijeras. *oo-say soh-loh lahs tee-HAIR-ahs*

Trim my ____.

Recórteme ____. *ray-KOHR-tay-may*

▩ beard	**la barba** *lah bahr-bah*
▩ moustache	**el bigote** *ehl bee-GOH-tay*
▩ sideburns	**las patillas** *lahs pah-TEE-yahs*

I'd like to look at myself in the mirror.

Quisiera mirarme al espejo. *kee-SYEHR-ah meer-AHR-may ahl ehs-PAY-hoh*

How much do I owe you?

¿Cuánto le debo? *KWAHN-toh lay DEH-boh*

AT THE BEAUTY PARLOR

Is there a beauty parlor (hairdresser) near the hotel?	**¿Hay un salón de belleza (una peluquería) cerca del hotel?** *AH-ee oon sah-LOHN day beh-YEH-sah (oo-nah pel-oo-kehr-EE-ah) SEHR-kah del oh-TEL*
I'd like an appointment for this afternoon (tomorrow).	**Quisiera hacer una cita para esta tarde (mañana).** *kee-SYEHR-ah ah-SEHR oo-nah SEE-tah pah-rah EHS-tah TAHR-day (mahn-YA-nah)*
Can you give me _____?	**¿Puede darme _____?** *PWEH-day DAHR-may*

▓ a color rinse   **un enjuague de color** *oon ehn-hoo-AH-gay day koh-LOHR*

▓ a facial massage   **un masaje facial** *oon mah-SAH-hay fah-see-AHL*

▓ a haircut   **un corte de pelo** *oon KOHR-tay day PEH-loh*

▓ a manicure   **una manicura** *oon-nah mah-nee-KOOR-ah*

▓ a pedicure   **una pedicura** *oo-nah ped-ee-KOOR-ah*

▓ a permanent	**una permanente**	*oon-nah pehr-mah-NEN-tay*
▓ a shampoo	**un champú**	*oon chahm-POO*
▓ a tint	**un tinte**	*oon TEEN-tay*
▓ a touch-up	**un retoque**	*oon ray-TOH-kay*
▓ a wash and set	**un lavado y peinado**	*oon lah-bah-doh ee pay-NAH-doh*
▓ just a trim	**sólo las puntas**	*soh-loh lahs POON-tahs*

I'd like to see a color chart. **Quisiera ver un muestrario.** *kee-SYEHR-ah behr oon mwehs-TRAHR-ee-oh*

I want a ____ color. **Quiero un color ____.** *kee YEHR-oh oon koh-LOHR*

▓ auburn	**rojizo**	*roh-HEE-soh*
▓ (light) blond	**un rubio (claro)**	*oon ROO-bee-oh (KLAHR-oh)*
▓ brunette	**castaño**	*kas-TAHN-yo*
▓ darker	**más oscuro**	*mahs oh-SKOOR-oh*
▓ lighter	**más claro**	*mahs KLAH-roh*
▓ the same color	**el mismo color**	*ehl MEES-moh koh-LOHR*

Don't apply any hairspray. **No me ponga laca.** *noh may POHN-gah LAH-kah*

Not too much hairspray. **Sólo un poco de laca.** *SOH-loh oon POH-koh day LAH-kah*

I want my hair ____. **Quiero el pelo ____.** *kee-YEHR-oh ehl peh-loh*

▓ with bangs	**con flequillo**	*kohn fleh-KEE-yoh*
▓ in a bun	**con un moño**	*kohn oon MOHN-yoh*
▓ in curls	**con bucles**	*kohn boo-KLAYS*
▓ with waves	**con ondas**	*kohn OHN-dahs*

I'd like to look at myself in the mirror.	**Quiero mirarme al espejo.** *kee-YEHR-oh meer-AHR-may ahl ehs-PAY-hoh*
How much do I owe you?	**¿Cuánto le debo?** *KWAHN-toh lay DEH-boh*
Is tipping included?	**¿Está incluída la propina?** *es-TAH een-kloo-EE-dah lah proh-PEE-nah*

LAUNDRY AND DRY CLEANING

Where is the nearest laundry (dry cleaners)?	**¿Dónde está la lavandería (la tintorería) más cercana?** *DOHN-day ehs-TAH lah lah-bahn-deh-REE-ah (lah teen-TOHR-ehr-EE-ah) mahs sehr-KAH-nah*
I have a lot of (dirty) clothes to be ____.	**Tengo mucha ropa (sucia) que ____.** *TEN-goh MOO-chah ROH-pah (SOO-see-ah) kay*
▥ (dry) cleaned	**limpiar (en seco)** *leem-pee-AHR (ehn SEH-koh)*
▥ washed	**lavar** *lah-BAHR*
▥ mended	**arreglar** *ah-ray-GLAHR*
▥ ironed	**planchar** *plahn-CHAHR*
Here's the list.	**Aquí tiene la lista.** *ah-KEE tee-EH-neh lah LEES-tah*
▥ 3 shirts (men's)	**tres camisas (de hombre)** *trays kah-mee-sahs (day OHM-bray)*
▥ 6 pairs of socks	**seis pares de calcetines** *sayss pah-rays day kahl-say-TEEN-ays*
▥ 1 blouse (nylon)	**una blusa (de nilón)** *oo-nah BLOO-sah (day nee-LOHN)*

4 shorts (under-wear)	**cuatro calzoncillos** *KWAH-troh kahl-sohn-SEEL-yohs*
2 pajamas	**dos pijamas** *dohs pee-HAHM-ahs*
2 suits	**dos trajes** *dohs TRAH-hays*
3 ties	**tres corbatas** *trays kohr-BAH-tahs*
2 dresses (cotton)	**dos vestidos (de algodón)** *dohs behs-tee-dohs (day ahl-go-DOHN)*
2 skirts	**dos faldas** *dohs FAHL-dahs*
1 sweater (wool)	**un suéter (de lana)** *oon soo-EH-tehr (day LAH-nah)*
I need them for ____.	**Las necesito para ____.** *lahs neh-seh-SEE-toh PAH-rah*
tonight	**esta noche** *EHS-tah NOH-chay*
tomorrow	**mañana** *mahn-YAH-nah*
next week	**la semana próxima** *lah seh-MAH-nah PROHK-see-mah*
the day after tomorrow	**pasado mañana** *pah-SAH-doh mahn-YAH-nah*
When will you bring it back?	**¿Cuándo la traerá?** *KWAHN-doh lah trah-ehr-AH*
When will it be ready?	**¿Cuándo estará lista?** *KWAHN-doh ehs-tah-RAH LEES-tah*
There's a button missing.	**Falta on botón.** *FAHL-tah oon boh-TOHN*
Can you sew it on?	**¿Puede usted coserlo?** *PWEH-deh oos-TEHD koh-SEHR-loh*
This isn't my laundry.	**Esta no es mi ropa.** *EHS-tah noh ehs mee ROH-pah*

MEDICAL CARE

The rule of thumb in any foreign country says that you will receive medical attention in an emergency and that you will be liable for payment. Your current health insurance may pay some or all of your medical bills once you return to your country of origin; therefore, make sure to keep copies of all the bills you paid and of all the documents you signed. If the state of your health is uncertain, you should consider taking international medical insurance.

In Spain, dial 122 free of charge if you have a medical emergency.

THE PHARMACY (CHEMIST)

A Spanish pharmacy (**la farmacia**—*lah fahr-MAH-see-ah*) can be recognized by its sign with a green cross. If it is closed, look for a list on the door indicating the nearest stores that are open (**farmacias de guardia**—*fahr-MAH-see-ahs deh GWAHR-dee-ah*). Note that in Spain a pharmacy mainly sells drugs; for toiletries you must go to a **perfumería** (*pehr-foo-meh-REE-ah*). Many Latin American pharmacies also use the green cross sign.

Where is the nearest (all-night) pharmacy (chemist)?	**¿Dónde está la farmacia (de guardia) más cercana?** *DOHN-day ehs-TAH lah fahr-MAH-see-ah (day GWAHR-dee-ah) mahs sehr-KAH-nah*
At what time does the pharmacy open (close)?	**¿A qué hora se abre (se cierra) la farmacia?** *ah kay OH-rah say AH-bray (say SYEHR-ah) lah fahr-MAH-see-ah*

I need something for _____.	**Necesito algo para _____.** *neh-seh-SEE-toh AHL-goh pah-rah*
■ allergy	**la alergia** *lah ah-LEHR-hee-ah*
■ a cold	**on catarro** *oon kah-TAH-roh*
■ constipation	**el estreñimiento** *ehl ehs-trayn-yee-MYEHN-toh*
■ a cough	**la tos** *lah tohs*
■ diarrhea	**la diarrea** *lah dee-ahr-RAY-ah*
■ a fever	**la fiebre** *lah fee-YEHB-ray*
■ flatulence	**flatulencia** *flah-too-LEN-see-ah*
■ a headache	**un dolor de cabeza** *oon doh-LOHR day kah-BAY-sah*
■ insomnia	**el insomnio** *ehl een-SOHM-nee-oh*
■ nausea	**náuseas** *NAH-oo-say-ahs*
■ sunburn	**la quemadura del sol** *lah kay-mah-DOOR-ah del SOHL*
■ a toothache	**un dolor de muelas** *oon doh-LOHR day MWEH-lahs*
■ an upset stomach	**la indigestión** *la een-dee-hes-TYOHN*
I do not have a prescription.	**No tengo la receta.** *noh TEN-goh lah reh-SAY-tah*
May I have it right away?	**¿Me la puede dar en seguida?** *May lah PWEH-day DAHR ehn seh-GHEE-dah*
It's an emergency!	**¡Es urgente!** *ehs oor-HEN-tay*
How long will it take?	**¿Cuánto tiempo tardará?** *KWAHN-toh tee-YEHM-poh tahr-dahr-AH*
When can I come for it?	**¿Cuándo puedo venir a recogerla?** *KWAHN-doh PWEH-doh ben-EER ah ray-koh-HAIR-lah*

How many do I take at once?	**¿Cuántas debo tomar de inmediato?** *KWAHN-tahs DEH-boh to-MAHR deh een-meh-dee-AH-toh*
How many times a day?	**¿Cuántas veces al día?** *KWAHN-tahs VEH-sehs ahl DEE-ah*
How long should I take this?	**¿Por cuánto tiempo debo tomar esto?** *pohr KWAHN-toh tee-EHM-poh DEH-boh to-MAHR EHS-toh*
Do I take them with food?	**¿Debo tomarlas con comida?** *DEH-boh toh-MAHR-lahs kohn koh-MEE-dah*
Will this make me drowsy?	**¿Me dejará esto soñoliento?** *meh deh-hah-RAH EHS-toh soh-nyoh-lee-EHN-toh*
I would like ____.	**Quisiera ____.** *kee-see-YEHR-ah*
■ adhesive tape	**esparadrapo** *ehs-pah-rah-DRAH-poh*
■ alcohol	**alcohol** *ahl-koh-OHL*
■ an antacid	**un antiácido** *oon ahn-tee-AH-see-doh*
■ an antihistamine	**un antihistamínico** *oon ahn-tee-ees-tah-MEEN-ee-koh*
■ an antiseptic	**un antiséptico** *oon ahn-tee-SEP-tee-koh*
■ aspirins	**aspirinas** *ahs-peer-EE-nahs*
■ Band-Aids	**curitas** *koor-EE-tahs*
■ contraceptives	**contraceptivos** *kohn-trah-sep-TEE-bohs*
■ corn plasters	**callicidas** *kah-yee-SEE-dahs*
■ cotton	**algodón** *ahl-goh-DOHN*
■ cough drops	**pastillas para la tos** *PAHS-TEE-yahs pah-rah lah TOHS*
■ cough syrup	**jarabe para la tos** *hah-RAH-bay PAH-rah lah TOHS*
■ ear drops	**gotas para los oídos** *GOH-tahs PAH-rah lohs oh-EE-dohs*

▨ eye drops	**gotas para los ojos**	*GOH-tahs PAH-rah lohs OH-hohs*
▨ iodine	**yodo**	*YOH-doh*
▨ a (mild) laxative	**un laxante (ligero)**	*oon lahk-SAHN-tay (lee-HEHR-oh)*
▨ milk of magnesia	**una leche de magnesia**	*oo-nah leh-chay day mahg-NAY-see-ah*
▨ prophylactics	**preservativos**	*preh-sehr-vah-TEE-vohs*
▨ sanitary napkins	**servilletas higiénicas**	*sehr-bee-YEH-tahs ee-HYEHN-ee-kahs*
▨ suppositories	**supositorios**	*soo-pohs-ee-TOHR-ee-ohs*
▨ talcum powder	**polvos de talco**	*POHL-bohs day TAHL-koh*
▨ tampons	**tampones**	*tahm-POHN-ays*
▨ a thermometer	**un termómetro**	*oon tehr-MOH-met-roh*
▨ tranquilizers	**un tranquilizante**	*oon trahn-kee-lee-SAHN-tay*
▨ vitamins	**vitaminas**	*bee-tah-MEE-nahs*

WITH THE DOCTOR

Call the United States embassy (see **United States Embassies in Spanish-Speaking Countries** on page 262) to obtain the address of an English-Speaking physician.

I don't feel well.	**No me siento bien.** *noh may SYEHN-toh BYEHN*
I need a doctor (right now).	**Necesito un médico (ahora mismo).** *neh-seh-SEE-toh oon MEH-dee-koh (ah-OHR-ah MEES-moh)*

Do you know a doctor (chiropractor) who speaks English?	**¿Conoce un médico (quiropráctico) que hable inglés?** *koh-NOH-say oon MEH-dee-koh (kee-rho-PRAHK-tee-koh) kay ah-blay een-GLAYSS*
Where is his office (surgery)?	**¿Dónde está su consultorio?** *DOHN-day ehs-TAH soo kohn-sool-TOHR-ee-oh*
Will the doctor come to the hotel?	**¿Vendrá el medico al hotel?** *ben-DRAH ehl MED-ee-koh ahl oh-TEL*
I feel dizzy.	**Estoy mareado.** *ehs-TOY mahr-ay-AH-doh*
I feel weak.	**Me siento débil.** *may SYEHN-toh DAY-beel*
My temperature is normal (37°C).	**Tengo la temperatura normal (treinta y siete grados).** *TEN-goh lah tem-pehr-ah-TOOR-ah nohr-MAHL (TRAYN-tah ee see-EH-tay GRAH-dohs)*
I (think I) have ____.	**(Creo que) tengo ____.** *KRAY-oh kay TEN-goh*
▪ an abscess	**un absceso** *oon ahb-SEHS-oh*
▪ a broken bone	**un hueso roto** *oon WAY-soh ROH-toh*
▪ a bruise	**una contusión** *oo-nah kohn-too-SYOHN*
▪ a burn	**una quemadura** *oo-nah kay-mah-DOOR-ah*
▪ something in my eye	**algo en el ojo** *AHL-goh ehn ehl OH-hoh*
▪ the chills	**escalofríos** *ehs-kah-loh-FREE-ohs*
▪ a chest (head) cold	**un catarro (resfriado)** *oon kah-TAHR-oh (res-free-AH-doh)*

■ constipation **estreñimiento** *ehs-trayn-yee-mee-YENT-oh*

■ stomach cramps **calambres** *kahl-AHM-brays*

■ a cut **una cortadura** *oo-nah kohr-tah-DOOR-ah*

■ diarrhea **diarrea** *dee-ah-RAY-ah*

■ a fever **fiebre** *fee-YEHB-bray*

■ a fracture **una fractura** *oo-nah frahk-TOOR-ah*

■ a backache **un dolor de espalda** *oon doh-LOHR day es-PAHL-dah*

■ an earache **un dolor de oído** *oon doh-LOHR day oh-EE-doh*

■ a headache **un dolor de cabeza** *oon doh-LOHR day kah-BAY-sah*

■ an infection **una infección** *oo-nah een-fek-SYOHN*

■ a lump **un bulto** *oon BOOL-toh*

■ a sore throat **un dolor de garganta** *oon doh-LOHR day gahr-GAHN-tah*

■ a stomachache **un dolor de estómago** *oon doh-LOHR day ehs-TOH-mah-goh*

It hurts me here. **Me duele aquí.** *may DWEH-lay ah-KEE*

My whole body hurts. **Me duele todo el cuerpo.** *may DWEH-lay toh-doh ehl KWEHR-poh*

Can you check my blood pressure (pulse, temperature)? **¿Puede verificar mi presión (pulso, temperatura)?** *PWEH-day behr-ee-fee-KAHR mee preh-SYOHN (POOL-soh tem-pehr-ah-TOOR-ah)*

I am allergic to _____.	**Soy alérgico a _____.** *SOH-ee ah-LEHR-hee-koh ah*
▨ antibiotics	**los antibióticos** *lohs ahn-tee-bee-OH-tee-kohs*
▨ anti-inflammatories	**los antiinflamatorios** *lohs ahn-tee-een-flah-mah-TOH-ree-ohs*
▨ bees	**las abejas** *lahs ah-BEH-hahs*
▨ codeine	**la codeína** *lah koh-deh-EE-nah*
▨ peanuts	**el maní** *ehl mah-NEE* **los cacahuates** (Mexico) *lohs kah-kah-HWAH-tehs*
▨ penicillin	**la penicilina** *lah peh-nee-see-LEE-nah*

PARTS OF THE BODY

ankle	**el tobillo** *ehl toh-BEE-yoh*
appendix	**el apéndice** *ehl ah-PEN-dee-say*
arm	**el brazo** *ehl BRAH-soh*
back	**la espalda** *lah ehs-PAHL-dah*
breast	**el pecho** *ehl PAY-choh*
cheek	**la mejilla** *lah meh-HEE-yah*
ear	**el oído** *ehl oh-EE-doh*
elbow	**el codo** *ehl KOH-doh*
eye	**el ojo** *ehl OH-hoh*
face	**la cara** *lah KAH-rah*
finger	**el dedo** *ehl DAY-doh*
foot	**el pie** *ehl pee-AY*
glands	**las glándulas** *lahs GLAHN-doo-lahs*

hand	**la mano**	*lah MAHN-oh*
head	**la cabeza**	*lah kah-BAY-sah*
heart	**el corazón**	*ehl kohr-ah-SOHN*
hip	**la cadera**	*lah kah-DEHR-ah*
knee	**la rodilla**	*lah roh-DEE-yah*
leg	**la pierna**	*lah pee-YEHR-nah*
lip	**el labio**	*ehl LAH-bee-oh*
liver	**el hígado**	*ehl EE-gah-doh*
mouth	**la boca**	*lah BOH-kah*
neck	**el cuello**	*ehl KWEH-yoh*
nose	**la nariz**	*lah nah-REES*
shoulder	**el hombro**	*ehl OHM-broh*
skin	**la piel**	*lah pee-YEHL*
thumb	**el pulgar**	*ehl pool-GAHR*
throat	**la garganta**	*lah gahr-GAHN-tah*
toe	**el dedo del pie**	*ehl DAY-doh del pee-YEH*
tooth	**el diente**	*ehl dee-YEHN-tay*
wrist	**la muñeca**	*lah moon-YEH-kah*

TELLING THE DOCTOR

I need a new prescription.	**Necesito una nueva receta.** *neh-seh-SEE-toh oo-nah NWEH-vah reh-SEH-tah*
I've had this pain since yesterday.	**Tengo este dolor desde ayer.** *TEN-goh EHS-tay doh-LOHR des-day ah-YEHR*

There's a (no) history of asthma (diabetes) in my family.	**(No) hay incidencia de asma (diabetes) en mi familia.** *(noh) AH-ee een-see-DEN-see-ah day AHS-mah (dee-ah-BEH-tays) ehn mee fah-MEEL-yah*
I'm (not) allergic to antibiotics (penicillin).	**(No) soy alérgico(a) a los antibióticos (penicilina).** *(noh) soy ah-LEHR-hee-koh(kah) ah lohs ahn-tee-bee-OH-tee-kohs (pen-ee-see-LEE-nah).*
I have a pain in my chest.	**Tengo dolor en el pecho.** *TEN-goh doh-LOHR ehn ehl PAY-choh*
I have heart trouble.	**Tengo problemas cardíacos** *TEN-goh pro-BLAY-mahs kahr-DEE-ah-kohs*
I had a heart attack ____ year(s) ago.	**Tuve on ataque al corazón hace ____ año(s).** *TOO-bay oon ah-TAH-kay ahl kohr-ah-SOHN ah-say ahn-yoh(s)*

I'm taking this medicine (insulin).	**Tomo esta medicina (insulina).** *TOH-moh EHS-tah med-ee-SEE-nah (een-soo-LEE-nah)*
I'm pregnant.	**Estoy embarazada.** *EHS-toy ehm-bahr-ah-SAH-dah*

I feel better (worse).	**Me siento mejor (peor).** *may see-YEN-toh may-HOHR (pay-OHR)*
Is it serious (contagious)?	**¿Es grave (contagioso)?** *ehs GRAH-bay (kohn-tah-hee-OH-soh)*
Do I have to go to the hospital?	**¿Tengo que ir al hospital?** *TEN-goh kay eer ahl ohs-pee-TAHL*
When can I continue my trip?	**¿Cuándo puedo continuer mi viaje?** *KWAHN-doh PWEH-doh kon-teen-oo-AHR mee bee-AH-hay*

FOLLOWING UP

Do I need ____?	**¿Necesito ____?**
■ an MRI	**una imagen por resonancia magnética** *oo-nah ee-MAH-hen pohr reh-soh-NAHN-see-ah mahg-NET-ee-kah*
■ a sonogram	**un sonograma** *oon soh-noh-GRAH-mah*
■ an angiogram	**un angiograma** *oon ahn-hee-oh-GRAH-mah*
■ an ECG	**un electrocardiograma** *oon eh-lek-tro-KAHR-dee-oh-GRAH-mah*
■ a CAT scan	**una tomografía computarizada** *oo-nah toh-moh-grah-FEE-ah kohn-poo-tahr-ee-SAH-dah*
■ x-rays	**rayos equis** *RAH-ee-ohs EH-kees*
■ a blood (urine, stool) test	**un examen de sangre (orina, excremento)** *oon ek-SAH-men day SAHN-gray (oh-REE-nah eks-cray-MEN-toh)*
Are you giving me a prescription?	**¿Va a darme una receta?** *bah ah DAHR-may oo-nah ray-SAY-tah*

How often must I take this medicine (these pills)?	**¿Cuántas veces al día tengo que tomar esta medicina (estas píldoras)?** *KWAHN-tahs BEH-says ahl DEE-ah TEN-goh kay toh-MAHR EHS-tah med-ee-SEE-nah (EHS-tahs PEEL-dohr-ahs)*
(How long) do I have to stay in bed?	**¿(Cuánto tiempo) tengo que quedarme en cama?** *(KWAHN-toh tee-YEHM-poh) TEN-goh kay kay-DAHR-may ehn KAH-mah*
Thank you (for everything), doctor.	**Muchas gracias (por todo), doctor.** *MOO-chahs GRAH-see-ahs (pohr TOH-doh) dohk-TOHR*
How much do I owe you for your services?	**¿Cuánto le debo?** *KWAHN-toh lay DEHB-oh*
Will you accept my medical insurance?	**¿Acepta mi seguro médico?** *ah-SEP-tah mee seh-GOOR-oh MED-ee-koh*

IN THE HOSPITAL (ACCIDENTS)

Help!	**¡Socorro!** *soh-KOH-roh*
Get a doctor, quick!	**¡Busque un médico, rápido!** *BOO-skay oon MED-ee-koh RAH-pee-doh*
Call an ambulance!	**¡Llame una ambulancia!** *YAH-may oo-nah ahm-boo-LAHN-see-ah*
Take me to the hospital!	**¡Lléveme al hospital!** *YEV-eh-may ahl ohs-pee-TAHL*

I've fallen.	**Me he caído.** *may ay kah-EE-doh*
I was knocked down (run over).	**Fui atropellado(a).** *fwee ah-troh-peh-YAH-doh*
I think I've had a heart attack.	**Creo que he tenido un ataque al corazón.** *KRAY-oh kay ay ten-EE-doh oon ah-TAH-kay ahl kohr-ah-SOHN*
I need my nitroglycerine.	**Necesito mi nitroglicerina** *neh-seh-SEE-toh mee nee-troh-glee-sehr-EE-nah*
I burned myself.	**Me quemé.** *may kay-MAY*
I cut myself.	**Me corté.** *may kohr-TAY*
I'm bleeding.	**Estoy sangrando.** *ehs-toy sahn-GRAHN-doh*
I think the bone is broken (dislocated).	**Creo que el hueso está roto (dislocado)** *KRAY-oh kay ehl WAY-soh ehs-TAH ROH-toh (dees-loh-KAH-doh)*
My leg is swollen.	**La pierna está hinchada.** *lah pee-EHR-nah ehs-TAH een-CHAH-dah*

I have sprained (twisted) my wrist (ankle).	**Me he torcido la muñeca (el tobillo).** *may ay tohr-SEE-doh lah moon-YEH-kah (ehl toh-BEE-yoh)*
I can't move my elbow (knee).	**No puedo mover el codo (la rodilla).** *noh pweh-doh moh-BEHR ehl KOH-doh (lah roh-DEE-yah)*
I don't have medical insurance.	**No tengo seguro médico.** *noh ten-goh seh-GOO-roh MED-ee-koh*

AT THE DENTIST

Can you recommend a dentist?	**¿Puede recomendar un dentista?** *PWEH-day reh-koh-men-DAHR oon den-TEES-tah*
I have a toothache that's driving me crazy.	**Tengo un dolor de muela que me vuelve loco.** *ten-goh oon doh-LOHR day MWEH-lah kay may BWEHL-bay loh-koh*
I've lost a filling.	**Se me ha caído un empaste.** *say may ah kah-EE-doh oon ehm-PAHS-tay*
I've broken a tooth.	**Me rompí un diente.** *may rohm-PEE oon dee-EHN-tay*
My gums hurt.	**Me duelen las encías.** *may DWEH-len lahs ehn-SEE-ahs*
Is there an infection?	**¿Hay una infección?** *AH-ee oo-nah een-fehk-SYOHN*
Will you have to extract the tooth?	**¿Tendrá que sacar la muela (el diente)?** *ten-DRAH kay sah-kahr lah MWEH-lah (ehl dee-EHN-tay)*
Can you fill it ____?	**¿Podría empastarlo ____?** *poh-DREE-ah ehm-pahs-TAHR-loh*

■ with amalgam	**con platino** *kohn plah-TEE-noh*
■ with gold	**con oro** *kohn OHR-oh*
■ with silver	**con plata** *kohn PLAH-tah*
■ for now	**por ahora** *pohr ah-OHR-ah*
Can you fix ____?	**¿Puede usted reparar ____?** *PWEH-day oo-STEHD ray-pah-RAHR*
■ this bridge	**este puente** *EHS-tay PWEHN-tay*
■ this crown	**esta corona** *EHS-tah kohr-OH-nah*
■ these dentures	**estos dientes postizos** *EHS-tohs dee-EHN-tays pohs-TEE-sohs*
When should I come back?	**¿Cuándo debo volver?** *KWAHN-doh DEH-boh bohl-BEHR*
How much do I owe you for your services?	**¿Cuánto le debo?** *KWAHN-toh lay DEH-boh*

SPECIAL NEEDS

Where can I get ____?	**¿Dónde puedo obtener ____?** *DOHN-deh PWEH-doh ohb-teh-NEHR*
■ a cane	**un bastón** *oon bahs-TOHN*
■ crutches	**unas muletas** *oo-nahs moo-LEH-tahs*
■ a hearing aid	**un audífono** *oon ow-DEE-foh-noh*
■ a walker	**una apoyatura para caminar** *oo-nah ah-poh-yah-TOO-rah PAH-rah kah-mee-NAHR*
■ a wheelchair	**una sila de ruedas** *oo-nah SEE-yah deh RWEH-dahs*

What services do you have for the handicapped?	**¿Qué servicios tienen para los minusválidos?** *keh sehr-VEE-see-ohs tee-EH-nehn PAH-rah lohs mee-noos-VAH-lee-dohs*
I need assistance.	**Necesito asistencia.** *neh-seh-SEE-toh ah-sees-TEHN-see-ah*
Is there wheelchair access?	**¿Hay acceso para sillas de rueda?** *AH-ee ahk-SEH-soh PAH-rah SEE-yahs deh RWEH-dah*
Are there toilet facilities for the handicapped?	**¿Hay dispositivos de asistencia para minusválidos en los baños?** *AH-ee dees-poh-see-TEE-vohs deh ah-sees-TEHN-see-ah PAH-rah mee-noos-VAH-lee-dohs ehn lohs BAHN-yohs*
Are there stairs?	**¿Hay escaleras?** *AH-ee ehs-kah-LEH-rahs*
Is there an elevator?	**¿Hay ascensor?** *AH-ee ahs-sehn-SOHR*
Is there a ramp?	**¿Hay rampa?** *AH-ee RAHM-pah*
Are guide dogs allowed?	**¿Se permiten perros lazarillo?** *seh pehr-MEE-tehn PEHR-rohs lah-sah-REE-yoh*

WITH THE OPTICIAN

Can you repair these glasses (for me)?	**¿Puede usted arreglar(me) estas gafas? (estos lentes)** *PWEH-day oos-TEHD ah-ray-GLAHR (may) EHS-tahs GAH-fahs (EHS-tohs LEN-tehs)*
I've broken a lens (the frame).	**Se me ha roto un cristal (la armadura).** *say may oh ROH-toh oon krees-TAHL (lah ahr-mah-DOOR-ah)*
Can you put in a new lens?	**¿Puede usted ponerme un cristal nuevo?** *PWEH-day oos-TEHD poh-NEHR-may oos krees-TAHL NWEH-boh*
I have transition lenses (bifocals).	**Tengo lentes polarizados (bifocales).** *TEN-go LEN-tehs poh-lahr-ee-SAH-dohs (bee-foh-KAH-lehs)*

Do you have (prescription) sunglasses?	**¿Tiene lentes (de receta) de sol?** *TYEH-neh LEN-tehs (day ray-SAY-tah) day sohl*
I (do not) have a prescription.	**(No) tengo receta.** *noh TEN-goh ray-SAY-tah*

I'm nearsighted (farsighted).

Soy miope (présbita) *soy mee-OH-peh (PREHS-bee-tah)*

Can you tighten the screws?

¿Puede usted apretar los tornillitos? *PWEH-day oos-TEHD ah-pray-tahr lohs tohr-NEE-yee-tohs*

I need the glasses as soon as possible.

Necesito las gafas urgentemente. *neh-seh-SEE-toh lahs GAH-fahs oor-hen-tay-MEN-tay*

I've lost a contact lens.

Se me ha perdido un lente de contacto. *say may ah pehr-DEE-doh oon LEN-tay day kohn-TAHK-toh*

Can you replace it quickly?

¿Puede reemplazarlo rápidamente? *PWEH-day ray-ehm-plah-SAHR-loh rah-pee-dah-MEN-tay*

COMMUNICATIONS

POST OFFICE

In Spain, postcards and stamps can be purchased at **estancos** (tobacconists) and kiosks (these can be distinguished by their red and yellow signs) in addition to the official post office (**Correos y Telégrafos**).

The post office is open from 9:00 to 1:30 and from 4:00 to 7:00 Monday to Saturday.

Hours may differ somewhat in Latin America, and postcards are seldom sold at post offices.

I want to mail a letter.	**Quiero echar una carta al correo.** *kee-YEHR-oh ay-CHAHR oo-nah KAHR-tah ahl kohr-AY-oh*
Where's the post office?	**¿Dónde está correos?** *DOHN-day ehs-TAH kohr-AY-ohs*
Where's a letterbox?	**¿Dónde hay un buzón?** *DOHN-day AH-ee oon boo-SOHN*
What is the postage on ____ to the United States (Canada, England, Australia)?	**¿Cuánto es el franqueo de ____ a los Estados Unidos (al Canadá, a Inglaterra, a Australia)?** *KWAHN-toh ehs ehl frahn-KAY-oh day ah lohs ehs-TAH-dohs oo-NEE-dohs (ahl kahn-ah-DAH ah eeng-lah-TEHR-ah ah ow-STRAHL-yah)*
▪ a letter	**una carta** *oo-nah KAHR-tah*
▪ a registered letter	**una carta certificada** *oo-nah KAHR-tah sehr-teef-ee-KAH-dah*
▪ a special delivery letter	**una carta urgente** *oo-nah KAHR-tah oor-HEN-tay*

■ a package	**un paquete postal** *oon pah-kay-tay pohs-TAHL*
■ a postcard	**una postal** *oo-nah pohs-TAHL*
When will it arrive?	**¿Cuándo llegará?** *KWAHN-doh yeh-gahr-AH*
Which is the _____ window?	**¿Cuál es la ventanilla de _____?** *kwahl ehs lah ben-tah-NEE-yah day*
■ general delivery	**la lista de correos** *lah LEES-tah day kohr-AY-ohs*
■ stamp	**los sellos** *lohs SEH-yohs*
I'd like _____.	**Quisiera _____.** *kee-see-YEHR-ah*
■ 10 envelopes	**diez sobres** *dee-EHS SOH-brays*
■ 6 postcards	**seis postales** *sayss pohs-TAHL-ays*
■ 5 (air mail) stamps	**cinco sellos (aéreos)** *SEEN-koh SEH-yohs (ah-EHR-ay-ohs)*
Do I fill out a customs receipt?	**¿Hay un recibo de adana?** *AH-ee oon ray-SEE-boh day ah-DWAHN-ah*

TELEPHONES

All calls from Spain and Latin America to the United States or Canada require that you dial 001 first, followed by the area code and number. To call Spain from the U.S. or Canada dial 011 34 followed by the city code and then the seven-digit number. Some Spanish city codes are:

- ■ Barcelona 93
- ■ Ibiza 971
- ■ Madrid 91

■ Seville 95

■ Valencia 96

To call the UK from Spain dial 00 44 and omit the zero from the area code. To call Spain from the UK dial 00 34 followed by the city code and then the seven digit number.

In Spain you can use a telephone card (**tarjeta telefónica**—*tahr-HEH-tah teh-leh-FOH-nee-kah*) for local and long distance calls. Cards may be purchased at post offices, tobacco shops, and newsstands. Public telephones take €1 and €2 coins and 2c, 5c, 10c, 20c, and 50c coins. Some phones accept credit cards, and some telephones are for local calls only. To call another city or country, you must find a booth with a green stripe across the top marked "**Interurbano.**"

Three important telephone numbers in Spain:

■ Emergency: 112

■ Information: 010

■ Operator assistance: 025

To call a Latin American country from the United States or Canada you must dial 011 followed by the Latin American country code followed by the city code followed by the telephone number.

Where is ____?	**¿Donde hay ____?** *DOHN-day AH-ee*
■ a public telephone	**un teléfono público** *oon tel-EHF-oh-noh POO-blee-koh*
■ a telephone booth	**una cabina telefónica** *oo-nah kah-BEE-nah tel-eh-FOHN-ee-kah*
May I use your phone?	**¿Me permite usar su teléfono?** *may pehr-MEE-tay oo-sahr soo tel-EHF-oh-noh*

I want to make a _____ call.	**Quiero hacer una llamada _____.** *kee-YEHR-oh ah-SEHR oo-nah yah-MAH-dah*
▓ local	**local** *loh-kahl*
▓ long distance	**a larga distancia** *ah LAHR-gah dees-TAHN-see-ah*
▓ person to person	**personal** *pehr-SOHN-ahl*
▓ collect	**a cobro revertido** *ah KOH-broh ray-behr-TEE-doh*
Hello.	**Diga.** *DEE-gah*
This is _____.	**Habla _____.** *AH-blah*
Who is this?	**¿Con quién hablo?** *kohn kee-YENN AH-bloh*
May I speak to _____?	**¿Puedo hablar con _____?** *PWEH-doh ah-BLAHR kohn*
Speak louder, please.	**Hable más alto, por favor.** *AH-blay mahs AHL-toh pohr fah-BOHR*
I want to leave a message.	**Quiero dejar un recado.** *kee-YEHR-oh day-HAHR oon ray-KAH-doh*
I'll call you.	**Le llamaré.** *ley yah-mah-RAY*
I'll text you.	**Le voy a textear.** *ley VOH-ee ah TEX-teh-ahr*
I was cut off.	**Me han cortado.** *may ahn kohr-TAH-doh*
What's your phone number?	**¿Cuál es su número de teléfono?** *kwahl ehs soo NOO-meh-roh day teh-LEH-foh-noh*
My phone number is _____.	**Mi número de teléfono es _____.** *mee NOO-meh-roh day teh-LEH-foh-noh ehs*
Do you text?	**¿Textea usted?** *tex-TEH-ah oos-TEHD*

Can I text you?	**¿Puedo textearle?** *PWEH-doh tex-teh-AHR-leh*
Do you have Bluetooth?	**¿Tiene Bluetooth?** *tee-EH-neh Bluetooth*
How do I get the operator?	**¿Cómo puedo conseguir la central?** *KOH-moh PWEH-doh kohn-seh-gheer lah sehn-TRAHL*
Operator, how much is a three-minute call to ____?	**Señorita, ¿cuánto vale una llamada de tres minutos a ____?** *Sehn-yohr-EE-tah KWAHN-toh VAH-leh oo-nah yah-MAH-dah ah*
How much does each additional minute cost?	**¿Cuánto cuesta cada minuto adicional?** *KWAHN-toh KWEHS-tah KAH-dah mee-NOO-toh ah-dee-see-oh-NAHL*
I would like to buy a ____.	**Quiero comprar ____.** *kee-EH-roh kohm-PRAHR*
■ a prepaid phone card	**una tarjeta telefónica prepagada** *oo-nah tahr-HEH-tah teh-leh-FOH-nee-kah preh-pah-GAH-dah*
■ a prepaid cell phone	**un teléfono celular prepagado** *oon teh-LEH-foh-noh seh-loo-LAHR preh-pah-GAH-doh*
■ a charger for my phone	**un cargador para mi teléfono** *oon kahr-gah-DOHR PAH-rah mee teh-LEH-foh-noh*

BUSINESS SERVICES AND ELECTRONIC COMMUNICATION

Deluxe hotels and other major cities usually can arrange secretarial services in English, French, and German for business guests.

FAX

Do you have a fax machine?	**¿Tiene usted una máquina de fax?** *TYEHN-eh oos-TED oo-nah MAH-kee-nah day-FAHKS*
What is your fax number?	**¿Cuál es su número de fax?** *KWAHL ehs soo NOO-mehr-oh day FAHKS*
I want to send a fax.	**Quiero mandar un fax.** *KYEHR-oh mahn-DAHR oon FAHKS*
Can I send a fax from here?	**¿Puedo enviar un fax desde aquí?** *PWEH-do en-bee-YAHR oon FAHKS DES-day ah-KEE*
Fax it to me.	**Mándemelo por fax.** *MAHN-day-may-loh pohr FAHKS*
I didn't get your fax.	**No recibí su fax.** *No reh-see-BEE soo fahks*

Did you receive my fax?	**¿Recibió usted mi fax?** *reh-see-BYOH oos-TED mee fahks*
Your fax is illegible.	**Su fax está ilegible.** *soo fahks ehs-TAH ee-leh-HEE-blay*
Please send it again.	**Por favor, mándelo de nuevo.** *Por fah-BOHR MAHN-day-lo day NWEH-boh*

COMPUTERS

Note that a computer in Latin America is a **computadora**, whereas in Spain it is an **ordenador**.

To get information on Spain or any Latin American country on the Internet:

1. Go to the location box in your net browser
2. Type **www.altavista.com** or **www.hotbot.com**
3. Click on **altavista** or **hotbot**
4. You will see a search screen. Type **Spain** or a Latin American country and click **Enter**
5. You can search for any subject.

Do you have ____?	**¿Tiene usted ____?** *TYEHN-eh oos-TED*	
a Macintosh computer	**una computadora (un ordenador) Macintosh** *oo-nah kohm-poo-tah-DOHR-ah (oon or-day-nah-DOHR) mah-keen-TOHS*	
a PC	**una computadora (un ordenador) PC** *oo-nah kohm-poo-tah-DOHR-ah (oon or-day-nah-DOHR) pay-say*	
Are there computers (laptops) available?	**¿Hay computadoras (computadoras portátiles) disponibles?** *AH-ee kohm-poo-tah-DOHR-ahs (kohm-poo-tah-DOHR-ahs por-TAH-tee-lehs) dees-poh-NEE-blehs*	

Does it have a (color) printer, scanner, floppy disk, modem, CD-ROM drive, antivirus software?	**¿Tiene una impresora (de color), un escáner, un diskette, un modulador, una disquetera de CD-ROM, datos de aplicación antivirus?** *TYEHN-eh oo-nah eem-preh-SOHR-ah (day ko-LOHR) oon es-KAHN-ehr oon dees-KET oon moh-doo-lah-DOHR oo-nah dees-ket-eh-rah day say-day-ROHM DAH-tos day ah-plee-kah-SYOHN AHN-tee-BEE-roos*
Is is possible to access the Internet from here?	**¿Es posible tener acceso al internet desde aquí?** *es poh-SEE-blay ten-EHR ahk-SES-oh ahl EEN-tehr-net DES-day ah-KEE*
Do you have WI-FI?	**¿Tiene WI-FI?** *tee-EH-neh oo-EE fee*
What's the closest hotspot?	**¿Dónde está el WI-FI más cercano?** *DOHN-deh ehs-TAH ehl oo-EE-fee mahs sehr-KAH-noh*
Who is the provider?	**¿Quién es el proveedor?** *kee-YEHN ehs ehl pro-beh-eh-DOHR*
What operating system are you using?	**¿Qué sistema operativo está usando?** *kay sees-TAY-mah boh-pehr-ah-TEE-boh ehs-TAH oo-SAHN-doh*
What word processing program are you using?	**¿Qué programa de procesamiento de texto está usando?** *kay pro-GRAH-mah day pro-sehs-ah-MYEN-toh day TEKS-toh es-TAH oo-SAHN-doh*
Are our systems compatible?	**¿Son compatibles nuestros sistemas?** *sohn kohm-pah-TEE-blays NWEHS-trohs sees-TAY-mahs*
What is the password?	**¿Cuál es la contraseña?** *kwahl ehs lah kohn-trah-SEHN-yah*

What is your e-mail address?	**¿Cuál es su dirección de correo electrónico?** *KWAHL es soo dee-rek-SYOHN day kohr-AY-oh eh-lek-TROHN-ee-koh*
The computer doesn't work.	**La computadora no funciona.** *Lah kohm-poo-tah-DOHR-ah no foon-SYOHN-ah*
Where can I have it repaired?	**¿Dónde me la pueden reparar?** *DOHN-day may lah PWEH-den reh-pah-RAHR*

COMPUTER MINI-DICTIONARY

access	**el acceso** *ehl ahk-SES-oh*
backup disk	**la copia de seguridad** *lah KOH-pee-yah day seh-goor-ee-DAHD*
byte	**byte** *BAH-eet*
cable	**el cable** *ehl KAH-blay*
CD-ROM disk	**el disco CD-ROM** *ehl DEES-koh seh deh ROHM*
chip	**el chip** *ehl CHEEP*
(to) click	**hacer clic** *ah-SEHR kleek*
clipboard	**el fichero temporal** *ehl fee-CHEH-roh tehm-poh-RAHL*
CPU	**la Unidad de Proceso Central** *lah oon-ee-DAHD day pro-SES-oh sen-TRAHL*
computer programmer	**el programador (de computación)** *ehl pro-grah-mah-DOHR (day kohn-poo-tah-SYOHN)*
(to) copy	**copiar** or **reproducir** *koh-pee-AHR, ray-pro-doo-SEER*

cursor	**el cursor**	*ehl koor-SOHR*
(to) cut	**cortar**	*kohr-TAHR*
database	**el banco de datos**	*ehl BAHN-koh day DAH-tohs*
disk	**el disco**	*ehl DEES-koh*
disk drive	**la disquetera**	*lah dees-kay-TEHR-ah*
document	**el documento**	*ehl do-koo-MEN-toh*
DOS	**el sistema operativo de disco**	*ehl sees-TAY-mah oh-pehr-ah-TEE-boh day DEES-koh*
(to) download	**bajar**	*bah-HAHR*
e-mail	**el correo electrónico**	*ehl kohr-AY-oh eh-lek-TROHN-ee-koh*
file	**el fichero**	*ehl fee-CHEHR-oh*
font	**el tipo de letra**	*ehl TEE-poh day LET-rah*
graphics	**los gráficos**	*lohs GRAH-fee-kohs*
hardware	**los elementos mecánicos**	*lohs eh-leh-MEHN-tohs meh-KAH-nee-kohs*
icon	**el ícono**	*ehl EE-koh-noh*
Internet	**el internet**	*ehl EEN-tehr-net*
joystick	**la palanca de juego**	*lah pah-LAHN-kah day WAY-goh*
key	**la tecla** *lah TEK-lah* (or **la llave**)	*(lah YAH-bay)*
keyboard	**el teclado**	*ehl tek-LAH-do*
(to) keyboard	**teclar**	*tek-LAHR*

laptop	**la computadora portátil** *lah kohm-poo-tah-DOHR-ah por-TAH-teel*
laser printer	**la impresora láser** *lah eem-pray-SOHR-ah LAH-sehr*
memory	**la memoria** *lah mem-OHR-ee-yah*
modem	**el módem** *ehl MOH-dem* (or **el modulador**) *el moh-doo-lah-DOHR*
mouse	**el ratón** *ehl rah-TOHN*
network	**la red** *lah red*
on-line service	**el servicio en-línea** *ehl sehr-BEE-syoh en-lee-nay-ah*
(to) paste	**pegar** *peh-GAHR*
printer	**la impresora** *lah eem-preh-SOHR-ah*
program	**el programa** *ehl pro-GRAH-mah*
(to) save	**guardar** *gwahr-DAHR*
scanner	**el escáner** *ehl es-KAHN-ehr*
screen	**la pantalla** *lah pahn-TAH-yah*
search engine	**el buscador** *ehl boos-kah-DOHR*
site	**el sitio** *ehl SEE-tyoh*
software	**los datos de aplicación** *lohs DAH-tohs day ah-plee-kah-SYOHN*

speed	**la velocidad** *lah behl-oh-see-DAHD*
spell checker	**el corrector ortográfico** *ehl kohr-ehk-TOHR or-toh-GRAH-fee-koh*
symbol	**el símbolo** *ehl-SEEM-boh-loh*
website	**el website** *ehl WEB-sah-eet*
zip disk	**el zip** *el zip*
zip drive	**la disquetera zip** *lah dees-kay-TEHR-ah zip*

PHOTOCOPYING

Where can I get photocopying done?	**¿Dónde puedo hacer una fotocopia?** *DOHN-day PWEH-doh ah-SEHR oo-nah foh-toh-KOH-pee-ah*
Do you have a photocopy machine?	**¿Tiene una fotocopiadora?** *TYEHN-eh oo-nah foh-toh-koh-pee-ah-DOHR-ah*

Does it make color copies?	**¿Hace copias en color?** *AH-say KOH-pee-ahs ehn koh-LOHR*
Does it enlarge (reduce)?	**¿Puede aumentar (reducir) el documento?** *PWEH-day ow-men-TAHR (reh-doo-SEER) ehl doh-koo-MEN-toh?*

GENERAL INFORMATION

TELLING TIME

What time is it?　　　　**¿Qué hora es?**　*kay OH-rah ehs*

When telling time in Spanish, *It is* is expressed by **Es la** for 1:00 and **Son las** for all other numbers.

It's 1:00.　　　　**Es la una.**　*ehs lah oo-nah*

It's 2:00.　　　　**Son las dos.**　*sohn lahs dohs*

It's 3:00, etc.　　　　**Son las tres, etc.**　*sohn lahs trehs*

The number of minutes after the hour is expressed by adding **y** (and) followed by the number of minutes.

It's 4:10.　　　　**Son las cuatro y diez.**　*sohn lahs KWAH-troh ee dyehs*

It's 5:20.　　　　**Son las cinco y veinte.**　*sohn lahs SEEN-koh ee BAYN-tay.*

A quarter after and half past are expressed by placing **y cuarto** and **y media** after the hour.

It's 6:15.　　　　**Son las seis y cuarto.**　*sohn lahs sayss ee KWAHR-toh*

It's 7:30.　　　　**Son las siete y media.**　*sohn lahs SYEH-tay ee MEH-dyah*

After passing the half-hour point on the clock, time is expressed in Spanish by *subtracting* the number of minutes from the next hour.

It's 7:35.	**Son las ocho menos veinticinco.** *sohn lahs OH-choh MEH-nohs bayn-tee-SEEN-koh*
It's 8:50.	**Son las nueve menos diez.** *sohn lahs NWEH-bay meh-nohs dyehs*
At what time?	**¿A qué hora?** *ah kay OH-rah*
At 1:00.	**A la una.** *ah lah OO-nah*
At 2:00 (3:00, etc.)	**A las dos (tres, etc.)** *ah lahs dohs (trehs)*
A.M.	**de la mañana (in the morning)** *day lah man-YAH-nah*
P.M.	**de la tarde (in the afternoon)** *day lah TAHR -day* **de la noche (at night)** *day lah NOH-chay*
It's noon.	**Es mediodía.** *ehs meh-dee-ohd-EE-oh*
It's midnight.	**Es medianoche.** *ehs MEH-dee-ah-NOH-chay*
It's early (late).	**Es temprano (tarde).** *ehs temp-RAH-noh (TAHR-day)*

Official time is based on the 24-hour clock. You will find train schedules and other such times expressed in terms of a point within a 24-hour sequence.

To convert from official time, subtract 12 and add P.M.

The train leaves at 15:30. (3:30 P.M.)	**El tren sale a las quince y media.** *ehl trehn SAH-lay ah lahs KEEN-say ee MEH-dee-ah*
The time is now 21:15. (9:15 P.M.)	**Son las veintiuna y cuarto.** *sohn lahs bayn-tee-OO-nah ee KWAHR-toh*

DAYS OF THE WEEK

What day is today?	**¿Qué día es hoy?**	*kay DEE-ah ehs oy*

The days are *not* capitalized in Spanish.

Today is ____.	**Hoy es ____.**	*oy ehs*
■ Monday	**lunes**	*LOO-nehs*
■ Tuesday	**martes**	*MAHR-tays*
■ Wednesday	**miércoles**	*MYEHR-kohl-ays*
■ Thursday	**jueves**	*HWEB-ays*
■ Friday	**viernes**	*bee-EHR-nays*

■ Saturday	**sábado**	*SAH-bah-doh*
■ Sunday	**domingo**	*doh-MEEN-goh*
yesterday	**ayer**	*ah-YEHR*
the day before yesterday	**anteayer**	*ant-ay-ah-YEHR*
tomorrow	**mañana**	*mahn-YAH-nah*
the day after tomorrow	**pasado mañana**	*pah-SAH-doh mahn-YAH-nah*
last week	**la semana pasada**	*ah seh-MAH-nah pah-SAH-dah*
next week	**la semana próxima**	*lah seh-MAH-nah PROHK-see-mah*
tonight	**esta noche**	*EHS-tah NOH-chay*
last night	**anoche**	*ahn-OH-chay*

MONTHS OF THE YEAR

The months are *not* capitalized in Spanish.

January	**enero**	*ay-NEHR-oh*
February	**febrero**	*fay-BREH-roh*
March	**marzo**	*MAHR-soh*
April	**abril**	*ah-BREEL*
May	**mayo**	*MAH-yoh*
June	**junio**	*HOO-nee-oh*
July	**julio**	*HOO-lee-oh*
August	**agosto**	*ah-GOHS-toh*

September	**septiembre** *sep-tee-EHMB-ray*
October	**octubre** *ohk-TOO-bray*
November	**noviembre** *noh-bee-EHMB-ray*
December	**diciembre** *dee-SYEHM-bray*
What's today's date?	**¿Cuál es la fecha de hoy?** *kwahl ehs lah FAY-chah day oy*

The first of the month is *el primero* (an ordinal number). All other dates are expressed with *cardinal* numbers.

Today is August ____.	**Hoy es ____ de agosto.** *oy ehs ____ day ah-GOHS-tah*
▇ first	**el primero** *ehl pree-MEHR-oh*
▇ second	**el dos** *ehl dos*
▇ fourth	**el cuatro** *ehl KWAH-troh*
▇ 25th	**el veinticinco** *ehl bayn-tee-SEENK-oh*
this month	**este mes** *EHS-tay mehs*
last month	**el mes pasado** *ehl mehs pah-SAH-doh*
next month	**el mes próximo** *ehl mehs PROHK-see-moh*
last year	**el año pasado** *ehl AHN-yoh pah-SAH-doh*
next year	**el año que viene** *ehl AHN-yoh kay bee-EN-ay*
May 1, 1876	**El primero de mayo de mil ochocientos setenta y seis.** *ehl pree-MEHR-oh day MAH-ee-oh day meel oh-choh-SYEHN-tohs say-TEN-tah ee SAYSS*

July 4, 2012   **El cuatro de julio de dos mil doce.**
*ehl KWAH-troh day HOOL-ee-oh day
dohs meel DOH-seh*

THE FOUR SEASONS

spring   **la primavera** *lah pree-mah-BEHR-ah*

summer   **el verano** *ehl behr-AH-noh*

fall   **el otoño** *ehl oh-TOHN-yoh*

winter   **el invierno** *ehl eem-BYEHR-noh*

THE WEATHER

How is the weather today?   **¿Qué tiempo hace hoy?** *kay TYEHM-poh ah-say oy*

It's nice (bad) weather.   **Hace buen (mal) tiempo.** *ah-say bwehn (mahl) TYEHM-poh*

It's raining.   **Llueve.** *YWEHB-ay*

It's snowing.   **Nieva.** *NYEHB-ah*

It's ____.   **Hace ____.** *AH-say*

- hot   **calor** *kah-LOHR*
- cold   **frío** *FREE-oh*
- cool   **fresco** *FREHS-koh*
- windy   **viento** *BYEHN-toh*
- sunny   **sol** *sohl*

RELIGIOUS SERVICES

In addition to viewing the churches and cathedrals, you may wish to attend services.

Is there a ____ near here?	**¿Hay una ____ cerca de aquí?** *AH-ee oo-nah SEHR-kah day ah-KEE*
■ Catholic church	**iglesia católica** *ee-GLAY-see-ah kah-TOHL-ee-kah*
■ Protestant church	**iglesia protestante** *ee-GLAY-see-ah pro-test-AHN-tay*
■ Synagogue	**sinagoga** *see-nah-GOH-gah*
■ Mosque	**mezquita** *mehs-KEE-tah*
When is the service (mass)?	**¿A qué hora es la misa?** *ah kay OH-rah ehs lah MEE-sah*
I want to speak to a ____.	**Quiero hablar con ____.** *kee-EHR-oh ah-BLAHR kohn*
■ priest	**un cura** *oon KOO-rah*
■ minister	**un ministro** *oon mee-NEES-troh*
■ rabbi	**un rabino** *oon rah-BEEN-oh*

COUNTRIES AND NATIONALITIES

COUNTRY		NATIONALITY
Argentina	**Argentina**	argentino
Bolivia	**Bolivia**	boliviano
Brazil	**Brasil**	brasileño
Canada	**Canadá**	canadiense
Chile	**Chile**	chileno
China	**China**	chino
Colombia	**Colombia**	colombiano
Costa Rica	**Costa Rica**	costarricense
Cuba	**Cuba**	cubano
Denmark	**Dinamarca**	danés
Dominican Republic	**República Dominicana**	dominicano
Ecuador	**Ecuador**	ecuatoriano
Egypt	**Egipto**	egipcio
England	**Inglaterra**	inglés
Europe	**Europa**	europeo
Finland	**Finlandia**	finlandés
France	**Francia**	francés
Germany	**Alemania**	alemán
Great Britain	**Gran Bretaña**	inglés

COUNTRY		NATIONALITY
Greece	**Grecia**	griego
Guatemala	**Guatemala**	guatemalteco
Iceland	**Islandia**	islandés
Holland	**Holanda**	holandés
Ireland	**Irlanda**	irlandés
Israel	**Israel**	israelí
Italy	**Italia**	italiano
Japan	**Japón**	japonés
Mexico	**México or Méjico**	mexicano
Nicaragua	**Nicaragua**	nicaragüense
Norway	**Noruega**	noruego
Panama	**Panamá**	panameño
Paraguay	**Paraguay**	paraguayo
Peru	**Perú**	peruano
Poland	**Polonia**	polaco
Portugal	**Portugal**	portugués
Puerto Rico	**Puerto Rico**	puertorriqueño
Russia	**Rusia**	ruso
El Salvador	**El Salvador**	salvadoreño
Spain	**España**	español
Sweden	**Suecia**	sueco
Switzerland	**Suiza**	suizo
Turkey	**Turquía**	turco
United States	**Estados Unidos**	estadounidense (norteamericano)
Uruguay	**Uruguay**	uruguayo
Venezuela	**Venezuela**	venezolano

IMPORTANT SIGNS

Abajo	Down
Abierto	Open
Alto	Stop
Arriba	Up
Ascensor	Elevator
Caballeros	Men's room
Caja	Cashier
Caliente or **"C"**	Hot
Carretera particular	Private road
Cerrado	Closed
Completo	Filled up
Cuidado	Watch out, caution
Damas	Ladies room
Empuje	Push
Entrada	Entrance
Frío or **"F"**	Cold
Libre	Vacant
No fumar	No smoking

No obstruya la entrada	Don't block entrance
No pisar el césped	Keep off the grass
No tocar	Hands off, don't touch
Ocupado	Busy, occupied
¡Pase!	Walk, cross
Peligro	Danger
Prohibido	Forbidden, No ____
■ **____ el paso**	No entrance, Keep out
■ **____ escupir**	No spitting
■ **____ fumar**	No smoking
■ **____ estacionarse**	No parking
■ **____ bañarse**	No bathing
Reservado	Reserved
Sala de espera	Waiting room
Salida	Exit
Se alquila	For rent
Señoras	Ladies room
Servicios	Toilets
Se vende	For sale
Tire	Pull
¡Veneno!	Poison!
Venta	Sale

COMMON ABBREVIATIONS

apdo.	**apartado de correos**	post office box
Av., Avda.	**avenida**	avenue
C., Cía	**compañía**	company
c.	**calle**	street
D.	**don**	title of respect used before a masculine first name: don Pedro
Da., Dᵃ	**doña**	title of respect used before a feminine first name: doña María
EE.UU	**Estados Unidos**	United States (U.S.)
F.C.	**ferrocarril**	railroad
Hnos.	**hermanos**	brothers
N°, num.	**número**	number
1°	**primero**	first
RENFE	**Red Nacional de Ferrocarriles**	Spanish National Railroad System
2°	**segundo**	second
S., Sta.	**San, Santa**	Saint
S.A.	**Sociedad Anónima**	Inc.
Sr.	**Señor**	Mr.
Sra.	**Señora**	Mrs.
Sres., Srs.	**Señores**	Gentlemen

Srta.	**Señorita**	Miss
Ud., Vd.	**Usted**	You (polite sing.)
Uds., Vds.	**Ustedes**	You (polite & familiar plural)

CENTIMETERS/INCHES

It is usually unnecessary to make exact conversions from your customary inches to the metric system, but to give you an approximate idea of how they compare, we give you the following guide.

1 **centímetro** (centimeter)	=	0.39 inches **(pulgadas)**
1 **metro**	=	39.37 inches
		3.28 feet **(pies)**
		1.09 yards **(yardas)**
1 inch	=	2.54 centimeters
1 foot	=	30.5 centimeters
		0. 3 meters
1 yard	=	91.4 centimeters
		0.91 meters

To convert **centímetros** into inches, multiply by .39.
To convert inches into **centímetros,** multiply by 2.54.

Centímetros

Pulgadas

METERS/FEET

How tall are you in meters? See for yourself.

FEET	METERS	FEET	METERS
5	1.52	5.7	1.70
5.1	1.54	5.8	1.73
5.2	1.57	5.9	1.75
5.3	1.59	5.10	1.78
5.4	1.62	5.11	1.80
5.5	1.64	6	1.83
5.6	1.68	5.1	1.85

WHEN YOU WEIGH YOURSELF

1 ____ (kilogram)	=	2.2 ____ (pounds)
1 pound	=	.45 kilograms

KILOS	POUNDS	KILOS	POUNDS
40	88	75	165
45	99	80	176
50	110	85	187
55	121	90	198
60	132	95	209
65	143	100	220
70	154	105	231

LIQUID MEASUREMENTS

1 **litro** (liter)	=	1.06 ____ (quarts)
4 liters	=	1.06 ____ (gallons)

For a quick approximate conversion, multiply the number of gallons by 4 to get liters. Divide the number of liters by 4 to get gallons.

Note: You'll find other conversion charts on pages 92–93, 174, 177, and 178.

MINI-DICTIONARY FOR THE BUSINESS TRAVELER

amount (value)	**el importe**	*ehl eem-POHR-tay*
appraise (to)	**valuar**	*bahl-WAHR*
authorize (to)	**autorizar**	*ow-tohr-ee-SAHR*
authorized edition	**la edición autorizada**	*lah eh-dee-SYOHN ow-tohr-ee-SAH-dah*
bill (noun)	**la cuenta**	*lah KWEHN-tah*
▪ bill of exchange	**la letra de cambio**	*lah LEH-trah day KAHM-bee-oh*
▪ bill of lading	**el conocimiento de embarque**	*ehl koh-noh-see-MYEHN-toh day ehm-BAHR-kay*
▪ bill of sale	**la escritura de venta**	*lah ehs-kree-TOOR-ah day BEN-tah*
business operation	**la operación comercial**	*lah oh-pehr-ah-SYOHN koh-mehr-SYAHL*
cash (money)	**el dinero contante**	*ehl-dee-NEHR-oh kohn-TAHN-tay*
▪ to buy for cash	**pagar al contado**	*pa-GAHR ahl kon-TAH-doh*
▪ to sell for cash	**vender al contado**	*ben-DEHR ahl kon-TAH-doh*

■ to cash a check	**cobrar un cheque** *koh-BRAHR oon CHEH-kay*
certified check	**el cheque certificado** *ehl CHEH-kay sehr-tee-fee-KAH-doh*
chamber of commerce	**la cámara de comercio** *lah KAH-mah-rah day koh-MEHR-see-oh*
compensation for damages	**la indemnización de daños y perjuicios** *lah een-dehm-nee-sah-SYOHN day DAHN-yohs ee pehr-WEE-see-ohs*
competition	**la competición** *la kohm-peh-tee-SYOHN*
■ competitive price	**el precio competidor** *ehl PREH-see-oh kohm-peh-tee-DOHR*
contract	**el contrato** *ehl kohn-TRAH-toh*
■ contractual obligations	**las obligaciones contractuales** *lahs oh-blee-gah-SYOHN-ays kohn-trahk TWAHL-ays*
controlling interest	**el interés predominante** *ehl een-tehr-AYS pray-doh-mee-NAHN-tay*
down payment	**el pago inicial** *ehl PAH-goh ee-nees-YAHL*
due	**vencido** *ben-SEE-doh*
enterprise	**la empresa** *lah ehm-PRAY-sah*
expedite (to) delivery (of goods)	**facilitar la entrega (de mercancía)** *fah-see-lee-TAHR lah ehn-TRAY-gah (day mehr-kahn-SEE-ah)*
■ expedite delivery (of letters)	**facilitar el reparto (de cartas)** *fah-seel-ee-TAHR ehl ray-PAHR-toh (day KAHR-tahs)*
expenses	**los gastos** *lohs GAHS-tohs*

goods	**las mercancías** *lahs mehr-kahn-SEE-ahs*
infringement of patent rights	**violación de derechos de patente** *bee-oh-lah-SYOHN day deh-RAY-chohs day pah-TEN-tay*
insurance against all risks	**seguros contra todo riesgo** *seh-GOOR-ohs kohn-trah TOH-doh ree-EHS-goh*
international law	**la ley internacional** *lah lay een-tehr-nah-syohn-AHL*
lawful possession	**la posesión legal** *lah poh-seh-SYOHN lay-GAHL*
lawsuit	**el pleito** *ehl PLAY-toh*
lawyer	**el abogado** *ehl ah-boh-GAH-doh*
letter of credit	**la carta de crédito** *lah KAHR-tah day KREH-dee-toh*
mail-order business	**el negocio de ventas par correo** *ehl neh-GOH-see-oh day BEN-tahs pohr kohr-AY-oh*
market-value	**el valor comercial** *ehl bah-LOHR koh-mehrs-YAHL*
manager	**el gerente** *ehl hehr-EN-tay*
owner	**el dueno** *ehl DWAYN-yoh*
partner	**el socio** *ehl SOH-see-oh*
payment	**el pago** *ehl PAH-goh*
partial payment	**el pago parcial** *ehl PAH-goh pahr-SYAHL*
past due	**vencido** *ben-SEE-doh*
post office box	**el apartado** *ehl ah-pahr-TAH-doh*
property	**la propiedad** *lah proh-pee-eh-DAHD*

purchasing agent	**el comprador** *ehl kohm prah-DOHR*
put (to) on the American market	**poner en el mercado norteamericano** *poh-NEHR ehn ehl mehr-KAH-doh nohr-tay-ah-mehr-ee-KAH-noh*
sale	**la venta** *lah BEN-tah*
sell (to)	**vender** *ben-DEHR*
send (to)	**mandar** *mahn-DAHR*
■ to send back	**devolver** *day-bohl-BEHR*
■ to send C. O. D.	**mandar contra reembolso** *mahn-DAHR kohn-trah ray-ehm-BOHL-soh*
shipment	**el envío** *ehl ehm-BEE-oh*
tax	**el impuesto** *ehl eem PWEHS-toh*
■ tax-exempt	**libre de impuestos** *LEE-bray day eem-PWEHS-tohs*
■ sales tax	**el impuesto sobre ventas** *ehl eem-PWEHS-toh soh-bray BEN-tahs*
■ value added tax	**el impuesto sobre el valor añadido** *ehl eem-PWEHS-toh soh-bray ehl bah-LOHR ahn-yah-DEE-doh*
trade	**el comercio** *ehl koh-MEHR-see-oh*
transact business (to)	**hacer negocios** *ah-SEHR neh-GOH-see-ohs*
transfer (noun)	**la transferencia** *lah trahns-fehr-EHN-see-ah*
transportation charges	**gastos de transporte** *GAHS-tohs day trahns-POHR-tay*
via	**por vía** *pohr BEE-ah*
yield a profit (to)	**rendir una ganancia** *rehn-DEER oo-nah gah-NAHN-see-ah*

QUICK GRAMMAR GUIDE

Your facility with Spanish will be greatly enhanced if you know a little of its grammar. Here are a few simple rules governing the use of the various parts of speech.

NOUNS

In contrast with English, in which inanimate objects are considered neuter, Spanish nouns are designated either masculine or feminine. In addition, if a noun represents a male being, it is masculine; if it is for a female being, it is feminine.

Examples of some masculine nouns are:

el hombre (the man)
el hermano (the brother)
el padre (the father)

Some feminine nouns are:

la mujer (the woman)
la hermana (the sister)
la madre (the mother)

As a general rule, nouns ending in *o* are masculine while nouns ending in *a* are feminine.

el minuto (the minute)	**la joya** (the jewel)
el médico (the doctor)	**la manzana** (the apple)

But there are some exceptions, such as:

la mano (the hand)	**el día** (the day)
la foto (the photograph)	**el mapa** (the map)

To make singular nouns plural, add *s* to nouns that end in a vowel and *es* to those that end in a consonant.

el muchacho	**los muchachos**
la rosa	**las rosas**
el tren	**los trenes**
la mujer	**las mujeres**

ARTICLES

Articles *(the, a, an)* agree in gender (masculine or feminine) and in number (singular or plural) with the nouns they modify.

el libro (the book)	**los libros** (the books)
la casa (the house)	**las casas** (the houses)
un libro (a book)	**unos libros** (some books)
una casa (a house)	**unas casas** (some houses)

Two contractions are formed when **el** *(the)* combines with either **a** *(to)* or **de** *(of* or *from)*.

a + el = al (to the)	**Voy al cine** (I'm going to the movies)
de + el = del (of or from the)	**Es el principio del año** (It's the beginning of the year)

ADJECTIVES

Adjectives agree in gender with the nouns they modify. Generally, descriptive adjectives follow the noun.

la casa blanca (the white house)
el hombre alto (the tall man)

Adjectives also agree in number with the nouns they modify. The plural of adjectives is formed in the same way as in the plural of nouns. For adjectives ending in a vowel, you add *s;* for adjectives ending in a consonant, add *es.*

el papel azul
(the blue paper)

los papeles azules
(the blue papers)

la casa roja
(the red house)

las casas rojas
(the red houses)

Limiting adjectives agree in number and gender with the nouns they modify, and usually precede the noun.

muchas cosas (many things)

pocos americanos (few Americans)

Demonstrative adjectives *(this, that, these, those)* are placed in front of the nouns they modify. They must agree in number and gender with the nouns, and in a series they are usually repeated before each noun. Use the following table to find the correct form of these demonstrative adjectives, then notice how they are used in context, agreeing with their nouns in gender and number.

SINGULAR (PLURAL)	MASCULINE	FEMININE
this (these)	este (estos)	esta (estas)
that (those)	ese (esos)	esa (esas)
that (those) (meaning far away)	aquel (aquellos)	aquella (aquellas)

Now, in context.

este zapato (this shoe)

estos zapatos (these shoes)

esa blusa (that blouse)

esas blusas (those blouses)

aquel edificio (that building—in the distance)

aquellos edificios (those buildings)

estos hombres y estas mujeres (these men and women)

Possessive adjectives must agree with the nouns they modify. Use the following table to locate the appropriate form to express what you mean.

	SINGULAR	**PLURAL**
my	mi	mis
your (familiar)	tu	tus
your (polite) his her its	su	sus
our	nuestro(a)	nuestros(as)
your (plural familiar)	vuestro(a)	vuestros(as)
your (plural polite) their	su	sus

Here are some examples of possessive adjectives, as they modify their nouns in number and gender.

mi amigo (my friend)	**mis amigos** (my friends)
nuestra casa (our house)	**nuestro coche** (our car)
nuestros libros (our books)	**tus zapatos** (your shoes)*

*This is the familiar form, used when talking to a friend, a child, or among members of the same family. **Sus zapatos** (your shoes) would be the polite form, always used when talking to strangers.

Since **su** and **sus** have six possible meanings, it is often necessary to use a prepositional phrase **(de usted, de ustedes, de él, de ellos, de ella, de ellas)** to avoid any possible ambiguity.

su casa (could mean your, her, his, its, or their house)
la casa de usted (your house)
la casa de ella (her house)

PRONOUNS

Subject pronouns (*I, you, he, she*, etc.) have both singular and plural forms.

SINGULAR		PLURAL	
I	yo	(we)	nosotros(as)
you	tú	you (familiar)	vosotros (as) (used in Spain)
you	usted	you (polite)	ustedes (used for both familiar and polite forms in Latin America)
he	él	they (m.)	ellos
she	ella	they (f.)	ellas

Direct object pronouns (*me, you, him, it, us, them*) are used as direct objects of verbs. They have both singular and plural forms, as the table below indicates.

SINGULAR		PLURAL	
me	me	us	nos
you	te	you (familiar)	os (used in Spain)
you	le, la	you (polite)	los, las
him	le, lo	them (m.)	los
		them (f.)	las
her	la		
it	lo		

Object pronouns precede the verb unless the sentence is an affirmative command or the verb is an infinitive.

Yo te veo (I see you)
Ella me habla (She talks to me)

But in a command or with an infinitive:

Dígame la verdad (Tell me the truth)
Déme el paquete (Give me the package)
Yo quiero verla (I want to see her)
Usted no puede hacerlo (You can't do it)

Indirect object pronouns are pronouns serving as indirect objects. They take either singular or plural forms, as the table below indicates.

SINGULAR		PLURAL	
to me	me	to us	nos
to you (familiar)	te	to you (familiar)	os (used in Spain)
to you (polite)	le	to you (polite)	les
him	le	to them (m.)	les
her	le	to them (f.)	les
it	le		

VERBS

In this phrase book, we limit the use of verbs to the present tense, since this is the most likely one for you to use as a tourist. All Spanish verbs in the infinitive end in either *ar*, *er*, or *ir*.

pas<u>ar</u> (to pass)
beb<u>er</u> (to drink)
viv<u>ir</u> (to live)

In order to conjugate a verb this infinitive ending must be removed and replaced by the appropriate ending. The following are three typical regular verbs.

VERB WITH *AR* ENDING (HABLAR—TO SPEAK)

yo	habl<u>o</u>	nosotros (as)	habl<u>amos</u>
tú	habl<u>as</u>	vosotros (as)	habl<u>áis</u> (used in Spain)
usted	habl<u>a</u>	ustedes	
él, ella	habl<u>a</u>	ellos ellas	habl<u>an</u>

VERB WITH *ER* ENDING (COMER—TO EAT)

yo	com<u>o</u>	nosotros (as)	com<u>emos</u>
tú	com<u>es</u>	vosotros (as)	com<u>éis</u> (used in Spain)
usted	com<u>e</u>	ustedes	
él, ella	com<u>e</u>	ellos ellas	com<u>en</u>

VERB WITH *IR* ENDING (ESCRIBIR—TO WRITE)

yo	escrib<u>o</u>	nosotros (as)	escrib<u>imos</u>
tú	escrib<u>es</u>	vosotros (as)	escrib<u>ís</u> (used in Spain)
usted	escrib<u>e</u>	ustedes	
él, ella	escrib<u>e</u>	ellos ellas	escrib<u>en</u>

Using the conjugation tables above, we give you some examples of verbs paired with the appropriate verb endings.

vender (to sell)   **Yo vendo** (I sell)

pasar (to pass)   **Ellos pasan** (They pass)

vivir (to live)   **Nosotros vivimos** (We live)

Many Spanish verbs are irregular. The following tables show the conjugations for commonly used irregular verbs.

DAR (TO GIVE)

doy	damos
das	dais
da	dan

DECIR (TO SAY, TO TELL)

digo	decimos
dices	decís
dice	dicen

HACER (TO DO, TO MAKE)

hago	hacemos
haces	hacéis
hace	hacen

IR (TO GO)

voy	vamos
vas	vais
va	van

OÍR (TO HEAR)

oigo	oímos
oyes	oís
oye	oyen

PODER (TO BE ABLE)

puedo	podemos
puedes	podéis
puede	pueden

PONER (TO PUT, TO PLACE)

pongo	ponemos
pones	ponéis
pone	ponen

QUERER (TO WISH, TO WANT)

quiero	queremos
quieres	queréis
quiere	quieren

SABER (TO KNOW)

sé	sabemos
sabes	sabéis
sabe	saben

SALIR (TO LEAVE, GO OUT)

salgo	salimos
sales	salís
sale	salen

TENER (TO HAVE)	
tengo	tenemos
tienes	tenéis
tiene	tienen

TRAER (TO BRING)	
traigo	traemos
traes	traéis
trae	traen

VENIR (TO COME)	
vengo	venímos
vienes	venís
viene	vienen

VER (TO SEE)	
veo	vemos
ves	veis
ve	ven

There are two verbs in Spanish that express the various forms of the verb to be.

SER (TO BE)	
soy	somos
eres	sois
es	son

ESTAR (TO BE)	
estoy	estamos
estás	estáis
está	están

The verb **estar** and its various forms are used in three major instances.

1. To tell about or inquire about location.
   Madrid está en España. (Madrid is in Spain.)
   ¿Dónde está el policía? (Where is the policeman?)
2. To tell or ask about health.
   ¿Cómo está usted hoy? (How are you today?)
   Estoy bien, gracias. (I'm fine, thank you.)
3. To describe a temporary or changeable condition.
   La puerta está abierta. (The door is open.)
   El café está caliente. (The coffee is hot.)
   Nosotros estamos contentos. (We are happy.)
   Ella está cansada. (She is tired.)

At all other times, use the forms of ser.

Yo soy norteamericano. (I am American.)
El coche es grande. (The car is big.)
El libro es importante. (The book is important.)
Los anillos son de oro. (The rings are (made) of gold.)

The verb **tener** *(to have)* is used in a number of Spanish idiomatic expressions.

tener frío (to be cold, literally to have cold)
tener calor (to be hot)
tener hambre (to be hungry)
tener sed (to be thirsty)
tener sueño (to be sleepy)
tener prisa (to be in a hurry)
tener miedo (to be afraid)
tener razón (to be right)
no tener razón (to be wrong)
tener ____ años (to be ____ years old)

Some examples.

No tengo calor. Tengo frío. (I'm not hot. I'm cold.)
¿Tiene usted hambre? (Are you hungry?)
No, tengo sed. (No, I am thirsty.)
Tenemos prisa. (We're in a hurry.)
Tengo razón. El tiene veinte años. (I'm right. He's 20 years old.)

PREPOSITIONS

The following is a listing of simple prepositions and their English equivalents.

a (to, at; with time)
con (with)
contra (against)
de (from, of, about)
en (in, on)
entre (between, among)
hacia (toward)
hasta (up to, until)
para (for, in order to, to)
por (for, by, through, because)
según (according to)
sin (without)
sobre (on, about)

And some compound prepositions:

además de (besides, in addition to)
al lado de (beside, at the side of)
antes de (before; references to time)
cerca de (near)
debajo de (under, underneath)
delante de (in front of)
dentro de (inside of, within)
después de (after)
detrás de (behind)
en vez de (instead of)
encima de (on top of)
enfrente de (facing, opposite, in front of)
fuera de (outside of)
lejos de (far from)

Here are some examples.

El policía está delante de la tienda. (The policeman is in front of the store.)

Voy con mi familia. (I'm going with my family.)
¿Está cerca de la estación? (It is near the station?)
Tomo el tren a las cinco. (I'm taking the train at 5:00.)

TO FORM QUESTIONS

Some common interrogative words in Spanish are the following.

¿Adónde (Where; to what place?)
¿Cómo? (How?)
¿Cuál? (Which?)
¿Cuándo? (When?)
¿Cuánto? (How much?)
¿Cuántos? (How many?)
¿Dónde? (Where?)
¿Para qué? (What for? Why?)
¿Por qué? (Why?)
¿Qué? (What?)
¿Quién? (Who?—singular)
¿Quiénes? (Who?—plural)

Notice that all interrogative words have a written accent.
To form a question in Spanish, place the subject *after* the verb. For example:

¿Habla usted español?	(Do you speak Spanish?)
¿Tiene María el billete?	(Does Maria have the ticket?)
¿Cuándo van ustedes al cine?	(When are you going to the movies?)

Note that in an interrogative sentence there is an inverted question mark before the sentence as well as the regular question mark after it.

TO FORM NEGATIVE WORDS

The most common negative word in Spanish is **no.** It always precedes the verb.

Yo no tengo dinero. (I have no money; I don't have any money.)

Other negative words are:

nadie (no one)
nada (nothing)
nunca (never)
ninguno (a) (none)
tampoco (neither)

Used in sentences, these would be:

Nadie viene. (No one is coming.)
No veo nada. (I don't see anything; I see nothing.)
Nunca comemos en casa. (We never eat at home.)
Ninguno me gusta. (I don't like any; I like none.)
Ella no tiene dinero, ni yo tampoco. (She has no money and neither do I.)

Any one of the negative words except **no** may be used either before or after the verb. If one is used after the verb, **no** is also used before the verb, making a double negative.

Nadie habla.   (Nobody is speaking.)
No habla nadie.

Nada veo.   (I don't see anything; I see nothing.)
No veo nada.

VOCABULARY VARIATIONS

Spanish is an international language spoken by over 300 million people in 19 independent countries and the commonwealth of Puerto Rico. Although there are some differences in pronunciation and a number of regional vocabulary variations, the basic language is remarkably free of mutually unintelligible dialects, and is universally understood in its written and spoken forms throughout the Spanish-speaking world.

The following is a list of some common words in English and their various equivalents in Spain and several Latin American countries.

car:	**el automóvil:** Universal
	el coche: Spain, Argentina
	el carro: Peru, Colombia, Venezuela, Puerto Rico, Mexico
	la máquina: Puerto Rico
	el auto: Peru, Chile
bus:	**el autobús:** Universal
	el camión: Mexico
	la guagua: Puerto Rico, Cuba, Canary Islands
	el ómnibus: Argentina
	el bus: Colombia, Chile
	el colectivo: Argentina, Uruguay
gas station:	**la estación de servicio:** Universal
	la gasolinera: Mexico
driver's license:	**la licencia de manejar:** Universal
	el carnet de conducir: Spain, Chile
	el brevete: Peru, Ecuador

to park:	**parquear:** Latin America **aparcar, estacionar (se):** Spain
swimming pool:	**la piscina:** Universal **la alberca:** Mexico **la pileta:** Argentina
sidewalk:	**la acera:** Universal **la banqueta:** Mexico **la vereda:** Argentina, Chile
police station:	**la estación de policía:** Universal **la comisaría:** Spain
apartment:	**el apartamento:** Universal **el departamento:** Mexico, Chile **el piso:** Spain
eyeglasses:	**los anteojos:** Latin America **los lentes:** Universal **las gafas:** Spain
bootblack:	**el limpiabotas:** Universal **el bolero:** Mexico
(drinking) straw:	**la paja:** Universal **la pajita:** Argentina
eggs:	**los huevos:** Universal **los blanquillos:** Mexico
sandwich:	**el sándwich:** Universal **el emparedado, el bocadillo:** Spain **la torta:** Mexico
potato:	**la patata:** Spain **la papa:** South America
beef:	**la carne de vaca:** Universal **la carne de res:** Mexico

string (green) beans:	**las judías verdes:** Spain **las habichuelas verdes:** Universal **las chauchas:** Argentina **los ejotes:** Mexico
peas:	**los guisantes:** Spain **los chícharos:** Mexico **los pitipuá:** Puerto Rico **los porotos:** Argentina
grocery store:	**la tienda de comestibles:** Universal **la tienda de abarrotes:** Mexico, Chile, Peru **la tienda de ultramarinos:** Spain **la pulpería:** South America **la bodega:** Puerto Rico, USA
room:	**la habitación:** Universal **el cuarto:** Mexico
bedroom:	**el dormitorio:** Universal **la recámara:** Mexico **la alcoba:** Spain
soft boiled egg:	**el huevo pasado por agua:** Universal **el huevo tibio:** Mexico **el huevo hervido:** Argentina
fried eggs:	**huevos fritos:** Universal **huevos estrellados:** Mexico
fruit juice	**el jugo:** Universal **el zumo:** Spain
orange juice:	**el jugo de naranja:** Universal **el jugo de china:** Puerto Rico
roll:	**el panecillo:** Universal **el bolillo:** Mexico

lemon:	**el limón:** Universal **la lima:** Mexico
peanut:	**el maní:** Caribbean (Puerto Rico, Cuba, Dominican Republic), Chile, Peru, Argentina **el cacahuate:** Mexico **el cacahuete:** Spain
tomato:	**el tomate:** Universal **el jitomate:** Mexico
jacket:	**el saco:** Universal **la americana, la chaqueta:** Spain **la campera:** Argentina
postage stamp:	**la estampilla:** Latin America **el sello:** Spain **el timbre:** Mexico
ticket:	**el billete, la entrada:** Universal **el boleto:** Mexico
elevator:	**el ascensor:** Universal **el elevador:** Mexico
rest room:	**los baños:** Universal **los servicios:** Spain
shower:	**la ducha:** Universal **la regadera:** Mexico
refrigerator:	**el frigorífico**: Spain **el refrigerador:** Universal **la heladera:** Argentina **la nevera:** Central America
to rent:	**rentar or arrendar:** Universal **alquilar:** Spain

UNITED STATES EMBASSIES IN SPANISH-SPEAKING COUNTRIES

Note: For calls from the United States dial numbers in parentheses first. For in-country calls do not dial numbers in parentheses.

United States Embassy in Buenos Aires, ARGENTINA
Avenida Colombia 4300
(011-54-11) 5777-4533

United States Embassy in La Paz, BOLIVIA
Avenida Arce 2780
(011-5912) 216-8000

United States Embassy in Santiago, CHILE
Avenida Andrés Bello 2800, Las Condes
(011-562) 330-3000

United States Embassy in Bogotá, COLOMBIA
Calle 24 Bis No. 48-50
(011-571) 315-1566

United States Embassy in San José, COSTA RICA
Calle 120, Avenida O, Pavas
(011-5062) 519-2000

United States Embassy in Santo Domingo, DOMINICAN REPUBLIC
American Embassy César Nicolás Pensón and esquina
Leopoldo Navarro
(011-1809) 221-2171

United States Embassy in Quito, ECUADOR
Avenida Avigiras E12-170 and Avenida Eloy Alfaro
(next to SOLCA)
(011-5932) 398-5000

United States Embassy in San Salvador, EL SALVADOR
Boulevard Santa Elena, Antiguo Cuscactlán
(011-5032) 501-2999

United States Embassy in Guatemala City, GUATEMALA
Avenida Reforma 7-01, Zona 10
(011-5022) 326-4000

United States Embassy in Tegucigalpa, HONDURAS
Avenida La Paz
(011-504) 236-9320

United States Embassy in Mexico City, MEXICO
Paseo de la Reforma 305, Colonia Cuauhtemoc
(011-5255) 5080-2000

United States Embassy in Managua, NICARAGUA
American Embassy Km 4½ Carretera Sur
(011-5052) 252-7100

United States Embassy in Panama City, PANAMA
Apartado 0816-02561, Zona 5
(011-507) 207-7000

United States Embassy in Asunción, PARAGUAY
1776 Mariscal López Avenue
(011-595-21) 213-715

United States Embassy in Lima, PERU
Avenida La Encalada cdra, 17 s/n, Surco
(011-511) 618-2000

United States Embassy in Madrid, SPAIN
C/Serrano, 75
(011-34-91) 587-2200

United States Embassy in Montevideo, URUGUAY
Lauro Muller 1776
(011-5982) 418-7777

United States Embassy in Caracas, VENEZUELA
Calle F with Calle Suapure, Colinas de Valle Arriba
(011-58-212) 975-6411

ENGLISH-SPANISH DICTIONARY

A

a, an un *oon*, una (f.) *oo-nah*

able (to be) poder *poh-DEHR*

about alrededor de *ahl-reh-deh-DOHR day*; **about two o'clock** a eso de las dos *ah EH-soh day lahs dohs*

above arriba *ahr-REE-bah*; encima (de) *ehn-SEE-mah (day)*

abscess el absceso *ahbs-SEH-soh*

accelerator el acelerador *ah-seh-leh-rah-DOHR*

accept (v.) aceptar *ah-sehp-TAHR*

accident el accidente *ahk-see-DEHN-teh*

accountant el contador *kohn-ta-DOHR*

ache (head) el dolor de cabeza *doh-LOHR day kah-BEH-sah*; **(stomach)** el dolor de estómago *doh-LOHR day ehs-TOH-mah-goh*; **(tooth)** el dolor de muelas *doh-LOHR day MWEH-lahs*

across a través (de) *ah trah-BEHS (day)*

adapter el adaptador *ah-dahp-tah-DOHR*

address la dirección *dee-rehk-SYOHN*

adhesive tape cinta adhesiva *SEEN-tah ahd-eh-SEE-vah*

adjust (v.) ajustar *ah-hoos-TAHR*, arreglar *ahr-reh-GLAHR*

admittance (no) se prohibe la entrada *seh proh-EE-beh lah ehn-TRAH-dah*

afraid (to be) tener miedo *teh-NEHR MYEH-doh*

after después (de) *dehs-PWEHS (day)*

afternoon la tarde *TAHR-deh*

afterward después *dehs-PWEHS*, luego *LWEH-goh*

again otra vez *OH-trah behs*, de nuevo *deh NWEH-boh*

against contra *KOHN-trah*

agree (v.) estar de acuerdo *ehs-TAHR deh ah-KWEHR-doh*

ahead adelante *ah-deh-LAHN-teh*

aid la ayuda *ah-YOO-dah*; **first aid** primeros auxilios *pree-mehr-ohs ah-ook-SEEL-yohs*

AIDS el SIDA *SEE-dah*

air aire *AHY-reh*; **air mail** el correo aéreo *kohr-REH-oh ah-EH-reh-oh*

airline la línea aérea *LEE-neh-ah ah-EH-reh-ah*

airplane el avión *ah-BYOHN*

airport el aeropuerto *ah-eh-roh-PWEHR-toh*

alarm clock el despertador *dehs-pehr-tah-DOHR*

all todo *TOH-doh*; **All aboard!** ¡A bordo! *ah BOHR-doh*, ¡Señores viajeros al tren! *sehn-YOH-rehs byah-HEH-rohs ahl TREHN*

allergy la alergia *ah-LEHR-hee-ah*

allow permitir *pehr-mee-TEER*

almond la almendra *ahl-MEHN-drah*

almost casi *KAH-see*

alone solo *SOH-loh*

already ya *yah*

also también *tahm-BYEHN*

always siempre *SYEHM-preh*

A.M. de (por) la mañana *deh (pohr) lah mahn-YAHN-nah*

am soy *soy*, estoy *ehs-TOY*

American norteamericano *NOHR-teh-ah-meh-ree-KAH-noh*; **American plan** la pensión completa *pehn-SYOHN kohm-PLEH-tah*, cuarto y comida *KWAHR-toh ee koh-MEE-dah*

among entre *EHN-treh*

and y *ee*; e *eh* [before i or hi]

ankle el tobillo *toh-BEE-yoh*

annoy (v.) molestar *moh-lehs-TAHR*

another otro *OH-troh*

answer (response) la respuesta *rehs-PWEHS-tah*, la contestación *kohn-tehs-tah-SYOHN*

antibiotic el antibiótico *ahn-tee-bee-OH-tee-koh*

any algún *ahl-GOON*

anybody (anyone) alguien *AHL-gyehn*

anything algo *AHL-goh*; **Anything else?** ¿Algo más? *AHL-goh MAHS*

apartment el piso *PEE-soh*, el apartamento *ah-pahr-tah-MEHN-toh*

aperitif el aperitivo *ah-peh-ree-TEE-boh*

appetizers los entremeses *ehn-treh-MEH-sehs*

apple la manzana *mahn-SAH-nah*

apricot el albaricoque *ahl-bah-ree-KOH-keh*

April abril *ah-BREEL*

Arab árabe *AH-rah-beh*

are son *sohn*, están *ehs-TAHN*

Argentinian argentino *ahr-hehn-TEEN-oh*

arm el brazo *BRAH-soh*

armchair el sillón *see-YOHN*

around alrededor (de) *ahl-reh-deh-DOHR (deh)*

arrival la llegada *yeh-GAH-dah*

article el artículo *ahr-TEE-koo-loh*

as como *KOH-moh*

ashtray el cenicero *seh-nee-SEH-roh*

ask (a question) preguntar *preh-goon-TAHR*; **ask for** pedir *peh-DEER*

asparagus el espárrago *ehs-PAHR-ah-goh*

aspirin la aspirina *ahs-pee-REE-nah*

assistance la asistencia *ah-sees-TEHN-see-ah*

at en *ehn*, a *ah*; **at her house** en casa de ella *ehn KAH-sah deh EH-yah*; **at once** en seguida *ehn seh-GHEE-dah*

ATM cajero automático *kah-HEHR-oh ow-to-MAH-tee-koh*

attention! ¡atención! *ah-tehn-SYOHN*, ¡cuidado! *kwee-DAH-doh*

August agosto (m.) *ah-GOHS-toh*

aunt la tía *TEE-ah*

Austrian austríaco *ows-TREE-ah-koh*

automobile el automóvil *ow-toh-MOH-beel*, el carro *KAHR-roh*, el coche *KOH-cheh*

autumn el otoño *oh-TOHN-yoh*

avoid (v.) evitar *eh-bee-TAHR*

awful terrible *tehr-REE-bleh*

B

baby el bebé *beh-BEH*, el nene *NEH-neh*, la nena *NEH-nah*

back (body part) la espalda *ehs-PAHL-dah*; **(behind)** detrás (de) *deh-TRAHS (deh)*; **(direction, movement)** atrás *ah-TRAHS*

bacon el tocino *toh-SEE-noh*

bad malo *MAH-loh;* **too bad!** ¡es lástima! *ehs LAHS-tee-mah*

badly mal *mahl*

bag, handbag cartera *kahr-TEHR-ah;* **valise** la maleta *mah-LEH-tah*

baggage el equipaje *eh-kee-PAH-heh;* **baggage room** la sala de equipajes *SAH-lah deh eh-kee-PAH-hehs*

baked al horno *ahl OHR-noh*

balcony (theater) la galería *gah-leh-REE-ah*

ball la pelota *peh-LOH-tah*

banana el plátano *PLAH-tah-noh*

bandage (covering) la venda *BEHN-dah;* **to bandage** vendar *behn-DAHR*

bank el banco *BAHN-koh*

barber el peluquero *peh-loo-KEH-roh,* el barbero *bahr-BEHR-roh*

barbershop la peluquería *peh-loo-keh-REE-ah,* la barbería *bahr-behr-EE-ah*

bargain la ganga *GAHN-gah*

basket la cesta *SEHS-tah,* la canasta *kah-NAHS-tah*

bath baño *BAHN-yoh;* **to bathe** bañarse *bahn-YAHR-seh*

bathing cap el gorro de baño *GOHR-roh deh BAHN-yoh*

bathing suit el traje de baño *TRAH-heh deh BAHN-yoh*

bathrobe el albornoz *ahl-bohr-NOHS*

bathroom el cuarto de baño *KWAHR-toh deh BAHN-yoh*

battery (automobile) el acumulador *ah-koo-moo-lah-DOHR,* la batería *bah-teh-REE-ah;* **(electronics)** la pila *PEE-lah*

be (v.) ser *sehr,* estar *ehs-TAHR;* **be back** estar de vuelta *ehs-TAHR deh BWEHL-tah*

beach la playa *PLAH-yah*

beautiful bello *BEH-yoh,* hermoso *ehr-MOH-soh*

beauty salon el salón de belleza *sah-LOHN deh beh-YEH-sah*

because porque *POHR-keh*

bed la cama *KAH-mah*

bedroom la alcoba *ahl-KOH-bah,* el dormitorio *dohr-mee-TOR-ryoh*

beef la carne de vaca *KAHR-neh deh BAH-kah;* **roast beef** el rosbif *rohs-BEEF*

beer la cerveza *sehr-BEH-sah*

beet la remolacha *reh-moh-LAH-chah*

before antes de *AHN-tehs deh*

begin comenzar *koh-mehn-SAHR,* empezar *ehm-peh-SAHR*

behind detrás de *deh-TRAHS deh*

Belgian belga *BEHL-gah*

believe (v.) creer *kreh-EHR*

bell (door) el timbre *TEEM-breh*

bellhop el botones *boh-TOH-nehs*

belong pertenecer *pehr-teh-neh-SEHR*

belt el cinturón *seen-too-ROHN*

best el mejor *ehl meh-HOHR*

bet (I'll ...) apuesto a que *ah-PWEHS-toh ah keh*

better mejor *meh-HOHR*

between entre *EHN-treh*

bicarbonate of soda el bicarbonato de soda *bee-kahr-boh-NAH-toh deh SOH-dah*

bicycle la bicicleta *bee-see-KLAY-tah*

big grande *GRAHN-deh*

bill (restaurant check) la cuenta *KWEHN-tah*

billion mil millones *meel mee-YOH-nehs*

bird el pájaro *PAH-hah-roh*

bite (get a ...) tomar un bocado *toh-MAHR oon boh-KAH-doh*

bitter amargo *ah-MAHR-goh*

black negro *NEH-groh*

blade (razor) la hoja de afeitar *OH-hah deh ah-fey-TAHR*

blank (form) el formulario *fohr-moo-LAHR-ee-oh*

bleach (clothes) el blanqueador *blahn-keh-ah-DOHR*

blender la licuadora *lee-kwah-DOHR-ah*

block (city) la cuadra *KWAH-drah*, la manzana *mahn-SAH-nah*

blood la sangre *SAHN-greh*

blood pressure la presión de sangre *preh-SYOHN day SAHN-greh*

blouse la blusa *BLOO-sah*

blue azul *ah-SOOL*

boardinghouse la casa de huéspedes *KAH-sah deh WEHS-peh-dehs*

boat el barco *BAHR-koh*, el buque *BOO-keh*, el bote *BOH-teh*

body el cuerpo *KWEHR-poh*

boiled hervido *ehr-BEE-doh*

bolt (automobile) el perno *PEHR-noh*

bone el hueso *WEH-soh*

book el libro *LEE-broh*; **guide-book** la guía *GHEE-ah*

bookstore la librería *lee-breh-REE-ah*

booth (phone) la cabina (telefónica) *kah-BEE-nah teh-leh-FOH-nee-kah*

boric acid el ácido bórico *AH-see-doh BOH-ree-koh*

born (to be) nacer *nah-SEHR*

borrow (v.) pedir prestado *peh-DEER prehs-TAH-doh*;

He borrowed $5 from me Me pidió cinco dólares prestados *meh pee-DYOH SEEN-koh DOH-lah-rehs prehs-TAH-dohs*

bother (v.) molestar *moh-lehs-TAHR*; **Don't bother** no se moleste *noh seh moh-LEHS-teh*

bottle la botella *boh-TEH-yah*

box la caja *KAH-hah*

box office (theater) la taquilla *tah-KEE-yah*

boy el muchacho *moo-CHAH-choh*, el chico *CHEE-koh*

bra, brassiere el sostén *sohs-TEHN*

bracelet la pulsera *pool-SEHR-ah*

brakes (automobile) los frenos *FREH-nohs*

Brazilian brasileño *brah-see-LEH-nyoh*

bread el pan *pahn*

break (v.) romper *rohm-PEHR*

breakdown (auto) la avería *ah-beh-REE-ah*

breakfast el desayuno *deh-sah-YOO-noh*

breathe (v.) respirar *rehs-pee-RAHR*

bridge el puente *PWEHN-teh*

bring traer *trah-EHR*

broiled a la parrilla *ah lah pahr-REE-yah*

broken roto *ROH-toh*, quebrado *keh-BRAH-doh*

brother el hermano *ehr-MAH-noh*

brown pardo *PAHR-doh*, castaño *kas-TAH-nyoh*, moreno *moh-REH-noh*

bruise (injury) la contusión *kohn-too-SYOHN*

brush el cepillo *seh-PEE-yoh*; **to brush** cepillar *seh-pee-YAHR*

building el edificio *eh-dee-FEE-soyh*

bulb (electric) la bombilla *bohm-BEE-yah*

bull el toro *TOH-roh*; **bullring** la plaza de toros *PLAH-sah deh TOH-rohs*

bullfight la corrida de toros *kohr-REE-dah deh TOH-rohs*

bumper (automobile) el parachoques *pah-rah-CHOH-kehs*

burn (injury) la quemadura *keh-mah-DOO-rah*; **to burn** quemar *keh-MAHR*

bus el autobús *ow-toh-BOOS*

busy ocupado *oh-koo-PAH-doh*

but pero *PEH-roh*

butter la mantequilla *mahn-teh-KEE-yah*

button el botón *boh-TOHN*

buy (v.) comprar *kohm-PRAHR*

by de, por *deh, pohr*

C

cab el taxi *TAHK-see*

cabaret el cabaret *kah-bah-REH*

cabbage la col *kohl*

cake la torta *TOHR-tah*

call (telephone) la llamada *yah-MAH-dah*, la comunicación *koh-moo-nee-kah-SYOHN*; **to telephone** llamar por teléfono *yah-MAHR pohr teh-LEH-foh-noh*

camera la cámara *KAH-mah-rah*

can (container) la lata *LAH-tah*; **be able** poder *poh-DEHR*; **can opener** el abrelatas *ah-breh-LAH-tahs*

Canadian canadiense *kah-nah-DYEHN-seh*

cancel (v.) cancelar *kahn-seh-LAHR*

candle la bujía *boo-HEE-ah*, la vela *BEH-lah*

candy los dulces *DOOL-sehs*, los bombones *bohm-BOH-nehs*

cane el bastón *bahs-TOHN*

cap la gorra *GOHR-rah*

captain el capitán *kah-pee-TAHN*

car (automobile) el automóvil *ow-toh-MOH-beel*, el coche *KOH-cheh*; **railroad car** el vagón *bah-GOHN*, **streetcar** el tranvía *trahn-BEE-ah*

card (playing) la carta *KAHR-tah*, el naipe *NAH-ee-peh*

care (caution) el cuidado *kwee-DAH-doh*

careful (to be) tener cuidado *teh-NEHR kwee-DAH-doh*

carefully con cuidado *kohn kwee-DAH-doh*

carrot la zanahoria *sah-nah-OH-ryah*

carry (v.) llevar *yeh-BAHR*

case (cigarette) la pitillera *pee-tee-YER-rah*; **in any case** en todo caso *ehn TOH-doh KAH-soh*

cash (money) el dinero contante *dee-NEH-roh kohn-TAHN-teh*; **to cash** cobrar *koh-BRAHR*

cashier el cajero *kah-HEH-roh*

castle el castillo *kahs-TEE-yoh*

castor oil el aceite de ricino *ah-SAY-teh deh ree-SEE-noh*

cat el gato *GAH-toh*

catch (v.) agarrar *ah-gahr-RAHR*

cathedral la catedral *kah-teh-DRAHL*

Catholic católico *kah-TOH-lee-koh*

cauliflower la coliflor *koh-lee-FLOHR*

caution la precaución *preh-kow-SYOHN;* **Caution!** ¡Cuidado! *kwee-DAH-doh*

ceiling el techo *TEH-choh*

celery el apio *AH-pyoh*

center el centro *SEHN-troh*

cell phone el celular *seh-LOO-lahr*

certainly ciertamente *syehr-tah-MEHN-teh*

certificate el certificado *sehr-tee-fee-KAH-doh*

chain la cadena *kah-DEH-nah*

chair la silla *SEE-lyah*

change (money) el cambio *KAHM-byoh;* **small change** la moneda suelta *moh-NEH-dah SWEHL-tah,* el suelto *SWEHL-toh;* **to change** cambiar *kahm-BYAHR*

charge (cover) el gasto mínimo *GAHS-toh MEE-nee-moh;* **to charge** cobrar *koh-BRAHR*

charger el cargador *kahr-gah-DOHR*

cheap barato *bah-RAH-toh*

check (baggage) el talón *tah-LOHN;* **traveler's check** el cheque de viajeros *CHEH-keh deh byah-HEH-rohs;* **to check (baggage)** facturar *fahk-too-RAHR*

checkroom la sala de equipajes *SAH-lah deh eh-kee-PAH-hehs*

cheek la mejilla *meh-HEE-yah*

cheese el queso *KEH-soh*

cherry la cereza *seh-REH-sah*

chest el pecho *PEH-choh*

chestnut la castaña *kahs-TAHN-yah*

chicken el pollo *POH-yoh*

child el niño *NEEN-yoh,* la niña *NEEN-yah*

Chilean chileno *chee-LEH-noh*

chill el escalofrío *ehs-kah-loh-FREE-oh*

chin la barbilla *bahr-BEE-yah*

Chinese chino *CHEE-noh*

chiropodist el pedicuro *peh-dee-KOO-roh*

chocolate el chocolate *choh-koh-LAH-teh;* **chocolate candies** los bombones *bohm-BOH-nehs*

choose (v.) escoger *ehs-koh-HEHR*

chop, cutlet la chuleta *choo-LEH-tah*

Christmas la Navidad *nah-bee-DAHD;* **(Merry Christmas!)** ¡Felices Pascuas! *feh-LEE-sehs PAHS-kwahs,* ¡Feliz Navidad! *feh-LEES nah-bee-DAHD*

church la iglesia *ee-GLEH-syah*

cigar el cigarro *see-GAHR-roh,* el puro *POO-roh;* **cigar store** la tabaquería *tah-bah-keh-REE-ah,* el estanco *ehs-TAHN-koh*

cigarette el cigarrillo *see-gahr-REE-yoh,* el pitillo *pee-TEE-yoh*

city la ciudad *syoo-DAHD;* **city hall** el ayuntamiento *ah-yoon-tah-MYEHN-toh*

class la clase *KLAH-seh*

clean (spotless) limpio *LEEM-pyoh;* **to clean** limpiar *leem-PYAHR*

cleaner's la tintorería *teen-toh-reh-REE-ah*

clear (transparent) claro *KLAH-roh*

climb (v.) trepar *treh-PAHR*

clipper (barber's) la maquinilla *mah-kee-NEE-yah*

clock el reloj *reh-LOH*

close (near) cerca *SEHR-kah;* **to close** cerrar *sehr-RAHR;* **closed** cerrado *sehr-RAH-doh*

cloth   la tela *TEH-lah*, el paño *PAHN-yoh*

clothes, clothing   la ropa *ROH-pah*, los vestidos *behs-TEE-dohs*; **evening clothes** el traje de etiqueta *TRAH-heh deh eh-tee-KEH-tah*; **clothes brush**   el cepillo de ropa *seh-PEEL-yoh deh ROH-pah*

cloud   la nube *NOO-beh*; **cloudy** nublado *noo-BLAH-doh*

club (night)   el cabaret *kah-bah-REH*

clutch (automobile)   el embrague *ehm-BRAH-gheh*

coach (railroad)   el coche *KOH-cheh*, el vagón *bah-GOHN*

coat   el saco *SAH-koh*, la americana *ah-meh-ree-KAH-nah*; **coat hanger**   el colgador *kol-gah-DOHR*

cocktail   el coctel *kohk-TEHL*

coffee   el café *kah-FEH*

coin (money)   la moneda *moh-NEH-dah*

cold (temperature)   frío *FREE-oh*; **(sickness)**   el resfriado *rehs-FRYAH-doh*; **(weather)**   hacer frío *ah-SEHR FREE-oh*

cold cuts   los fiambres (m. pl.) *FYAHM-brehs*

collar   el cuello *KWEHL-yoh*

collect   (v.) cobrar *koh-BRAHR*

cologne   el agua de colonia *AH-gwah deh koh-LOH-nyah*

color   el color *koh-LOHR*

comb   el peine *PAY-neh*

come   (v.) venir *beh-NEER*; **to come in**   entrar *ehn-TRAHR*; **Come in!**   ¡Pase usted! *PAH-seh oo-STEHD*, ¡Adelante! *Ah-deh-LAHN-teh*

comedy   la comedia *koh-MEH-dyah*

comfortable   cómodo *KOH-moh-doh*

compact disc   el disco *DEES-koh*

company   la compañía *kohm-pahn-YEE-ah*

compartment   el compartimiento *kohm-pahr-tee-MYEHN-toh*

complaint   la queja *KEH-hah*

computer   la computadora (Latin Am.), el ordenador (Spain) *kohm-poo-tah-DOH-rah, ohr-deh-nah-DOHR*

concert   el concierto *kohn-SYEHR-toh*

condoms   condones *kohn-DOH-nehs*

conductor (train)   el revisor *reh-bee-SOHR*

congratulations   las felicitaciones *feh-lee-see-tah-SYOHN-ehs*, la enhorabuena *ehn-oh-rah-BWEH-nah*

connected (to be ___ by telephone)   estar en comunicación *ehs-TAHR ehn koh-moo-nee-kah-SYOHN*

consul   el cónsul *KOHN-sool*

consulate   el consulado *kohn-soo-LAH-doh*

continue   (v.) continuar *kohn-tee-NWAHR*, seguir *seh-GHEER*

convent   el convento *kohn-BEHN-toh*

cooked   cocido *koh-SEE-doh*

cool   fresco *FREHS-koh*

corkscrew   el sacacorchos *sah-kah-KOHR-chohs*

corn   el maíz *mah-EES*

corner   la esquina *ehs-KEE-nah*

cost (amount)   el precio *PREH-syoh*, el costo *KOHS-toh*; **to cost**   costar *kohs-TAHR*

cotton   el algodón *ahl-goh-DOHN*

cough   (v.) toser *toh-SEHR*; **cough syrup**   el jarabe para la tos *hah-RAH-beh pah-rah lah TOHS*

count (v.) contar *kohn-TAHR*

country (nation) el país *pah-EES;* **countryside** el campo *KAHM-poh*

course (in meal) el plato *PLAH-toh*

cover charge el gasto mímimo *GAHS-toh MEE-nee-moh*

crazy loco *LOH-koh*

cream la crema *KREH-mah*

credit card la tarjeta de crédito *tahr-HEH-tah day KREH-dee-toh*

crutch la muleta *moo-LEH-tah*

crystal el cristal *krees-TAHL*

Cuban cubano *koo-BAH-noh*

cucumber el pepino *peh-PEE-noh*

cuff links los gemelos *heh-MEH-lohs*

cup la taza *TAH-sah*

curtain la cortina *kohr-TEE-nah,* el telón *teh-LOHN*

curve la curva *KOOR-bah*

customs la aduana *ah-DWAH-nah*

cut (v.) cortar *kohr-TAHR;* **Cut it out!** ¡Basta! *BAHS-tah*

cutlet la chuleta *choo-LEH-tah*

Czech checo *CHEH-koh*

D

daily (by the day) por día *pohr DEE-ah*

damp húmedo *OO-meh-doh*

dance el baile *BAH-ee-lay;* **to dance** bailar *bah-ee-LAHR*

danger el peligro *peh-LEE-groh;* **dangerous** peligroso *peh-lee-GROH-soh*

Danish danés *dah-NEHS*

dark oscuro *ohs-KOO-roh*

Darn it! ¡Caramba! *kah-RAHM-bah*

date (today's) la fecha *FEH-chah*

daughter la hija *EE-hah*

day el día *DEE-ah*

dead muerto *MWEHR-toh*

death la muerte *MWEHR-teh*

December diciembre (m.) *dee-SYEHM-breh*

declaration la declaración *deh-klah-rah-SYOHN*

declare (v.) declarar *deh-klah-RAHR*

deep profundo *proh-FOON-doh*

deliver (v.) entregar *ehn-treh-GAHR*

delivery la entrega *ehn-TREH-gah;* **special delivery** el correo urgente *kohr-REH-oh oor-HEHN-teh*

dental dental *dehn-TAHL*

dentist el dentista *dehn-TEES-tah*

denture la dentadura *dehn-tah-DOO-rah*

deodorant el desodorante *deh-soh-doh-RAHN-teh*

department store la tienda de departamentos *tee-EHN-dah day deh-pahr-tah-MEHN-tohs*

desk (information) el despacho de informes (información) *dehs-PAH-choh deh een-FOHR-mehs (een-fohr-mah-SYOHN)*

dessert el postre *POHS-treh*

detour la desviación *dehs-byah-SYOHN,* el desvío *dehs-BEE-oh*

develop (film) (v.) revelar *reh-beh-LAHR*

devil el diablo *DYAH-bloh,* el demonio *deh-MOH-nyoh*

diapers los pañales *pah-NYAH-lehs*

diarrhea la diarrea *dee-arh-REH-ah*

dictionary el diccionario *deek-syoh-NAH-ryoh*

different diferente *dee-feh-REHN-teh*

difficult difícil *dee-FEE-seel*

difficulty la dificultad *dee-fee-kool-TAHD*, el apuro *ah-POO-roh*

digital digital *dee-hee-TAHL*

dining car el coche comedor *KOH-cheh koh-meh-DOHR*

dining room el comedor *koh-meh-DOHR*

dinner la comida *koh-MEE-dah*

direct (v.) indicar *een-dee-KAHR*, dirigir *dee-ree-HEER*

direction la dirección *dee-rehk-SYOHN*

dirty sucio *soo-SYOH*

discount el descuento *dehs-KWEHN-toh*

dish el plato *PLAH-toh*

disposable desechable *deh-seh-CHAB-leh*

district el barrio *BAHR-ryoh*

disturb (v.) molestar *moh-lehs-TAHR*

dizzy (to feel) (v.) estar aturdido *ehs-TAHR ah-toor-DEE-doh*

do (v.) hacer *ah-SEHR*

dock el muelle *MWEH-yeh*

doctor el médico *MEH-dee-koh*, el doctor *dohk-TOHR*

document el documento *doh-koo-MEHN-toh*

dog el perro *PEHR-roh*

dollar el dólar *DOH-lahr*

domestic nacional *nah-syoh-NAHL*, del país *dehl-pah-EES*

door la puerta *PWEHR-tah*; **door handle** el tirador de puerta *tee-rah-DOHR deh PWEHR-tah*

doorman el portero *pohr-TEH-roh*

double room la habitación para dos personas *ah-bee-tah-SYOHN PAH-rah dohs pehr-SOH-nahs*

down abajo *ah-BAH-hoh*

download bajar *bah-HAHR*

dozen la docena *doh-SEH-nah*

draft (current of air) la corriente de aire *kohr-RYEHN-teh deh AH-ee-ray*

draw (v.) dibujar *dee-boo-HAHR*

drawer el cajón *kah-HOHN*

dress (garment) el vestido *behs-TEE-doh*; **to dress** vestirse *behs-TEER-seh*

dressing gown la bata *BAH-tah*

drink (beverage) la bebida *beh-BEE-dah*; **to drink** beber *beh-BEHR*

drinkable potable *poh-TAH-bleh*

drive (ride) el paseo en coche *pah-SEH-oh ehn KOH-cheh*; **to drive** guiar, conducir *ghee-AHR, kohn-doo-SEER* [first p. sing. (present), conduzco *(kohn-DOOS-koh)*]

driver el chófer *CHOH-fehr*

dropper (eye) el cuentagotas *kwehn-tah-GOH-tahs*

drown (v.) ahogarse *ah-oh-GAHR-say*

drug (legal) el medicamento *meh-dee-kah-MEHN-toh*; **(illegal)** la droga *DROH-gah*

drugstore la farmacia *fahr-MAH-syah*

drunk borracho *bohr-RAH-choh*

dry seco *SEH-koh*; **dry cleaning** la limpieza en seco *leem-PYEH-sah ehn SEH-koh*

duck el pato *PAH-toh*

Dutch holandés *oh-lahn-DEHS*

dysentery la disentería *dee-sehn-teh-REE-ah*

E

each cada *KAH-dah;* **each one** cada uno *KAH-dah oo-noh*

ear la oreja *oh-REH-hah*

earache el dolor de oído *doh-LOHR deh oh-EE-doh*

early temprano *tehm-PRAH-noh*

earpiece el auricular *ow-ree-koo-LAHR*

earring el arete *ah-REH-teh,* pendiente *pehn-DYEHN-teh*

east el este *EHS-teh*

easy fácil *FAH-seel;* **Take it easy!** ¡No se preocupe! *noh seh preh-oh-KOO-peh,* ¡Tómelo con calma! *TOH-meh-loh kohn KAHL-mah*

eat (v.) comer *koh-MEHR*

egg el huevo *WEH-boh*

eight ocho *OH-choh*

eighteen dieciocho *dyeh-see-OH-choh*

eighth octavo *ohk-TAH-boh*

eighty ochenta *oh-CHEHN-tah*

elbow el codo *KOH-doh*

electric eléctrico *eh-LEHK-tree-koh*

elevator el ascensor *ahs-sehn-SOHR*

eleven once *OHN-seh*

else (nothing else) nada más *NAH-dah mahs;* **What else?** ¿Qué más? *KEH MAHS*

e-mail el correo electrónico *kohr-REH-oh eh-lehk-TROH-nee-koh*

empty vacío *bah-SEE-oh*

end (conclusion) el fin *feen;* **to end** terminar *tehr-mee-NAHR*

endorse endosar *ehn-doh-SAHR*

engine el motor *moh-TOHR,* la máquina *MAH-kee-nah*

English inglés *een-GLEHS*

enlargement la ampliación *ahm-plyah-SYOHN*

enough bastante *bahs-TAHN-teh*

euro el euro *EH-oo-roh*

evening la tarde *TAHR-deh;* **evening clothes** el traje de etiqueta *TRAH-heh deh eh-tee-KEH-tah*

every cada *KAH-dah*

everybody, everyone todo el mundo *TOH-doh ehl MOON-doh,* todos *TOH-dohs*

everything todo *TOH-doh*

examine examinar *ehk-sah-mee-NAHR*

exchange (v.) cambiar *kahm-BYAHR;* **exchange office** la oficina de cambio *oh-fee-SEE-nah deh KAHM-byoh*

excursion la excursión *ehs-koor-SYOHN*

excuse (v.) perdonar *pehr-doh-NAHR,* dispensar *dees-pehn-SAHR*

exhaust (automobile) el escape *ehs-KAH-peh*

exit la salida *sah-LEE-dah*

expect (v.) esperar *eha-peh-RAHR,* aguardar *ah-gwahr-DAHR*

expensive caro *KAH-roh*

express (train) el expreso *ehs-PREH-soh*

extra extra *EHS-trah*

extract (v.) sacar *sah-KAHR*

eye el ojo *OH-hoh*

eyebrow la ceja *SEH-hah*

eyeglasses las gafas *GAH-fahs,* los anteojos *ahn-teh-OH-hohs*

eyelash la pestaña *pehs-TAHN-yah*

eyelid el párpado *PAHR-pah-doh*

F

face (body part) la cara *KAH-rah;* **face powder** los

facecloth el paño de lavar *PAHN-yoh deh lah-BAHR*

facial el masaje facial *mah-SAH-heh fah-SYAHL*

fall (autumn) el otoño *oh-TOHN-yoh*; (injury) la caída *kah-EE-dah*; to fall caer *kah-EHR*

false falso *FAHL-soh*

family la familia *fah-MEEL-yah*; family name el apellido *ah-peh-YEE-doh*

fan (car or electric) el ventilador *behn-tee-lah-DOHR*; (hand) el abanico *ah-bah-NEE-koh*; fan belt la correa de ventilador *kohr-REH-ah deh behn-tee-lah-DOHR*

far lejos *LEH-hohs*, lejano *leh-HAH-noh*

fare (fee) la tarifa *tah-REE-fah*

fast rapido *RAH-pee-doh*, pronto *PROHN-toh*; The watch is fast El reloj va adelantado *reh-LOH bah ah-deh-lahn-TAH-doh*

faster más rapido *mahs RAH-pee-doh*

father el padre *PAH-dreh*

faucet el grifo *GREE-foh*

fax el fax *FAHKS*

fear (dread) el miedo *MYEH-doh*; to fear tener miedo *teh-NEHR MYEH-doh*

February febrero (m.) *feh-BREH-roh*

feel (v.) sentirse *sehn-TEER-seh*; to feel like tener ganas de (+ infinitive) *teh-NEHR GAH-nahs deh*

felt (cloth) el fieltro *FYEHL-troh*

fender el guardabarro *gwahr-dah-BAHR-roh*

festival la fiesta *FYEHS-tah*

fever la fiebre *FYEH-breh*

few pocos *POH-kohs*; a few unos cuantos *oo-nohs KWAHN-tohs*

fifteen quince *KEEN-seh*

fifth quinto *KEEN-toh*

fifty cincuenta *seen-KWEHN-tah*

fig el higo *EE-goh*

fill, fill out (v.) llenar *yeh-NAHR*; to fill a tooth empastar *ehm-pahs-TAHR*; Fill it up! ¡llénelo! *YEH-neh-loh*

filling el empaste *ehm-PAHS-teh*

film la película *peh-LEE-koo-lah*

find (v.) hallar *ah-YAHR*, encontrar *ehn-kohn-TRAHR*

fine (good) fino *FEE-noh*, bello *BEH-yo*, bueno *BWEH-noh*

fine (fee) la multa *MOOL-tah*

finger el dedo *DEH-doh*

finish (v.) acabar *ah-kah-BAHR*, terminar *tehr-mee-NAHR*

fire el fuego *FWEH-goh*; (destructive) el incendio *een-SEHN-dyoh*

first primero *pree-MEH-roh*; first aid los primeros auxilios *pree-MEH-rohs ah-ook-SEEL-yohs*

fish (in water) el pez *pehs*; (when caught) el pescado *pehs-KAH-doh*

fit (v.) calzar *KAHL-sahr*, vestir *behs-TEER*

fix (v.) componer *kohm-poh-NEHR*, reparar *reh-pah-RAHR*, arreglar *ahr-reh-GLAHR*; fixed-price meal la comida corrida (completa) *koh-MEE-dah kohr-REE-dah (kohm-PLEH-tah)*

flashlight   la linterna eléctrica *leen-TEHR-nah eh-LEHK-tree-kah*

flat (level)   llano *YAH-noh*; **flat tire**   el pinchazo *peen-CHAH-soh*

flight (plane)   el vuelo *BWEH-loh*

floor   el piso *PEE-soh*, el suelo *SWEH-loh*

flower   la flor *flohr*

fluid (lighter)   la bencina *behn-SEE-nah*

fog   la niebla *NYEH-blah*

follow (v.) seguir *seh-GHEER*

foot   el pie *pyeh*

for (purpose, destination)   para *PAH-rah*; **(exchange)** por *pohr*

forbidden   prohibido *proh-ee-BEE-doh*

forehead   la frente *FREHN-teh*

forget (v.) olvidar *ohl-bee-DAHR*

fork   el tenedor *teh-neh-DOHR*

form (document)   el formulario *fohr-moo-LAH-ree-oh*

forty   cuarenta *kwah-REHN-tah*

forward (direction)   adelante *ah-deh-LAHN-teh*; **to forward**   reexpedir *reh-ex-peh-DEER*

fountain   la fuente *FWEHN-teh*; **fountain pen**   la pluma fuente *PLOO-mah FWEHN-teh*

four   cuatro *KWAH-troh*

fourteen   catorce *kah-TOHR-seh*

fourth   cuarto *KWAHR-toh*

fracture (injury)   la fractura *frahk-TOO-rah*

free (unattached)   libre *LEE-breh*; **free of charge**   gratis *GRAH-tees*

French   francés *frahn-SEHS*

frequent flyer miles   bonos de vuelo *BOH-nohs day BWEH-loh*

Friday   el viernes *BYEHR-nehs*

fried   frito *FREE-toh*

friend   amigo *ah-MEE-goh*, amiga *ah-MEE-gah*

from   de *deh*, desde *DEHS-deh*

front (position)   delantero *deh-lahn-TEH-roh*, que da a la calle *keh dah ah lah KAH-yeh*

fruit   la fruta *FROO-tah*

fuel pump   la bomba de combustible *BOHM-bah deh kohm-boos-TEE-bleh*

full (as in bus)   lleno *YEH-noh*; **(complete)** completo *kohm-PLEH-toh*

furnished   amueblado *ah-mweh-BLAH-doh*

G

game   el juego *HWEH-goh*, la partida *pahr-TEE-dah*

garage   el garage *gah-RAH-heh*

garden   el jardin *hahr-DEEN*

garlic   el ajo *AH-hoh*

gas (fuel), petrol   la gasolina *gah-soh-LEE-nah*; **gas station**   la estación de gasolina *ehs-tah-SYOHN deh gah-soh-LEE-nah*

gate (railroad station)   la barrera *bahr-REH-rah*

gauze   la gasa *GAH-sah*

gay   el gay *GEH-ee*

gear (car)   el engranaje *ehn-grah-NAH-heh*

general delivery   la lista de correos *LEES-tah deh kohr-REH-ohs*

gentleman   el señor *sehn-YOHR*, el caballero *kah-bah-YEH-roh*

German   alemán *ah-leh-MAHN*

get (obtain) (v.) conseguir *kohn-seh-GHEER*; **to get back (recover)**   recobrar *reh-koh-BRAHR*; **to get dressed**

vestirse *behs-TEER-seh;* **to
get off** bajarse *bah-HAHR-
seh;* **to get out** irse *EER-
seh,* salir *sah-LEER;* **to get
up** levantarse *leh-bahn-
TAHR-seh;* **Get out!** ¡Fuera!,
¡Fuera de aquí! *FWEH-rah
deh ah-KEE*

gift el regalo *reh-GAH-loh*
gin la ginebra *hee-NEH-brah*
girdle la faja *FAH-hah*
girl la muchacha *moo-CHAH-
chah,* la chica *CHEE-kah*
give (v.) dar *dahr;* **to give back**
devolver *deh-bohl-BEHR*
glad contento *kohn-TEHN-toh,*
alegre *ah-LEH-greh*
gladly con mucho gusto *kohn
MOO-choh GOOS-toh*
glass (drinking) el vaso *BAH-
soh;* **(material)** el vidrio
BEE-dryoh
glasses (eye) las gafas (f. pl.)
GAH-fahs, los anteojos (m.
pl.) *ahn-teh-OH-hohs*
glove el guante *GWAHN-teh*
go (v.) ir *eer;* **to go away** irse
EER-seh, marcharse *mahr-
CHAHR-seh;* **to go shopping**
de compras (de tiendas) *eer
deh KOHM-prahs (deh
TYEHN-dahs);* **to go down**
bajar *bah-HAHR;* **to go
home** ir a casa *eer ah KAH-
sah;* **to go in** entrar *ehn-
TRAHR;* **to go out** salir
sah-LEER; **to go to bed**
acostarse *ah-kohs-TAHR-seh;*
to go up subir *soo-BEER*
gold el oro *OH-roh*
good bueno *BWEH-noh;*
good-bye hasta la vista
AHS-tah lah BEES-tah, adiós
ah-DYOHS
goose el ganso *GAHN-soh*
grade (on road) la cuesta
KWEHS-tah; **grade crossing**

el paso a nivel *PAH-soh ah
nee-BEHL*
gram el gramo *GRAH-moh*
grapefruit la toronja *toh-
ROHN-hah,* el pomelo *poh-
MEHL-oh*
grapes las uvas *OO-bahs*
grass la hierba *YEHR-bah*
grateful agradecido *ah-grah-
deh-SEE-doh*
gravy, sauce la salsa *SAHL-sah*
gray gris *grees*
grease (lubricate) (v.)
engrasar *ehn-grah-SAHR*
Greek griego *GRYEH-goh*
green verde *BEHR-deh*
greeting el saludo *sah-LOO-doh*
guide el guia *GHEE-ah;* **guide-
book** la guía *GHEE-ah*
gum (chewing) el chicle
CHEE-kleh
gums las encías *ehn-SEE-ahs*
guy el tipo *TEE-poh*

H

hair el pelo *PEH-loh,* el
cabello *kah-BEH-yoh;* **hair
bleach** el descolorante
dehs-koh-loh-RAHN-teh; **hair
lotion** la loción para el
pelo *loh-SYOHN PAH-rah ehl
PEH-loh;* **hair net** la
redecilla *rah-deh-SEEL-yah;*
hair tonic el tónico para el
pelo *TOH-ne-koh PAH-rah
ehl PEH-loh;* **hair wash** el
enjuague *ehn-HWAH-gheh*
hairbrush el cepillo del pelo
seh-PEE-yoh dehl PEH-loh
haircut el corte de pelo
KOHR-teh deh PEH-loh
hairpin el gancho *GAHN-choh,*
la horquilla *ohr-KEE-yah*
half (adj.) medio *MEH-dyoh,*
(n.) la mitad *mee-TAHD*
Halt! ¡Alto! *AHL-toh*
ham el jamón *hah-MOHN*

hammer el martillo *mahr-TEE-yoh*

hand la mano *MAH-noh*; **hand lotion** la loción para las manos *loh-SYOHN PAH-rah lahs MAH-nohs*

handbag la bolsa *BOHL-sah*

handicapped minusválido *mee-noos-VAH-lee-doh*

handkerchief el pañuelo *pah-NYWEH-loh*

handmade hecho a mano *EH-choh ah MAH-noh*

hanger (coat) el colgador *kohl-gah-DOHR*

happen (v.) pasar *pah-SAHR*, suceder *soo-seh-DEHR*, ocurrir *oh-koor-REER*, resultar *reh-sool-TAHR*

happy feliz *feh-LEES*

Happy New Year! ¡Feliz Año Nuevo! *Feh-LEES AHN-yoh NWEH-boh*

harbor el puerto *PWEHR-toh*

hard (difficult) difícil *dee-FEE-seel;* **(tough)** duro *DOO-roh*

hard-boiled egg el huevo duro *WEH-boh DOO-roh*

hat el sombrero *sohm-BREH-roh;* **hat shop** la sombrerería *sohm-breh-reh-REE-ah*

have (v.) tener *teh-NEHR;* **to have to** deber *deh-BEHR*, tener que *teh-NEHR-keh*

hazelnut la avellana *ah-beh-YAH-nah*

he el *ehl*

head la cabeza *kah-BEH-sah*

headache el dolor de cabeza *doh-LOHR deh kah-BEH-sah*

headlight el farol *fah-ROHL*

headwaiter el jefe de comedor *HEH-feh deh koh-meh-DOHR*

health la salud *sah-LOOD;* **health certificate** el certificado de sanidad *sehr-tee-fee-KAH-doh deh sah-nee-DAHD*

hear (v.) oír *oh-EER;* **to hear from** tener (recibir) noticias de *teh-NEHR (reh-see-BEER) noh-TEE-syahs deh*

heart el corazón *koh-rah-SOHN*

heat el calor *kah-LOHR*

heaven el cielo *SYEH-loh*

heavy pesado *peh-SAH-doh*

heel (of foot) el talón *tah-LOHN;* **(of shoe)** et tacón *tah-KOHN*

hell el infierno *een-FYEHR-noh*

Hello! ¡Hola! *OH-lah,* ¡Qué tal! *KEH TAHL;* **(on phone)** ¡Diga! *DEE-gah*

help (v.) ayudar *ah-yoo-DAHR;* **May I help you?** ¿Qué desea? *KEH deh-SEH-ah,* ¿En qué puedo servirle? *EHN KEH PWEH-doh sehr-BEER-leh;* **Help yourself** Sírvase usted *SEER-bah-seh oo-STEHD;* **Help!** ¡Auxilio! ¡Socorro! *owk-SEEL-yoh, soh-KOHR-oh*

here aquí *ah-KEE*

high alto *AHL-toh*

highway (auto) la carretera *kahr-reh-TEH-rah*

hip la cadera *kah-DEH-rah*

hire (v.) alquilar *ahl-kee-LAHR*

his su *soo*

Hold the wire No cuelgue *noh KWEHL-geh*

home la casa *KAH-sah*, el hogar *oh-GAHR;* **to go home** ir a casa *eer ah KAH-sah;* **to be at home** estar en casa *ehs-TAHR ehn KAH-sah*

hood (car) el capó *kah-POH*

hook el gancho *GAHN-choh*

hope (v.) esperar *ehs-peh-RAHR*

horn (car) la bocina *boh-SEE-nah*

hors d'oeuvre los entremeses *ehn-treh-MEH-sehs*

horse el caballo *kah-BAH-yoh*

hospital el hospital *ohs-pee-TAHL*

hostel (youth) albergue de jóvenes *ahl-BEHR-geh deh HOH-ben-ehs*

hostess (plane) la azafata *ah-sah-FAH-tah*

hot caliente *kah-LYEHN-teh*

hotel el hotel *oh-TEL*

hour la hora *OH-rah;* **by the hour** por hora *pohr OH-rah*

house la casa *KAH-sah*

how cómo *KOH-moh;* **how far?** ¿a qué distancia? *ah KEH dees-TAHN-syah;* **how long?** ¿cuánto tiempo? *KWAHN-toh TYEHM-poh,* ¿desde cuándo? *DEHS-deh KWAHN-doh;* **how many?** ¿cuántos? *KWAHN-tohs;* **how much?** ¿cuánto? *KWAN-toh*

hundred ciento *SYEHN-toh* [*Cien* is used immediately before the noun: $100, cien dólares *(syehn DOH-lah-rehs)*, but: $160, ciento sesenta dólares *(SYEHN-toh seh-SEHN-tah DOH-lah-rehs)*

Hungarian húngaro *OON-gah-roh*

hungry (to be) tener hambre *teh-NEHR AHM-breh*

hurry (v.) darse prisa *DAHR-seh PREE-sah;* **to be in a hurry** tener prisa *teh-NEHR PREE-sah*

hurt (v.) lastimar *lahs-tee-MAHR,* hacer(se) daño *ah-SEHR-(seh) DAHN-yoh*

husband el marido *mah-REE-doh*

I

I yo *yoh*

ice el hielo *YEH-loh;* **ice cream** el helado *eh-LAH-doh;* **ice water** el agua helada *AH-gwah eh-LAH-dah*

identification la identificación *ee-dehn-tee-fee-kah-SYOHN*

if si *see*

ignition (car) el encendido *ehn-sehn-DEE-doh*

ill enfermo *ehn-FEHR-moh*

illness la enfermedad *ehn-fehr-meh-DAHD*

imported importado *eem-pohr-TAH-doh*

in en *ehn*

included incluido *een-kloo-EE-doh*

indigestion indigestión *een-dee-hes-TYOHN*

indisposed indispuesto *een-dees-PWEHS-toh*

information la información *een-fohr-mah-see-OHN;* **information desk** la oficina de información *oh-fee-SEE-nah deh een-fohr-mah-see-OHN*

injection la inyección *en-yehk-SYOHN*

ink la tinta *TEEN-tah*

inquire preguntar *preh-goon-TAHR,* averiguar *ah-beh-ree-GWAHR*

insect el insecto *een-SEHK-toh*

insecticide el insecticida *een-sehk-tee-SEE-dah*

inside dentro (de) *DEHN-troh (deh)*

instead en vez *ehn BEHS*

insurance el seguro *seh-GOO-roh*

insure (v.) asegurar *ah-seh-goo-RAHR*

interest el interés *een-teh-REHS*

Internet el internet *een-tehr-NEHT*

interpreter el intérprete *een-TEHR-preh-teh*

intersection la bocacalle *boh-koh-KAH-yeh,* el cruce *KROO-seh*

into en *ehn*, dentro de *DEHN-troh deh*

introduce (v.) presentar *preh-sehn-TAHR*

iodine el yodo *YOH-doh*

iron (metal) el hierro *YEHR-roh*; **flat iron** la plancha *PLAHN-chah*; **to iron** planchar *plahn-CHAHR*

is es *ehs*, está *ehs-TAH*

Italian italiano *ee-tah-LYAH-noh*

J

jack (for car) el gato *GAH-toh*; **to jack up (car)** alzar (levantar) con el gato *ahl-SAHR (leh-bahn-TAHR) kohn ehl GAH-toh*; **(electrical)** el enchufe hembra *ehn-CHOO-feh EHM-brah*

jam (fruit) la mermelada *mehr-meh-LAH-dah*

January enero (m.) *eh-NEH-roh*

Japanese japonés *hah-poh-NEHS*

jaw la quijada *kee-HAH-dah*

jeweler el joyero *hoh-YEH-roh*

jewelry las joyas *HOH-yahs*, las alhajas *ahl-AH-has*; **jewelry store** la joyería *hoh-yeh-REE-ah*

Jewish judío *hoo-DEE-oh*

journey (trip) el viaje *BYAH-heh*

juice el jugo *HOO-goh*, el zumo *SOO-moh*

July julio (m.) *HOO-lyoh*

June junio (m.) *HOO-nyoh*

K

keep (v.) guardar *gwahr-DAHR*, quedarse con *keh-DAHR-seh kohn*; **to keep**

right seguir la derecha *seh-GHEER lah deh-REH-chah*

key la llave *YAH-beh*

keyboard el teclado *tehk-LAH-doh*

kilogram el kilogramo *kee-loh-GRAH-moh*

kilometer el kilómetro *kee-LOH-meh-troh*

kind (nice) bueno *BWEH-noh*, amable *ah-MAH-bleh*; **(type)** la clase *KLAH-seh*, el género *HEH-neh-roh*

kiss el beso *BEH-soh*; **to kiss** besar *beh-SAHR*

kitchen la cocina *koh-SEE-nah*

knee la rodilla *roh-DEE-yah*

knife el cuchillo *koo-CHEE-yoh*

knock (v.) llamar *yah-MAHR*

know (v.) **(fact, know-how)** saber *sah-BEHR*; **(person or thing)** conocer *koh-noh-SEHR*

L

label la etiqueta *eh-tee-KEH-tah*

lace el encaje *ehn-KAH-heh*

laces (shoe) los cordones para los zapatos (m. pl.) *kohr-DOH-nehs PAH-rah lohs sah-PAH-tohs*

ladies' room el tocador de señoras *toh-kah-DOHR deh sehn-YOH-rahs*

lady la señora *sehn-YOR-rah*

lamb la carne de cordero *KAHR-neh deh kohr-DEH-roh*

lamp la lámpara *LAHM-pah-rah*

land (ground) la tierra *TYEHR-rah*; **to land** desembarcar *deh-sehm-bahr-KAHR*

language el idioma *ee-DYOH-mah*, la lengua *LEHN-gwah*

laptop la computadora portátil *kohm-poo-tah-DOH-rah pohr-TAH-teel*

large   grande *GRAHN-deh*

last (final)   pasado *pah-SAH-doh*, último *OOL-tee-moh;* **to last**   durar *doo-RAHR*

late   tarde *TAHR-deh*

latest (at the latest)   a más tardar *ah mahs tahr-DAHR*

laugh   (v.) reír *reh-EER*, reírse *reh-EER-seh*

laundress   la lavandera *lah-bahn-DEH-rah*

laundry   la lavandería *lah-bahn-deh-REE-ah*

lavatory   el lavabo *lah-BAH-boh*, el retrete *reh-TREH-teh*

laxative   el laxante *lahk-SAHN-teh*

leak (drip)   el escape *ehs-KAH-peh;* **to leak**   escapar *ehs-kah-PAHR*

lean   (v.) apoyarse en *ah-poh-YAHR-seh ehn;* **to lean out**   asomarse a *ah-soh-MAHR-seh ah*

learn   (v.) aprender *ah-prehn-DEHR*

least (at least)   al (por lo) (a lo) menos *ahl (pohr loh) (ah loh) MEH-nohs*

leather   el cuero *KWEH-roh*

leave (behind)   (v.) dejar *deh-HAHR;* **to depart**   salir *sah-LEER*

left (opposite of right)   izquierdo *ees-KYEHR-doh*

leg   la pierna *PYEHR-nah*

lemon   el limón *lee-MOHN*

lemonade   la limonada *lee-moh-NAH-dah*

lend   (v.) prestar *prehs-TAHR*

length   el largo *LAHR-goh*

lens   el lente *LEHN-teh*

lesbian   la lesbiana *lehs-bee-AH-nah*

less   menos *MEH-nohs*

let   (v.) dejar *deh-HAHR*, permitir *pehr-mee-TEER*

letter   la carta *KAHR-tah*

letterbox   el buzón *boo-SOHN*

lettuce   la lechuga *leh-CHOO-gah*

library   la biblioteca *bee-blyoh-TEH-kah*

lie (down)   (v.) acostarse *ah-kohs-TAHR-seh*

life   la vida *BEE-dah;* **life preserver**   el salvavidas *sahl-bah-BEE-dahs*

lifeboat   el bote salvavidas *BOH-teh sahl-bah-BEE-dahs*

lift (of shoe)   la tapa *TAH-pah;* **to lift**   levantar *leh-bahn-TAHR*, alzar *ahl-SAHR*

light (color)   claro *KLAH-roh;* **(brightness)**   la luz *loos;* **taillight**   el farol de cola *fah-ROHL deh KOH-lah;* **(weight)**   ligero *lee-HEH-roh;* **Give me a light**   Déme usted fuego *DEH-meh oo-STEHD FUEH-goh;* **to light**   encender *ehn-sehn-DEHR*

lighter (cigarette)   el encendedor *ehn-sehn-deh-DOHR*

lightning   el relámpago *reh-LAHM-pah-goh*

like (as)   como *KOH-moh;* **to like**   gustar *goos-TAHR*

limit (speed)   la velocidad máxima *beh-loh-see-DAHD MAHK-see-mah*

line   la línea *LEE-neh-ah*

linen   el lino *LEE-noh*, la ropa blanca *ROH-pah BLAHN-kah*

lip   el labio *LAH-byoh*

lipstick   el lápiz de labios *LAH-pees deh LAH-byohs*

liqueur   licor *lee-KOHR*

liquor   la bebida alcohólica *beh-BEE-dah ahl-koh-OH-lee-kah*

list (wine, food)   la lista *LEES-tah*

listen, listen to   (v.) escuchar *ehs-koo-CHAHR*

liter   el litro *LEE-troh*

little pequeño *peh-KEHN-yoh;* **a little** un poco *oon POH-koh*

live (v.) vivir *bee-BEER*

liver el hígado *EE-gah-doh*

living room la sala *SAH-lah*

lobby el vestíbulo *behs-TEE-boo-loh,* el salón de entrada *sah-LOHN deh ehn-TRAH-dah*

lobster la langosta *lahn-GOHS-tah*

local (train) el tren ómnibus *trehn OHM-nee-boos;* **(phone call)** la llamada local *yah-MAH-dah loh-KAHL*

lock (fastening) la cerradura *sehr-rah-DOO-rah*

long largo *LAHR-goh;* **how long?** ¿cuánto tiempo? *KWAHN-toh TYEHM-poh,* desde cuándo *dehs-deh KWAHN-doh;* **long-distance call** la llamada a larga distancia *yah-MAH-dah ah LAHR-gah dees-TAHN-syah,* la conferencia interurbana *kohn-feh-REHN-syah een-tehr-oor-BAH-nah*

look, look at (v.) mirar *mee-RAHR;* **to look for** buscar *boos-KAHR;* **Look out!** ¡Cuidado! *kwee-DAH-doh*

lose (v.) perder *pehr-DEHR*

lost and found la oficina de objetos perdidos *oh-fee-SEE-nah deh ohb-HEH-tohs pehr-DEE-dohs*

lotion la loción *loh-SYOHN*

lots (of), many mucho *MOO-choh,* muchos *MOO-chohs*

lounge el salón *sah-LOHN*

low bajo *BAH-hoh*

lower berth la litera baja *lee-TEH-rah BAH-hah*

luck la suerte *SWEHR-teh*

lunch el almuerzo *ahl-MWEHR-soh;* **to lunch** almorzar *ahl-mohr-SAHR*

lung el pulmón *pool-MOHN*

M

maid (chamber) la camarera *kah-mah-REH-rah*

mail el correo *kohr-REH-oh*

mailbox el buzón *boo-SOHN*

magazine la revista *reh-BEES-tah*

make (v.) hacer *ah-SEHR*

man el hombre *OHM-breh*

manager el director *dee-rehk-TOHR,* el gerente *heh-REHN-teh,* el administrador *ahd-mee-nees-trah-DOHR*

manicure la manicura *mah-nee-KOO-rah*

many muchos *MOO-chohs*

map (road) el mapa de carreteras *MAH-pah deh kahr-reh-TEHR-ahs,* el mapa itinerario *MAH-pah ee-tee-neh-RAH-ryoh*

March marzo (m.) *MAHR-soh*

market el mercado *mehr-KAH-doh*

mashed majado *mah-HAH-doh*

mass la misa *MEE-sah;* **high mass** la misa cantada (mayor) *MEE-sah kahn-TAH-dah (mah-YOHR)*

massage el masaje *mah-SAH-heh*

match el fósforo *FOHS-foh-roh*

matter (It doesn't matter.) No importa *noh eem-POHR-tah;* **What's the matter?** ¿Qué pasa? *keh PAH-sah,* ¿qué hay? *key-AH-ee*

mattress el colchón *kohl-CHOHN*

May mayo (m.) *MAH-yoh*

maybe quizá *kee-SAH*, quizás *kee-SAHS*, tal vez *tahl BEHS*, acaso *ah-KAH-soh*

meal la comida *koh-MEE-dah*; **fixed-price meal** la comida a precio fijo *koh-MEE-dah ah PREH-syoh FEE-hoh*, la comida corrida (completa) *koh-MEE-dah kohr-REE-dah (kohm-PLEH-tah)*

mean (v.) significar *seeg-nee-fee-KAHR*, querer decir *keh-REHR deh-SEER*

measurement la medida *meh-DEE-dah*

meat la carne *KAHR-neh*

mechanic el mecánico *meh-KAH-nee-koh*

medical médico *MEH-dee-koh*

medication el medicamento *meh-dee-kah-MEHN-toh*

medicine la medicina *meh-dee-SEE-nah*

meet (v.) encontrar *ehn-kohn-TRAHR*; **(socially)** (v.) conocer *koh-noh-SEHR*

melon el melón *meh-LOHN*

memory la memoria *meh-MOH-ree-ah*

memory card la tarjeta de memoria *tahr-HEH-tah deh meh-MOH-ree-ah*

mend (v.) remendar *reh-mehn-DAHR*

men's room el lavabo de señores *lah-BAH-boh deh sehn-YOH-rehs*

mention (don't mention it) no hay de qué *noh ah-ee deh keh*

menu el menú *meh-NOO*, la lista de platos *LEES-tah deh PLAH-tohs*

merry alegre *ah-LEH-greh*

Merry Christmas! ¡Felices Pascuas! *feh-LEE-sehs pah-kwahs*, ¡Feliz Navidad! *feh-LEES nah-bee-DAHD*

message el mensaje *mehn-SAH-heh*, el recado *reh-KAH-doh*

meter (length) el metro *MEH-troh*

meter (taxi) el taxímetro *tahk-SEE-meh-troh*

Mexican mexicano, mejicano *meh-hee-KAH-noh*

middle (center) el medio *MEH-dyoh*, el centro *SEHN-troh*

midnight la medianoche *meh-dyah-NOH-cheh*

mild ligero *lee-HEH-roh*, suave *SWAH-beh*

milk la leche *LEH-cheh*

million el millón *mee-YOHN*

mind (understanding) la mente *MEHN-teh*; **Never mind.** No importa. *noh eem-POHR-tah*

mine mío *MEE-oh*, los míos (pl.) *MEE-ohs*

mineral water el agua mineral *AH-gwah mee-neh-RAHL*

minister el ministro *mee-NEES-troh*

minute el minuto *mee-NOO-toh*

mirror el espejo *ehs-PEH-hoh*

Miss (woman) la señorita *sehn-yoh-REE-tah*

miss (a train) (v.) perder *pehr-DEHR*

missing (to be) (v.) faltar *fahl-TAHR*

mistake el error *ehr-ROHR*, la falta *FAHL-tah*

monastery el monasterio *moh-nahs-TEH-ryoh*

Monday el lunes *LOO-nehs*

money el dinero *dee-NEH-roh*; **money order** el giro (postal) *HEE-roh (pohs-TAHL)*

month el mes *mehs*

monument el monumento *moh-noo-MEHN-toh*

moon la luna *LOO-nah*

more más *mahs*

morning   la mañana *mahn-YAH-nah*

mosquito   el mosquito *mohs-KEE-toh*; **mosquito netting** el mosquitero *mohs-kee-TEH-roh*

mother   la madre *MAH-dreh*

motion picture   el cine *SEE-neh*

motor (car)   el motor *moh-TOHR*

mouth   la boca *BOH-kah*; **mouthwash** el enjuague *ehn-HWAH-gheh*

move   (v.) mover *moh-BEHR*; **(change residence)** mudarse de casa *moo-DAHR-seh deh KAH-sah*

movie   la película *peh-LEE-koo-lah*

Mr.   el señor *sehn-YOHR*; **(with first name only)** don *dohn*

Mrs.   la señora *sehn-YOHR-rah*; **(with first name only)** doña *DOHN-yah*

much   mucho *moo-choh*

museum   el museo *moo-SEH-oh*

mushroom   la seta *SEH-tah*, el hongo *OHN-goh*

must   (v.) deber *deh-BEHR*, tener que *teh-NEHR keh*

my   mi *mee*, mis *mees*

N

nail (finger or toe)   la uña *OON-yah*; **nail file** la lima de uñas *LEE-mah deh OON-yahs*; **nail polish** el esmalte *ehs-MAHL-teh*

name   el nombre *NOHM-breh*; **family name** el apellido *ah-peh-YEE-doh*

napkin   la servilleta *sehr-bee-YEH-tah*

narrow   estrecho *ehs-TREH-choh*, angosto *ahn-GOHS-toh*

nationality   la nacionalidad *nah-syoh-nah-lee-DAHD*

nauseated (to be)   (v.) tener náuseas *teh-nehr NOW-seh-ahs*

near   (adj.) cercano *sehr-KAH-noh*; (prep.) cerca de *SEHR-kah deh*

nearly   casi *KAH-see*

necessary   necesario *neh-seh-SAH-ryoh*

neck   el cuello *KWEHL-yoh*

necklace   el collar *koh-YAHR*

necktie   la corbata *kohr-BAH-tah*

need   (v.) necesitar *neh-seh-see-TAHR*

needle   la aguja *ah-GOO-hah*

nerve   el nervio *NEHR-byoh*

net (communication)   la red *REHD*; **(hair)** la redecilla *reh-deh-SEE-yah*; **mosquito net** el mosquitero *mohs-kee-TEH-roh*

never   nunca *NOON-kah*

new   nuevo *NWEH-boh*

New Year   el día de año nuevo *ehl DEE-ah deh ahn-yoh NWEH-boh*; **Happy New Year!** ¡Feliz Año Nuevo! *feh-LEES ahn-yoh NWEH-boh*

newspaper   el periódico *peh-RYOH-dee-koh*

newsstand   el quiosco *KYOHS-koh*

next   próximo *PROHK-see-moh*, siguiente *see-GYEHN-teh*

night   la noche *NOH-cheh*

nightclub   el cabaret *kah-bah-REHT*, el club nocturno *ehl KLOOB nohk-TOOR-noh*

nightgown   el camisón *kah-mee-SOHN*

nightlife   la vida nocturna *bee-dah nohk-TOOR-nah*

night rate   la tarifa nocturna *tah-REE-fah nohk-TOOR-nah*

nine   nueve *NWEH-beh*

nineteen   diecinueve *dyeh-see-NWEH-beh*

ninety   noventa *noh-BEHN-tah*

ninth noveno *noh-BEH-noh*

no (adj.) ninguno *neen-GOON-noh*, ningún *neen-GOON* [before m. sing. noun]; (adv.) **no** *noh*; **no one** nadie *NAH-dyeh*

noise el ruido *RWEE-doh*

noisy ruidoso *rwee-DOH-soh*

none ninguno *neen-GOO-noh*

noon el mediodía *meh-dyoh-DEE-ah*

north el norte *NOHR-teh*

Norwegian noruego *noh-RWEH-goh*

nose la nariz *nah-REES*

not no *noh*

nothing nada *NAH-dah*; **nothing else** nada más *nah-dah-MAHS*

notice (announcement) el aviso *ah-BEE-soh*

novel (book) la novela *noh-BEH-lah*

November noviembre (m.) *noh-BYEHM-breh*

now ahora *ah-OHR-ah*

number el número *NOO-meh-roh*

nurse la enfermera *ehn-fehr-MEH-rah*

nut (walnut) la nuez *nwehs*; **(mechanical)** la tuerca *TWEHR-kah*

O

occupied ocupado *oh-koo-PAH-doh*

October octubre (m.) *ohk-TOO-breh*

oculist el oculista *oh-koo-LEES-tah*

of de *deh*; **of course** naturalmente *nah-too-rahl-MEHN-teh*, desde luego *dehs-deh LWEH-goh*, por supuesto *pohr soo-PWEHS-toh*

office la oficina *oh-fee-SEE-nah*; **box office** la taquilla *tah-KEE-yah*; **exchange office** la oficina de cambio *oh-fee-SEE-nah deh KAHM-byoh*; **post office** el correo *kohr-REH-oh*

often a menudo *ah meh-NOO-doh*

oil el aceite *ah-SEY-teh*; **castor oil** el aceite de ricino *ah-SEY-teh deh ree-SEE-noh*; **olive oil** el aceite de oliva *ah-SEY-teh deh oh-LEE-bah*

okay (It's) Está bien *ehs-STAH BYEHN*, Conforme *kohn-FOHR-meh*

old viejo *BYEH-hoh*, anciano *ahn-SYAH-noh*; **How old are you?** ¿Qué edad tiene usted? *keh eh-DAHD TYEH-neh oo-STEHD*, ¿Cuántos años tiene usted? *KWAHN-tohs AHN-yohs TYEH-neh oo-STEHD*; **I am 20 years old.** Tengo veinte años *TEHN-goh BEYN-teh AHN-yohs*

olive la aceituna *ah-sey-TOO-nah*

omelet la tortilla *tohr-TEEL-yah*

on en *ehn*, sobre *SOH-breh*

once una vez *OO-nah behs*; **at once** en seguida *ehn seh-GHEE-dah*

one un *oon*, uno *oo-noh*, una *oo-nah*; **one-way traffic** la dirección única *dee-rehk-SYOHN OO-nee-kah*

onion la cebolla *seh-BOH-yah*

only sólo *SOH-loh*, solamente *soh-lah-MEHN-teh*

open abierto *ah-BYEHR-toh*; **to open** abrir *ah-BREER*

opera la ópera *OH-peh-rah*; **opera glasses** los gemelos de teatro *heh-MEH-los deh teh-AH-troh*

operator (phone) la telefonista *teh-leh-foh-NEES-tah*

optician el óptico *OHP-tee-koh*

or o *oh*, u *oo* [before word beginning with vowel sound *o*]

orange la naranja *nah-RAHN-hah*

orangeade la naranjada *nah-rahn-HAH-dah*

orchestra (band) la orquesta *ohr-KEHS-tah*; **orchestra section** la platea *plah-TEH-ah*; **orchestra seat** la butaca *boo-TAH-kah*

order el encargo *ehn-KAHR-goh*; **to order** encargar *ehn-kahr-GAHR*

other otro *OH-troh*

our, ours nuestro *NWEHS-troh*

out afuera *ah-FWEH-rah*

outlet (electric) el tomacorriente *TOH-mah-kohr-RYEHN-teh*, el enchufe *ehn-CHOO-feh*

outside fuera *FWEH-rah*, afuera *ah-FWEH-rah*

over (above) encima (de) *ehn-SEE-mah (deh)*; **(finished)** acabado *ah-kah-BAH-doh*

overcoat el abrigo *ah-BREE-goh*, el sobretodo *soh-breh-TOH-doh*, el gabán *gah-BAHN*

overdone requemado *reh-keh-MAH-doh*

overheat (motor) (v.) recalentar *reh-kah-lehn-TAHR*

overnight por la noche *pohr lah NOH-cheh*

owe (v.) deber *deh-BEHR*

own (v.) poseer *poh-seh-EHR*

oyster la ostra *OHS-trah*

P

pack (luggage) (v.) hacer las maletas *ah-SEHR lahs mah-LEH-tahs*

package el bulto *BOOL-toh*

packet el paquete *pah-KEH-teh*

page (of book) la página *PAH-hee-nah*; **to page** llamar *yah-MAHR*

pain el dolor *doh-LOHR*

paint (wet) recién pintado *reh-SYEHN peen-TAH-doh*

pair el par *pahr*

pajamas el pijama *pee-HAH-mah*

palace el palacio *pah-LAH-syoh*

panties las bragas *BRAH-ghahs*

pants los pantalones *pahn-tah-LOH-nehs*

paper el papel *pah-PEHL*; **toilet paper** el papel higiénico *pah-PEHL ee-HYEH-nee-koh*; **wrapping paper** el papel de envolver *pah-PEHL deh ehn-bohl-BEHR*; **writing paper** el papel de cartas *pah-PEHL deh KAHR-tahs*

parasol el quitasol *kee-tah-SOHL*

parcel el paquete *pah-KEH-teh*; **parcel post** el paquete postal *pah-KEH-teh pohs-TAHL*

pardon (v.) perdonar *pehr-doh-NAHR*, dispensar *dees-pehn-SAHR*; **Pardon me!** ¡Perdón! *pehr-DOHN*, ¡Dispénseme usted! *dees-PEHN-seh-meh oo-STEHD*

park (car) (v.) parquear *pahr-keh-AHR*, estacionar *ehs-tah-syohn-AHR*; **(garden)** el parque *PAHR-keh*

parking (no) prohibido estacionar *proh-ee-BEE-doh ehs-tah-syoh-NAHR*

part (section) la parte *PAHR-teh*; **to part hair** hacer la raya *ah-SEHR lah RAH-yah*; **to separate** separar *seh-pah-RAHR*, dividir *dee-bee-DEER*

parts (spare) las piezas de repuesto (f. pl.) *PYEH-sahs deh reh-PWEHS-toh*

pass (permit) el permiso *pehr-MEE-soh;* **to pass** pasar *pah-SAHR*

passenger el pasajero *pah-sah-HEH-roh*

passport el pasaporte *pah-sah-POHR-teh*

password la contraseña *kohn-trah-SEHN-yah*

past el pasado *pah-SAH-doh*

pastry los pasteles *lohs pahs-TEH-lehs*

pay (v.) pagar *pah-GAHR*

pea el guisante *ghee-SAHN-teh*

peach el melocotón *meh-loh-koh-TOHN,* el durazno *doo-RAHS-noh*

pear la pera *PEH-rah*

pedestrian el peatón *peh-ah-TOHN*

pen la pluma *PLOO-mah;* **fountain pen** la pluma fuente *ploo-mah FWEHN-teh*

pencil el lápiz *LAH-pees*

people la gente *HEN-teh*

pepper (black) la pimienta *pee-MYEHN-tah*

peppers los pimientos *pee-MYEHN-tohs*

per por *pohr*

performance la función *foon-SYOHN*

perfume el perfume *pehr-FOO-meh;* **perfume shop** la perfumería *pehr-foo-meh-REE-ah*

perhaps quizá *kee-SAH,* tal vez *tahl BEHS*

permanent (wave) la permanente *pehr-mah-NEHN-teh*

permit (pass) el permiso *pehr-MEE-soh;* **to permit** permitir *pehr-mee-TEER*

Persian persa *PEHR-sah*

personal personal *pehr-soh-NAHL*

pharmacy la farmacia *fahr-MAH-see-ah*

phone el teléfono *teh-LEH-foh-noh;* **to phone** telefonear *teh-leh-foh-neh-AHR*

phone card la tarjeta telefónica *tahr-HEH-tah teh-leh-FOH-nee-kah*

photograph la fotografía *foh-toh-grah-FEE-ah;* **to photograph** fotografiar *foh-toh-grah-fee-AHR*

pickle el encurtido *ehn-koor-TEE-doh*

picnic la jira *HEE-rah,* la comida campestre *koh-MEE-dah kahm-PEHS-treh*

picture (art) el cuadro *KWAH-droh,* la pintura *peen-TOO-rah;* **(motion)** la película *peh-LEE-koo-lah,* el cine *SEE-neh*

pie el pastel *pahs-TEHL*

piece el pedazo *peh-DAH-soh*

pier el muelle *MWEH-yeh*

pill la píldora *PEEL-doh-rah*

pillow la almohada *ahl-moh-AH-dah*

pillowcase la funda *FOON-dah*

pilot el piloto *pee-LOH-toh*

pin el alfiler *ahl-fee-LEHR;* **safety pin** el imperdible *eem-pehr-DEE-bleh*

pineapple la piña *PEEN-yah*

pink rosado *roh-SAH-doh,* color de rosa *koh-LOHR deh ROH-sah*

pipe (smoking) la pipa *PEE-pah*

pitcher el jarro *HAHR-roh,* el cántaro *KAHN-tah-roh*

pity (What a ... !) Qué lástima! *keh LAHS-tee-mah*

place (site) el sitio *SEE-tyoh,* el lugar *loo-GAHR;* **to place** colocar *koh-loh-KAHR*

plane (air) el avión *ah-BYOHN*

plate el plato *PLAH-toh*

platform el andén *ahn-DEHN*, la plataforma *plah-tah-FOHR-mah*

play el drama *DRAH-mah*, la pieza *PYEH-sah;* **to play (game)** jugar *hoo-GAHR;* **to play (instrument)** tocar *toh-KAHR*

playing cards los naipes *NAH-ee-pehs*, las cartas *KAHR-tahs*

pleasant agradable *ah-grah-DAH-bleh;* **(referring to a person)** simpático *seem-PAH-tee-koh*

please por favor *pohr fah-BOHR*, haga el favor (de) (+ infinitive) *AH-gah ehl fah-BOHR (deh)*

pleasure el gusto *GOOS-toh*, el placer *plah-SEHR*

pliers los alicates *ah-lee-KAH-tehs*, las tenazas *teh-NAH-sahs*

plug (spark) la bujía *boo-HEE-ah*

plum la ciruela *see-RWEH-lah*

P.M. de la tarde *deh lah TAHR-deh*, de la noche *deh lah NOH-cheh*

pocket (n.) el bolsillo *bohl-SEE-yoh;* **(adj.)** de bolsillo *deh bohl-SEE-yoh*

pocketbook la bolsa *BOHL-sah*

point (place) el punto *POON-toh*, el lugar *loo-GAHR;* **(sharp end)** la punta *POON-tah*

poison el veneno *beh-NEH-noh*

police la policía *poh-lee-SEE-ah;* **police station** la comisaría *koh-mee-sah-REE-ah*

police officer el policía *poh-lee-SEE-ah*, el agente de policía *ehl ah-HEHN-teh deh poh-lee-SEE-ah*

Polish polaco *poh-LAH-koh*

polish (nail) el esmalte *ehs-MAHL-teh;* **polish remover** el acetón *ah-seh-TOHN*

polite cortés *kohr-TEHS*

politeness la cortesía *kohr-teh-SEE-ah*

pomade la pomada *poh-MAH-dah*

poor pobre *POH-breh*

pork la carne de cerdo *KAHR-neh deh SEHR-doh*

port (harbor) el puerto *PWEHR-toh*

porter el mozo *MOH-soh*

portion la porción *pohr-SYOHN*, la ración *rah-SYOHN*

Portuguese portugués *pohr-too-GHEHS*

possible posible *poh-SEE-bleh*

postage el porte *POHR-teh*, el franqueo *frahn-KEH-oh*

postcard la tarjeta postal *tahr-HEH-tah pohs-TAHL;* **post office** la casa de correos *KAH-sah dehl kohr-REH-ohs*, el correo *kohr-REH-oh*

potato la patata *pah-TAH-tah*, la papa *PAH-pah*

pour (rain) (v.) llover a cántaros *lyoh-BEHR ah KAHN-tah-rohs*

powder el polvo *POHL-boh;* **face powder** los polvos para la cara *POHL-bohs PAH-rah lah KAH-rah;* **powder puff** la borla *BOHR-lah;* **powder room** el (cuarto) tocador *(KWAHR-toh) toh-kah-DOHR*

prefer (v.) preferir *preh-feh-REER*

prepaid prepagado *preh-pah-GAH-doh*

prepare (v.) preparar *preh-pah-RAHR*

prescription la receta *reh-SEH-tah*

press (iron) (v.) planchar *plahn-CHAHR*

pretty bonito *boh-NEE-toh*, lindo *LEEN-doh*

price el precio *PREH-syoh*

priest el cura *KOO-rah*

print (photo) la copia *KOH-pyah*

program el programa *proh-GRAH-mah*

promise (v.) prometer *proh-meh-TEHR*

prostitute la prostituta *prohs-tee-TOO-tah*

Protestant protestante *proh-tehs-TAHN-teh*

provide (v.) proveer *proh-beh-EHR*

prune la ciruela pasa *see-RWEH-lah PAH-sah*

pudding el budín *boo-DEEN*

pump (fuel) la bomba de combustible *BOHM-bah deh kohm-boos-TEE-bleh*

puncture (tire) el pinchazo *peen-CHAH-soh*

purchase (item) la compra *KOHM-prah*; **to purchase** comprar *kohm-PRAHR*

purple morado *moh-RAH-doh*

purse la bolsa *BOHL-sah*

purser el sobrecargo *soh-breh-KAHR-goh*

push (v.) empujar *ehm-poo-HAHR*

put (v.) poner *poh-NEHR*; **put in** meter en *meh-TEHR ehn*; **put on** ponerse *poh-NEHR-seh*

Q

quarter el cuarto *KWAHR-toh*

quick, quickly pronto *PROHN-toh*

quiet quieto *KYEH-toh*, tranquilo *trahn-KEE-loh*

quinine la quinina *kee-NEE-nah*

quite bastante *bahs-TAHN-teh*

R

rabbi el rabino *rah-BEE-noh*

rack (train) la red, la rejilla *rehd, reh-HEE-yah*

radiator el radiador *rah-dyah-DOHR*

radio la radio *RAH-dyoh*

radish el rábano *RAH-bah-noh*

railroad el ferrocarril *fehr-roh-kahr-REEL*

rain la lluvia *LYOO-byah*; **to rain** llover *lyoh-BEHR*

raincoat el impermeable *eem-pehr-meh-AH-bleh*

rare (meat) poco asado (hecho) *poh-koh ah-SAH-doh (EH-choh)*

rate of exchange el tipo de cambio *TEE-poh deh KAHM-byoh*; **hourly rate** la tarifa por hora *tah-REE-fah pohr OH-rah*

rather (have) (v.) preferir *preh-feh-REER*

razor la navaja de afeitar *nah-BAH-hah deh ah-fey-TAHR*; **safety razor** la maquinilla de afeitar *mah-kee-NEE-yah deh ah-fey-TAHR*; **razor blade** la hojita de afeitar *oh-HEE-lah deh ah-fey-TAHR*

read (v.) leer *leh-EHR*

ready (to be) estar listo *ehs-TAHR LEES-toh*

real verdadero *behr-dah-DEH-roh*

really de veras, verdaderamente *deh BEH-rahs, behr-dah-DEH-rah-mehn-teh*

reasonable (price) razonable *rah-soh-NAH-bleh*

receipt el recibo *reh-SEE-boh*

receiver (of packages) el destinatario *dehs-tee-nah-TAH-ryoh*

recommend (v.) recomendar *reh-koh-mehn-DAHR*

recover (v.) **(get back)** recobrar *reh-koh-BRAHR;* **(health)** reponerse *reh-poh-NEHR-seh*

red rojo *ROH-hoh*

refund (payment) el reembolso *reh-ehm-BOHL-soh;* **to refund** reembolsar *reh-ehm-bohl-SAHR*

refuse (v.) rehusar *reh-oo-SAHR,* rechazar *reh-chah-SAHR*

regards recuerdos *reh-KWEHR-dohs,* saludos *sah-LOO-dohs*

registered mail certificado *sehr-tee-fee-KAH-doh*

registry window la ventanilla de los certificados *behn-tah-NEE-yah deh lohs sehr-tee-fee-KAH-dohs*

regular (ordinary) ordinario *ohr-dee-NAH-ryoh*

remedy el remedio *reh-MEH-dyoh*

remember (v.) recordar *reh-kohr-DAHR,* acordarse de *ah-kohr-DAHR-seh deh*

rent el alquiler *ahl-kee-LEHR;* **to rent** alquilar *ahl-kee-LAHR;* **for rent** se alquila *seh ahl-KEE-lah*

repair la reparación *reh-pah-rah-SYOHN,* la compostura *kohm-pohs-TOO-rah;* **to repair** reparar *reh-pah-RAHR,* componer *kohm-poh-NEHR*

repeat (v.) repetir *reh-peh-TEER*

reply (v.) responder *rehs-pohn-DEHR,* contestar *kohn-tehs-TAHR*

reservation la reservaición *reh-sehr-bah-SYOHN,* la reserva *reh-SEHR-bah*

reserve (v.) reservar *reh-sehr-BAHR*

reserved seat el asiento reservado *ah-SYEHN-toh reh-sehr-BAH-doh*

rest (v.) descansar *dehs-kahn-SAHR*

restaurant el restaurante *rehs-tow-RAHN-teh*

rest room el lavabo *lah-BAH-boh,* el retrete *reh-TREH-teh*

retired jubilado(a) *hoo-bee-LAH-doh(dah)*

return (v.) **(give back)** devolver *deh-bohl-BEHR;* **(go back)** volver *bohl-BEHR*

rib la costilla *kohs-TEE-yah*

ribbon la cinta *SEEN-tah*

rice el arroz *ahr-ROHS*

rich rico *REE-koh*

ride el paseo *pah-SEH-oh;* **to ride** pasear en *pah-seh-AHR ehn,* ir en *EER ehn*

right (opposite of left) derecho *deh-REH-choh;* **to be right** tener razón *teh-NEHR-reh-SOHN;* **all right** está bien *ehs-TAH byehn;* **right now** ahora mismo *ah-OH-rah MEES-moh*

ring (on finger) el anillo *ah-NEE-yoh,* la sortija *sohr-TEE-hah;* **to ring (call)** llamar *yah-MAHR*

rinse el enjuague *ehn-HWAH-gheh*

river el río *REE-oh*

road el camino *kah-MEE-noh,* la carretera *kahr-reh-TEH-rah,* la vía *BEE-ah;* **road map** el mapa de carretera *MAH-pah deh kahr-reh-TEH-rah,* el mapa itinerario *MAH-pah ee-tee-neh-RAH-ryoh*

roast   asado *ah-SAH-doh;* **roast beef**   el rosbif *rohs-BEEF*

rob   (v.) robar *roh-BAHR*

robe   la bata *BAH-tah*

roll (bread)   el panecillo *pah-neh-SEE-yoh,* el bollito *boh-YEE-toh;* **(film)**   el rollo *ROH-yoh,* el carrete *kah-REH-teh*

Romanian   rumano *roo-MAH-noh*

room   el cuarto *KWAHR-toh,* la habitación *ah-bee-tah-SYOHN*

root   la raíz *rah-EES*

rope   la cuerda *KWEHR-dah*

rouge   el colorete *koh-loh-REH-teh*

round   redondo *reh-DOHN-doh;* **round trip**   el viaje de ida y vuelta *BYAH-heh deh EE-dah ee BWEHL-tah*

royal   real *reh-AHL*

row (theater)   la fila *FEE-lah*

rubber   el caucho *KOW-choh,* la goma *GOH-mah;* **rubber band**   el elástico *eh-LAHS-tee-koh,* la liga de goma *LEE-gah deh GOH-mah;* **rubber heels**   los tacones de goma *tah-KOH-nehs deh GOH-mah*

rubbers   los chanclos *CHAHN-klohs*

rug   la alfombra *ahl-FOHM-brah*

run   (v.) correr *kohr-REHR*

running water   el agua corriente *AH-gwah kohr-RYEHN-teh*

runway (plane)   la pista *PEES-tah*

Russian   ruso *ROO-soh*

S

safe (strongbox)   la caja fuerte *KAH-hah FWEHR-teh*

safety pin   el imperdible *eem-pehr-DEE-bleh;* **safety razor**   la maquinilla de afeitar *mah-kee-NEE-yah deh ah-fey-TAHR*

sake (For heaven's sake!)   ¡Por Dios! *pohr-DYOHS*

salad   la ensalada *ehn-sah-LAH-dah*

salami   el salchichón *sahl-chee-CHOHN*

sale   la venta *BEHN-tah*

salesperson   el vendedor *ben-deh-DOHR*

salon (beauty)   el salón de belleza *sah-LOHN deh beh-YEH-sah*

saloon   la cantina *kahn-TEE-nah,* la taberna *tah-BEHR-nah*

salt   la sal *sahl*

salty   salado *sah-LAH-doh*

same   mismo *MEES-moh*

sand   la arena *ah-REH-nah*

sandal   la sandalia *sahn-DAH-lyah*

sandwich   el emparedado *ehm-pah-reh-DAH-doh*

sardine   la sardina *sahr-DEE-nah*

Saturday   el sábado *SAH-bah-doh*

sauce   la salsa *SAHL-sah*

saucer   el platillo *plah-TEE-yoh*

sausage   la salchicha *sahl-CHEE-chah,* el chorizo *choh-REE-soh*

say   (v.) decir *deh-SEER*

scalp massage   el masaje de cabeza *mah-SAH-heh deh kah-BEH-sah*

scarf   la bufanda *boo-FAHN-dah*

school   la escuela *ehs-KWEH-lah*

scissors   las tijeras *tee-HEH-rahs*

Scram!   ¡Váyase! *BAH-yah-seh,* ¡Fuera de aquí! *FWEH-rah deh ah-KEE*

screen la pantalla *pahn-TAH-yah*

screwdriver el destornillador *dehs-tohr-nee-yah-DOHR*

sea el mar *mahr*

seafood los mariscos *mah-REES-kohs*

seasickness el mareo *mah-REH-oh*

season la estación *ehs-tah-SYOHN*

seasoned sazonado *sah-soh-NAH-doh*

seat (in conveyance) el asiento *ah-SYEHN-toh*

second segundo *seh-GOON-doh*

secretary el secretario *seh-kreh-TAH-ryoh*, la secretaria *seh-kreh-TAH-ryah*

security la seguridad *seh-goo-ree-DAHD*; **security check** el control de seguridad *kohn-TROHL deh seh-goo-ree-DAHD*

see (v.) ver *behr*

seem (v.) parecer *pah-reh-SEHR*; **it seems to me** me parece *meh pah-REH-seh*

select (v.) escoger *ehs-koh-HEHR*

sell (v.) vender *behn-DEHR*

send (v.) mandar, enviar *mahn-DAHR, ehn-BYAHR*; **to send for** enviar por *ehn-BYAHR pohr*

sender (of mail) el remitente *reh-mee-TEHN-teh*

September septiembre, setiembre (m.) *seh-TYEHM-breh*

serve (v.) servir *sehr-BEER*

service el servicio *sehr-BEE-syoh*; **at your service** a sus órdenes *ah soos OHR-deh-nehs*

set (hair) (v.) arreglarse *ahr-reh-GLAHR-seh*

seven siete *SYEH-teh*

seventeen diecisiete *dyeh-see-SYEH-teh*

seventh séptimo *SEHP-tee-moh*

seventy setenta *seh-TEHN-tah*

several varios *BAH-ryohs*

shade (in the shade) A la sombra *ah lah SOHM-brah*; **window shade** persianas *pehr-SYAH-nahs*

shampoo el champú *chahm-POO*

shave (v.) afeitar *ah-fay-TAHR*

shaving cream la crema de afeitar *KREH-mah deh ah-fay-TAHR*

shawl el chal *chahl*

she ella *EH-yah*

sheet la sábana *SAH-bah-nah*

shine (v.) **(shoes)** lustrar *loos-TRAHR*; **(stars)** brillar *bree-YAHR*

ship el buque *BOO-keh*, el barco *BAHR-koh*, el vapor *bah-POHR*; **to ship** enviar *ehn-BYAHR*

shirt la camisa *kah-MEE-sah*

shoe el zapato *sah-PAH-toh*; **shoe store** la zapatería *sah-pah-teh-REE-ah*

shoelaces los cordones de zapato *kohr-DOH-nehs deh sah-PAH-toh*

shop la tienda *TYEHN-dah*

shopping (to go) (v.) ir de compras *eer deh KOHM-prahs*, ir de tiendas *TYEHN-dahs*

shopping mall la galería comercial *gah-leh-REE-ah koh-mehr-see-AHL*

short corto *KOHR-toh*

shorts (underwear) los calzoncillos *kahl-sohn-SEE-yohs*

shoulder el hombro *ohm-broh*

show (v.) mostrar *mohs-TRAHR*, enseñar *ehn-sehn-YAHR*

showcase la vitrina *bee-TREE-nah*

shower la ducha *DOO-chah*

shrimp el camarón *kah-mah-ROHN*, la gamba *GAHM-bah*

shrine el santuario *sahn-TWAH-ryoh*

shut (v.) cerrar *sehr-RAHR*

shutter la contraventana *kohn-trah-behn-TAH-nah*

shuttle el transbordo *trahns-BOHR-doh;* **shuttle bus** el autobús de transbordo *ow-toh-BOOS day trahns-BOHR-doh*

sick enfermo *ehn-FEHR-moh*

sickness la enfermedad *ehn-fehr-meh-DAHD*

side el lado *LAH-doh*

sidewalk la acera *ah-SEH-rah*

sightseeing el turismo *too-REES-moh*

sign (display) el letrero *leh-TREH-roh*, el aviso *ah-BEE-soh;* **to sign (a letter)** (v.) firmar *feer-MAHR*

silk la seda *SEH-dah*

silver la plata *PLAH-tah*

since desde *DEHS-deh*

sing (v.) cantar *kahn-TAHR*

single room la habitación para uno (habitación individual) *ah-bee-tah-SYOHN pah-rah OO-noh (ah-bee-tah-SYOHN een-dee-bee-DWAHL)*

sink (basin) el lavabo *lah-BAH-boh*

sir el señor *sehn-YOHR*

sister la hermana *ehr-MAH-nah*

sit (down) (v.) sentarse *sehn-TAHR-seh*

six seis *seys*

sixteen dieciseis *dyeh-see-SEYS*

sixth sexto *SEHS-toh*

sixty sesenta *seh-SEHN-tah*

size el tamaño *tah-MAHN-yoh*

skates patines *pah-TEEN-ehs*

skin la piel *pyehl*

skirt la falda *FAHL-dah*

sky el cielo *SYEH-loh*

sleep (v.) dormir *dohr-MEER*

sleeping car el coche-cama *KOH-cheh KAH-mah*

sleepy (to be) (v.) tener sueño *teh-NEHR SWEHN-yoh*

sleeve la manga *MAHN-gah*

slip (garment) la combinación *kohm-bee-nah-SYOHN*

slippers las zapatillas *sah-pah-TEE-yahs*

slow lento *LEHN-toh;* **the watch is slow** el reloj va atrasado *reh-LOH bah ah-trah-SAH-doh*

slowly despacio *dehs-PAH-syoh*, lentamente *lehn-tah-MEHN-teh*

small pequeño *peh-KEHN-yoh*, chiquito *chee-KEE-toh*

smelling salts las sales aromáticas *SAH-lehs ah-roh-MAH-tee-kahs*

smoke (v.) fumar *foo-MAHR*

smoking car el (coche) fumador *(KOH-cheh) foo-mah-DOHR*

snow la nieve *NYEH-beh;* **to snow** nevar *neh-BAHR*

so así *ah-SEE*

soap el jabón *hah-BOHN;* **soap flakes** los copos de jabón *KOH-pohs deh hah-BOHN*

soccer el fútbol *FOOT-bohl*

socks los calcetines *kahl-seh-TEE-nehs*

soda (bicarbonate) el bicarbonato (de soda) *bee-kahr-boh-NAH-toh (deh-SOH-dah)*

sofa el sofá *soh-FAH*

soft blando *BLAHN-doh*, suave *SWAH-beh;* **soft drink** el

refresco *reh-FREHS-koh,* la bebida no alcohólica *beh-BEE-dah noh ahl-koh-OH-lee-kah*

sole (shoe) la suela *SWEH-lah*

some algún *ahl-GOON*

someone alguien *AHL-gyehn*

something algo *AHL-goh*

sometimes a veces *ah BEH-sehs,* algunas veces *ahl-goo-nahs BEH-sehs*

son el hijo *EE-hoh*

song la canción *kahn-SYOHN*

soon pronto *PROHN-toh*

sore throat el dolor de garganta *doh-LOHR deh gahr-GAHN-tah*

sorry (to be) (v.) sentir *sehn-TEER;* **I am sorry** Lo siento. *loh-SYEHN-toh*

soup la sopa *SOH-pah;* **soup dish** el plato sopero *PLAH-toh soh-PEH-roh*

sour agrio *AH-gryoh*

south el sur *soor,* el sud *sood*

souvenir el recuerdo *reh-KWEHR-doh*

Spanish español *ehs-pahn-YOHL*

spare tire el neumático de repuesto *neh-oo-MAH-tee-koh deh reh-PWEHS-toh,* la goma de recambio *GOH-mah deh reh-KAHM-byoh*

spark plug la bujía *boo-HEE-ah*

sparkling wine el vino espumante (espumoso) *BEE-noh ehs-poo-MAHN-teh (ehs-poo-MOH-soh)*

speak (v.) hablar *ah-BLAHR*

special especial *ehs-peh-SYAHL;* **special delivery** el correo urgente *kohr-REH-oh oor-HEHN-teh;* **today's special** el plato del día *ehl plah-toh dehl DEE-ah*

speed limit la velocidad máxima *beh-loh-see-DAHD MAHK-see-mah*

spend (v.) **(money)** gastar *gahs-TAHR;* **(time)** pasar *pah-SAHR*

spice la especia *ehs-PEH-see-yah*

spicy picante *pee-KAHN-teh*

spinach la espinaca *ehs-pee-NAH-kah*

spitting forbidden prohibido escupir *proh-ee-BEE-doh ehs-koo-PEER*

spoon la cuchara *koo-CHAH-rah*

sprain la torcedura *tohr-seh-DOO-rah*

spring (mechanical) el muelle *MWEH-yeh,* el resorte *reh-SOHR-teh;* **(season)** la primavera *pree-mah-BEH-rah*

square (adj.) cuadrado *kwah-DRAH-doh;* **plaza** la plaza *PLAH-sah*

stairs la escalera *ehs-kah-LEH-rah*

stop (v.) parar *pah-RAHR*

stamp (postage) el sello *SEH-yoh*

stand (v.) estar de pie *ehs-TAHR deh pyeh;* **stand in line** hacer cola *ah-SEHR KOH-lah*

star la estrella *ehs-TREH-yah,* el astro *AHS-troh*

starch (laundry) el almidón *ahl-mee-DOHN;* **to starch** almidonar *ahl-mee-doh-NAHR*

start (v.) empezar *ehm-peh-SAHR,* comenzar *koh-mehn-SAHR,* principiar *preen-see-PYAHR*

starter (car) el arranque *ahr-RAHN-keh*

stateroom el camarote *kah-mah-ROH-teh*

station (gasoline) la estación de gasolina *ehs-tah-SYOHN deh gah-soh-LEE-nah,* la gasolinera *gah-soh-lee-NEH-rah;* **(railroad)** la estación de ferrocarril *ehs-tah-SYOHN deh fehr-roh-kahr-REEL*

stationery store la papelería *pah-peh-leh-REE-ah*

stationmaster el jefe de estación *heh-feh deh ehs-tah-SYOHN*

stay (a visit) la estancia *ehs-TAHN-syah,* la morada *moh-RAH-dah,* la permanencia *pehr-mah-NEHN-syah;* **to stay** quedar(se) *keh-DAHR-(seh)*

steak el bistec *bees-TEHK,* el biftec *beef-TEHK*

steal (v.) robar *roh-BAHR*

steel el acero *ah-SEH-roh*

steep grade la cuesta *KWEHS-tah*

steering wheel el volante *boh-LAHN-teh*

stew el guisado *ghee-SAH-doh,* el estofado *ehs-toh-FAH-doh*

steward (deck) el camarero (de cubierta) *kah-mah-REH-roh (deh koo-BYEHR-tah)*

stewardess (airplane) la azafata *ah-sah-FAH-tah*

stockings las medias *MEH-dyahs*

stomach el estómago *ehs-TOH-mah-goh;* **stomachache** el dolor de estómago *doh-lohr deh ehs-TOH-mah-goh*

stop (bus) la parada *pah-RAH-dah*

stoplight la luz de parada *loos deh pah-RAH-dah,* el semáforo *seh-MAH-foh-roh*

store la tienda *TYEHN-dah*

straight derecho *deh-REH-choh,* seguido *seh-GHEE-doh*

strap la correa *kohr-REH-ah*

straw la paja *PAH-hah*

strawberry la fresa *FREH-sah*

street la calle *KAH-yeh*

streetcar el tranvía *trahn-BEE-ah*

string la cuerda *KWEHR-dah*

string (green) bean la habichuela verde *ah-bee-CHWEH-lah BEHR-deh*

strong fuerte *FWEHR-teh*

style el estilo *ehs-TEE-loh;* **(fashion)** la moda *MOH-dah*

sudden repentino *reh-pehn-TEE-noh,* súbito *SOO-bee-toh*

suddenly de repente *deh reh-PEHN-teh*

sugar el azúcar *ah-SOO-kahr*

suit el traje *TRAH-heh*

suitcase la maleta *mah-LEH-tah*

summer el verano *beh-RAH-noh*

sun el sol *sohl*

Sunday el domingo *doh-MEEN-goh*

sunglasses las gafas de sol *GAH-fahs deh SOHL*

sunny asoleado *ah-soh-leh-AH-doh,* de sol *deh sohl*

suntan lotion la loción contra quemadura de sol *loh-SYOHN kohn-trah keh-mah-DOO-rah deh SOHL*

supper la cena *SEH-nah*

surgeon el cirujano *see-roo-HAH-noh*

sweater el suéter *SWEH-tehr*

Swedish sueco *SWEH-koh*

sweet dulce *DOOL-seh;* **sweet wine** vino dulce *BEE-noh DOOL-seh*

swell (v.) hinchar *een-CHAHR*

swim (v.) nadar *nah-DAHR*

swimming pool la piscina *pees-SEE-nah*

Swiss suizo *SWEE-soh*

switch (electric) el interruptor *een-tehr-roop-*

TOHR, el conmutador *kohn-moo-tah-DOHR*

swollen hinchado *een-CHAH-doh,* inflamado *een-flah-MAH-doh*

synagogue la sinagoga *see-nah-GOH-gah*

syrup (cough) el jarabe para la tos *hah-RAH-beh pah-rah lah tohs*

T

table la mesa *MEH-sah*

tablecloth el mantel *mahn-TEHL*

tablespoon la cuchara *coo-CHAH-rah*

tablespoonful la cucharada *koo-chah-RAH-dah*

tablet la pastilla *pahs-TEE-yah*

taillight (car) el farol de cola *fah-ROHL deh KOH-lah,* el farol trasero *fah-ROHL trah-SEH-roh*

tailor el sastre *SAHS-treh*

take (v.) **(carry)** llevar *yeh-BAHR;* **(person)** conducir *kohn-doo-SEER,* llevar *yeh-BAHR;* **(thing)** tomar *toh-MAHR;* **will take time** tomará (llevará) tiempo *toh-mah-RAH TYEHM-poh (yeh-bah-RAH) TYEHM-poh*

taken (occupied) ocupado *oh-koo-PAH-doh*

take off (garment) (v.) quitarse *kee-TAHR-seh*

talcum powder el polvo de talco *POHL-boh deh TAHL-koh*

tall alto *AHL-toh*

tan (color) el color de canela *koh-LOHR deh kah-NEH-lah,* café claro *kah-FEH KLAH-roh*

tangerine la mandarina *mahn-dah-REE-nah*

tank (car) el depósito *deh-POH-see-toh*

tap el grifo *GREE-foh*

tape (adhesive, skin) el esparadrapo *ehs-pah-rah-DRAH-poh*

tasty sabroso *sah-BROH-soh,* rico *REE-koh*

tax el impuesto *eem-PWEHS-toh*

taxi el taxi *TAHK-see*

tea el té *teh*

teaspoon la cucharita *koo-chah-REE-tah,* la cucharilla *koo-chah-REE-yah*

teaspoonful la cucharadita *koo-chah-rah-DEE-tah*

telephone el teléfono *teh-LEH-foh-noh;* **to telephone** telefonear *teh-leh-foh-neh-AHR*

tell (v.) decir *deh-SEER*

teller (bank) el cajero *kah-HEH-roh*

temporarily temporalmente *tehm-poh-rahl-MEHN-teh,* provisionalmente *proh-bee-syoh-nahl-MEHN-teh*

ten diez *dyes*

tension (high-tension wires) los cables de alta tensión *KAH-blehs deh AHL-tah tehn-SYOHN*

tenth décimo *DEH-see-moh*

terminal (bus, plane) la terminal *tehr-mee-NAHL*

terrorism el terrorismo *tehr-roh-REES-moh*

terrorist el terrorista *tehr-roh-REES-tah*

thank (v.) dar las gracias a *dahr lahs GRAH-syahs ah*

Thank you Gracias *GRAH-syahs*

that (conj.) que *keh;* (adj.) aquel *ah-KEHL,* ese *EH-seh,* aquella *ah-KEH-yah,* esa *EH-sah*

the el *ehl*, los *lohs*, la *lah*, las *lahs*

theater el teatro *teh-AH-troh*

their su *soo*

there ahí *ah-EE*, allí *ah-YEE*, allá *ah-YAH*; **there is (are)** hay *AH-ee*

thermometer el termómetro *tehr-MOH-meh-troh*

these estos *EHS-tohs*, estas *EHS-tahs*

they ellos *EH-yohs*, ellas *EH-yahs*

thick espeso *ehs-PEH-soh*, denso *DEHN-soh*, grueso *GRWEH-soh*

thief el ladrón *lah-DROHN*

thigh el muslo *MOOS-loh*

thing la cosa *KOH-sah*

think (v.) pensar *pehn-SAHR*

third tercero *tehr-SEH-roh*

thirsty (to be) tener sed *teh-NEHR sehd*

thirteen trece *TREH-seh*

thirty treinta *TREYN-tah*

this este *EHS-teh*, esta *EHS-tah*

those esos *EH-sohs*, aquellos *ah-KEH-yohs*, esas *EH-sahs*, aquellas *ah-KEH-yahs*

thousand mil *meel*

thread el hilo *EE-loh*

three tres *trehs*; **three times** tres veces *trehs BEH-sehs*

throat la garganta *gahr-GAHN-tah*

through por *pohr*, a través de *a trah-BEHS deh*

thumb el pulgar *pool-GAHR*

thunder el trueno *TRWEH-noh*; **to thunder** tronar *troh-NAHR*

Thursday el jueves *HWEH-behs*

ticket el billete *bee-YEH-teh*; **ticket window** la ventanilla *behn-tah-NEE-yah*

tie (neck) la corbata *kohr-BAH-tah*

tighten (car, brakes) apretar *ah-preh-TAHR*

till hasta (que) *ahs-tah KEH*

time el tiempo *TYEHM-poh*, la hora *OH-rah*; **on time** a tiempo *ah-TYEHM-poh*; **at what time?** ¿a qué hora? *ah-keh-OH-rah*

timetable el horario *oh-RAH-ryoh*

tint (hair) (v.) teñir *tehn-YEER*

tip (gratuity) la propina *proh-PEE-nah*

tire (car) la llanta *YAHN-tah*, el neumático *neh-oo-MAH-tee-koh*

tired (to be) (v.) cansado (estar) *kahn-SAH-doh (ehs-TAHR)*

tissue paper el papel de seda *pah-PEHL deh SEH-dah*

to a *ah*, por *pohr*, para *PAH-rah*

toast (bread) la tostada *tohs-TAH-dah*; **(drink)** el brindis *BREEN-dees*

toaster el tostador *tohs-tah-DOHR*

tobacco el tabaco *tah-BAH-koh*

today hoy *oy*

toe el dedo del pie *DEH-doh dehl pyeh*

together juntos *HOON-tohs*

toilet el retrete *reh-TREH-teh*; **toilet paper** el papel higiénico *pah-PEHL ee-HYEH-nee-koh*

token (bus or phone) la ficha *FEE-chah*

tomato el tomate *toh-MAH-teh*

tomorrow mañana *mahn-YAH-nah*

tongue la lengua *LEHN-gwah*

tonic (hair) el tónico para el pelo *TOH-nee-koh pah-rah ehl PEH-loh*

tonight esta noche *ehs-tah NOH-cheh*

too (also) también *tahm-BYEHN*; **Too bad!** ¡Es lástima! *ehs LAHS-tee-mah*; **Too much.** Demasiado. *deh-mah-SYAH-doh*

tooth el diente *DYEHN-teh*, la muela *MWEH-lah*

toothache el dolor de muelas *doh-LOHR deh MWEH-lahs*

toothbrush el cepillo de dientes *seh-PEE-yoh deh DYEHN-tehs*

toothpaste la pasta dentífrica *PAHS-tah dehn-TEE-free-kah*

top la cima *SEE-mah*

touch (v.) tocar *toh-KAHR*

tough duro *DOO-roh*

tourist el (la) turista *too-REES-tah*

tow (car) (v.) remolcar *reh-mohl-KAHR*

toward hacia *AH-syah*

towel la toalla *toh-AH-yah*

town el pueblo *PWEH-bloh*, la población *poh-blah-SYOHN*

track (R.R.) los rieles *RYEH-lehs*

traffic light la luz de parada *loos deh pah-RAH-dah*, la luz de tráfico *loos deh TRAH-fee-koh*, el semáforo de circulación *seh-MAH-foh-roh deh seer-koo-lah-syohn*

train el tren *trehn*

transfer (ticket) el transbordo *trahns-BOHR-doh*; **to transfer** transbordar *trahns-bohr-DAHR*

translate (v.) traducir *trah-doo-SEER*

travel (v.) viajar *byah-HAHR*; **travel insurance** el seguro de viaje *seh-GOO-roh deh BYAH-heh*

traveler el viajero *byah-HEH-roh*; **traveler's check** el cheque de viajeros *CHEH-keh deh byah-HEH-rohs*

tree el árbol *AHR-bohl*

trip (voyage) el viaje *BYAH-heh*

trolley car el tranvía *trahn-BEE-ah*

trouble (to be in) tener dificultades *teh-NEHR dee-fee-kool-TAH-dehs*, estar en un apuro *ehs-TAHR ehn oon ah-POO-roh*

trousers los pantalones *pahn-tah-LOH-nehs*

truck el camión *kah-MYOHN*

true verdadero *behr-dah-DEH-roh*

trunk (car) el portaequipaje *pohr-tah-eh-kee-PAH-heh*, el baúl *bah-OOL*

try on (v.) probarse *proh-BAHR-seh*

try to (v.) tratar de (+ infinitive) *trah-TAHR deh*

Tuesday el martes *MAHR-tehs*

Turkish turco *TOOR-koh*

turn (n.) la vuelta *BWEHL-tah*; **to turn** doblar *doh-BLAHR*, volver *bohl-BEHR*

tuxedo el smoking *SMOH-keeng*

twelve doce *DOH-seh*

twenty veinte *BEYN-teh*

twice dos veces *dohs BEH-sehs*

twin beds las camas gemelas *KAH-mahs heh-MEH-lahs*

two dos *dohs*

U

ugly feo *FEH-oh*

umbrella el paraguas *pah-RAH-gwahs*

uncle el tío *TEE-oh*

uncomfortable incómodo *een-KOH-moh-doh*

under debajo de *deh-BAH-hoh deh*, bajo *BAH-hoh*

undershirt la camiseta *kah-mee-SEH-tah*

understand comprender *kohm-prehn-DEHR*, entender *ehn-tehn-DEHR*

underwear la ropa interior *ROH-pah een-teh-RYOHR*

university la universidad *oo-nee-behr-see-DAHD*

until hasta *AHS-tah*

up arriba *ahr-REE-bah*

upon sobre *SOH-breh*, encima de *ehn-SEE-mah deh*

upper alto *AHL-toh*

upstairs arriba *ahr-REE-bah*

U.S.A. los Estados Unidos de América *ehs-TAH-dohs oo-NEE-dohs deh ah-MEH-ree-kah* [abbreviate EE.UU.]

use (purpose) el uso *OO-soh*, el empleo *ehm-PLEH-oh*; **to use** usar *oo-SAHR*, emplear *ehm-pleh-AHR*

V

valise la maleta *mah-LEH-tah*

veal la ternera *tehr-NEH-rah*

vegetables las legumbres *leh-GOOM-brehs*; **green vegetables** las verduras *behr-DOO-rahs*

velvet el terciopelo *tehr-syoh-PEH-loh*

very muy *mooy*

vest el chaleco *chah-LEH-koh*

veterinarian el veterinario *beh-teh-ree-NAH-ryoh*

video el video *vee-DEH-oh*

video recorder la filmadora de video *feel-mah-DOH-rah deh vee-DEH-oh*

view la vista *BEES-tah*

vinegar el vinagre *bee-NAH-greh*

visit la visita *bee-SEE-tah*; **to visit** visitar *bee-see-TAHR*, hacer una visita *ah-SEHR oo-nah bee-SEE-tah*

visitor el visitante *bee-see-TAHN-teh*

W

waist la cintura *seen-TOO-rah*, el talle *TAH-yeh*

wait (for) (v.) esperar *ehs-peh-RAHR*

waiter el camarero *kah-mah-REH-roh*; **headwaiter** el jefe de comedor *HEH-feh deh koh-meh-DOHR*

waiting room la sala de espera *SAH-lah deh ehs-PEH-rah*

waitress la camarera *kah-mah-REH-rah*

wake up (v.) despertarse *dehs-pehr-TAHR-seh*

walk (take a) (v.) dar un paseo *dahr oon pah-SEH-oh*

wall el muro *MOO-roh*, la pared *pah-REHD*

wallet la cartera (de bolsillo) *kahr-TEH (deh bohl-SEE-yoh)*

want (v.) querer *keh-REHR*

warm caliente *kah-LYEHN-teh*

was era *EH-rah*, estaba *ehs-TAH-bah*

wash (v.) lavarse *lah-BAHR-seh*

washroom el lavabo *lah-BAH-boh*

watch (clock) el reloj *reh-LOH*; **to watch** mirar *mee-RAHR*; **Watch out!** ¡Cuidado! *kwee-DAH-doh*

water el agua (f.) *AH-gwah*

watermelon la sandía *sahn-DEE-ah*

way (path, mode) la vía *BEE-ah*, la manera *mah-NEH-rah*, el modo *MOH-doh*; **by way of** (por) vía (de) *(pohr) BEE-ah (deh)*, pasando por *pah-SAHN-doh pohr*; **one way** dirección única *dee-rehk-SYOHN OO-nee-kah*; **this way** por aquí *pohr ah-KEE*;

which way? ¿por dónde? *pohr DOHN-deh*; **wrong way** rumbo equivocado *ROOM-boh eh-kee-boh-KAH-dah*

we nosotros *noh-SOH-trohs*

weak débil *DEH-beel*

wear (v.) llevar *yeh-BAHR*

weather el tiempo *TYEHM-poh*

Wednesday el miércoles *MYEHR-koh-lehs*

week la semana *seh-MAH-nah*

weigh (v.) pesar *peh-SAHR*

weight el peso *PEH-soh*

welcome. (You're) De nada. *deh NAH-dah*

well bien *byehn*; **well-done (steak)** bien hecho *byehn EH-choh*

west el oeste *oh-EHS-teh*

wet mojado *moh-HAH-doh*; **wet paint** recién pintado *reh-SYEHN peen-TAH-doh*

what qué *keh*

wheel la rueda *RWEH-dah*; **steering wheel** el volante *boh-LAHN-teh*

wheelchair la silla de ruedas *SEE-yah deh RWEH-dahs*

when cuando *KWAHN-doh*

where donde *DOHN-deh*

which cual *kwahl*

whiskey el whiskey *WEES-kee*

white blanco *BLAHN-koh*

who quién *kyehn*, quiénes (pl.) *KYEH-nehs*

whom a quién *ah kyehn*, a quiénes (pl.) *ah KYEHN-ehs*

whose de quién *deh kyehn*, de quiénes (pl.) *deh KYEHN-ehs*

why por qué *pohr KEH*

wide ancho *AHN-choh*

width la anchura *ahn-CHOO-rah*

wife la señora *sehn-YOH-rah*, la esposa *ehs-POH-sah*

wind el viento *BYEHN-toh*

window la ventana *behn-TAH-nah*; **display window** el

escaparate *ehs-kah-pah-RAH-teh*; **(train, post office, bank)** la ventanilla *behn-tah-NEE-yah*

windshield el parabrisas *pah-rah-BREE-sahs*

windy ventoso *behn-TOH-soh*; **it is windy** hace viento *ah-seh BYEHN-toh*

wine el vino *bee-noh*; **wine list** la lista de vinos *LEES-tah deh BEE-nohs*

winter el invierno, *een-BYEHR-noh*

wiper (windshield) el limpiaparabrisas *leem-pyah-pah-rah-BREE-sahs*

wire (high-tension) el cable de alta tensión *KAH-bleh deh AHL-tah tehn-SYOHN*; **Hold the wire. (telephone)** No se retire. *noh seh reh-TEE-reh*

wish (v.) querer *keh-REHR*, desear *deh-seh-AHR*

wishes (best) saludos *sah-LOO-dohs*

with con *kohn*

without sin *seen*

woman la mujer *moo-HEHR*

wood la madera *mah-DEH-rah*

wool la lana *LAH-nah*

word la palabra *pah-LAH-brah*

work el trabajo *trah-BAH-hoh*; **(creative work)** la obra *OH-brah*; **to work** trabajar *trah-bah-HAHR*

worry (v.) preocuparse *preh-oh-koo-PAHR-seh*; **Don't worry.** No se preocupe. *noh seh preh-oh-KOO-peh*

worse peor *peh-OHR*

worst el peor *ehl peh-OHR*

worth (to be) (v.) valer *bah-LEHR*

wound (injury) la herida *eh-REE-dah*

wounded herido *eh-REE-doh*

wrap up (v.) envolver *ehn-bohl-BEHR*

wrapping paper el papel de envolver *pah-PEHL deh ehn-bohl-BEHR*

wrench (tool) la llave inglesa (de tuercas) *YAH-beh een-GLEH-sah (deh TWEHR-kahs)*

wrist la muñeca *moon-YEH-kah;* **wristwatch** el reloj de pulsera *reh-LOH-deh pool-seh-rah*

write (v.) escribir *ehs-kree-BEER*

writing paper el papel de cartas *pah-PEHL deh KAHR-tahs,* el papel de escribir *deh ehs-kree-BEER*

wrong (to be) equivocarse *eh-kee-boh-KAHR-seh,* no tener razón *noh teh-NEHR rah-SOHN*

Y

year el año *AHN-yoh*

yellow amarillo *ah-mah-REE-yoh*

yes sí *see*

yesterday ayer *ah-YEHR*

yet todavía *toh-dah-BEE-ah;* **not yet** todavía no *toh-dah-BEE-ah noh*

you usted *oo-STEHD,* ustedes *oo-STEH-dehs,* tú *too*

young joven *HOH-behn*

your su, sus *soo, soos,* de usted *deh oo-STEHD,* de ustedes *deh oo-STEH-dehs*

youth hostel albergue juvenil *ahl-behr-gheh hoo-ben-EEL*

X

x-ray la radiografía *rah-dyoh-grah-FEE-ah,* los rayos X *lohs rah-yohs EH-kees*

Z

zipper la cremallera *kreh-mah-YEH-rah,* el cierre relámpago *syehr-reh reh-LAHM-pah-goh*

zoo el jardín zoológico *hahr-DEEN soh-oh-LOH-hee-koh*

SPANISH-ENGLISH DICTIONARY

Only masculine forms of adjectives are given here; in most cases, the feminine form requires dropping the "o" at the end and replacing it with "a." Gender is given by "**m.**" or "**f.**"

A

a to, at, in, on, upon

abajo down, downstairs

abierto open

¡Abran paso! Make way!

abrelatas m. can opener

abrigo m. overcoat

abril April

abrir to open

acabado over, finished

acabar to finish; **acabar de** to have just (done something)

aceite m. oil; **aceite de oliva** olive oil; **aceite de ricino** castor oil

aceituna f. olive

acera f. sidewalk

acero m. steel

acetona f. nail-polish remover

aclarar to clear up (weather)

acordarse to remember

acostarse to lie down, to go to bed

acuerdo m. agreement; **estar de acuerdo** to agree

acumulador m. battery

adelante ahead, forward, onward; **¡Adelante!** Come in!

adiós good-bye, farewell

aduana f. customs, customs house

afuera out, outside

agosto August

agradable pleasant

agradecido grateful

agrio sour

agua m. water; **agua corriente** running water; **agua de Colonia** Cologne; **agua mineral** mineral water

aguardar to expect, to wait for

aguja f. needle

agujero m. hole

ahí there

ahora now; **ahora mismo** right now

ajo m. garlic

ajustar to adjust

albaricoque m. apricot

albornoz m. bathrobe

alcachofa f. artichoke

alcoba f. bedroom

alegrarse to be glad, to rejoice

alegre glad, merry

alemán m. German

alergia f. allergy

alfiler m. pin

aflombra f. rug

algo something, anything; **¿Algo más?** Anything else?

algodón m. cotton

alguien someone, somebody, anyone, anybody

algún, alguno some, any; **algunas veces** sometimes

alicates m. pl. pliers

allá there, over there

allí there, right there

almacén m. warehouse

almendra f. almond

almidón m. starch

almidonar to starch

almohada f. pillow
almorzar to lunch
almuerzo m. lunch
alquilar to rent
alquiler m. rent (payment)
alrededor de around, about;
(los) alrededores
environs, outskirts
alto tall
¡Alto! Halt! Stop!
amargo bitter
amarillo yellow
amigo m. friend
ampliación f. enlargement
amueblado furnished
ancho wide
anchura f. width
andén m. platform
angosto narrow
anillo m. ring
año m. year
anteojos m. pl. eyeglasses
antes de before
antibiótico m. antibiotic
antipático unpleasant, not
likable (person)
apearse to get off
apellido m. family name,
surname
apio m. celery
aprender to learn
apretar to tighten
apuro m. trouble, difficulty
aquel that
aquí here
árabe Arab
árbol m. tree
arena f. sand
arete m. earring
armario m. closet
arranque m. starter (car)
arreglar to fix, to repair
arriba up, above
arroz m. rice
asado m. roast
asar to roast
ascensor m. elevator

asegurar to insure, to ensure,
to assure
así so, thus
asiento m. seat (on
conveyance); **asiento
reservado** reserved seat
asistencia f. assistance
asoleado sunny
asomarse a to lean out
atrás back, backward, behind
aturdido (estar) to feel dizzy
auricular m. earpiece
austríaco Austrian
autobús m. bus; **autobús de
transbordo m.** shuttle bus
avellana f. hazelnut
avería f. breakdown
avión f. airplane
aviso m. notice, sign, warning
ayer yesterday
ayudar to help
ayuntamiento m. city hall
azafata f. stewardess
azúcar m. sugar
azul blue

B

bailar to dance
baile m. dance
bajada f. downgrade
bajar to go down, to come
down; **(computers)** to
download
bajo low
bañarse to bathe, to take a
bath
baraja f. deck of cards
barato cheap
barba f. beard
barco m. boat
barrera f. gate, barrier
barrio m. district
¡Basta! Enough!. Cut it out!;
bastante enough (plenty)
bastón m. cane
bata f. robe, dressing gown
baúl m. trunk

beber   to drink
bebida f.   drink
belga   Belgian
bello   beautiful
bencina f.   gasoline
besar   to kiss
beso m.   kiss
biblioteca f.   library
bien   well; **Bien hecho.**   Well done.
billete m.   ticket, bill (banknote); **billete de ida y vuelta**   round-trip ticket
blanco   white
blando   soft
boca f.   mouth
bocacalle f.   intersection
bocado m.   mouthful, bite; **tomar un bocado**   to have or get a bite
bocina f.   car horn
bolsa f.   purse
bolsillo m.   pocket
bollito m.   roll
bombilla f.   electric bulb
bonito   pretty
bordo: a bordo   on board; **¡A bordo!**   All aboard!
borla f.   powder puff
borracho   drunk
bote m.   boat; **bote salvavidas m.**   lifeboat
botón m.   button
botones m.   bellboy, bellhop
bragas f. pl.   panties
brasileño   Brazilian
brazo m.   arm
brillar   to shine
brindis m.   toast (drink)
bueno   good
bufanda f.   scarf
bujía f.   sparkplug, candle
bulto m.   package
buque m.   ship, boat
buscar   to look for, to search
buzón m.   letterbox, mailbox

C

caballero m.   gentleman
caballo m.   horse
cabello m.   hair
cabeza f.   head
cabina f.   phone booth
cables de alta tensión m. pl.   high-tension wires
cada   each; **cada uno**   each one
cadena f.   chain
cadera f.   hip
caer   to fall
café m.   coffee, café; **café solo**   black coffee
caja f.   box, case; **Pague en la caja.**   Pay the cashier.
caja fuerte f.   safe (strongbox)
cajero m.   teller, cashier
cajón m.   drawer
caliente   warm, hot
calle f.   street
calor m.   heat, warmth; **Hace color.**   It's warm, hot.
calzoncillos m. pl.   shorts (underwear)
cama f.   bed
cámara fotográfica f.   camera
camarera f.   waitress, maid
camarero m.   waiter, valet; **camarero de cubierta m.**   deck steward
camarón m.   shrimp
camarote m.   stateroom
camas gemelas f. pl.   twin beds
cambiar   to change, to exchange
cambio m.   change
camino   road; **camino equivocado**   wrong way
camión m.   truck
camisa f.   shirt
camiseta f.   undershirt
camisón m.   nightgown
campo m.   countryside
canción f.   song
cansado (estar)   to be tired
cantar   to sing

cantina f. saloon
capó m. hood (car), bonnet
cara f. face
¡Caramba! Darn it!
cargador m. charger
caro expensive
carne f. meat, flesh; **carne de cerdo** f. pork; **carne de cordero** f. lamb; **carne de vaca** f. beef
carretera f. highway
carta f. letter; playing card
cartera (de bolsillo) f. pocketbook (wallet)
casa f. house, home; **en casa** at home; **casa de correos** f. post office; **casa de huéspedes** f. boardinghouse
casi almost
caso case
castaña f. chestnut
castaño brown
castillo m. castle
catarro m. cold (respiratory)
catorce fourteen
caucho rubber
cebolla onion
ceja f. eyebrow
celular m. cell phone
cena f. supper
cenicero m. ashtray
cepillar to brush
cepillo m. brush; toothbrush; **cepillo de ropa** clothes brush
cerca de near, close
cerdo m. pig, hog; **carne de cerdo** pork
cereza f. cherry
cerilla f. match
cerrado closed
cerradura f. lock
cerrajero m. locksmith
cerrar to close, to shut
certificado registered (mail)
cerveza f. beer
cesta f. basket
chal m. shawl

chaleco m. vest
chanclos m. pl. rubbers
checo Czech
cheque m. check (bank); **cheque de viajero** m. traveler's check
chileno Chilean
chino Chinese
chirrido m. squeak
chorizo m. sausage
chuleta f. chop, cutlet
cielo m. sky, heaven
cien, ciento hundred
cierre relámpago m. zipper
cima f. top
cincuenta fifty
cine m. movie house, movie show
cinta f. ribbon
cinta adhesiva f. adhesive tape, bandage
cintura f. waist
cinturón m. belt
ciruela f. plum; . . . **pasa** f. prune
cirujano m. surgeon
ciudad f. city
claro light (color), clear; **¡Claro!** Of course!
cobrar to collect, to cash
cocido cooked meat-vegetable stew
cocina f. kitchen
cocinar to cook
coche m. coach, auto, R.R. car; **coche-cama** m. sleeping car; **coche-comedor** m. dining car; **coche-fumador** m. smoking car
cochero m. coachman
codo m. elbow
coger to catch, take
cojinete m. bearing (car)
col f. cabbage
colchón m. mattress
colgador m. coat hanger
color de canela tan
colorete m. rouge
collar m. necklace

combinación f.   slip (garment)
comenzar   to begin, to start
comer   to eat
comida f.   meal; **comida a precio fijo, comida corrida** (or **completa**) f.   fixed-price meal
comisaría f.   police station
como   as, like
cómo   how
cómodo   comfortable
compañía f.   company
componer   to fix
composturas f. pl.   repairs
compota f.   preserve; stewed fruit
compra f.   purchase (item)
comprar   to buy, to purchase
comprender   to understand
computadora f.   computer; **computadora portátil** laptop
con   with; **con mucho gusto** gladly
condones   condoms
conducir   to drive
conferencia interurbana f.   long-distance phone call
conocer   to know, to make acquaintance of
conseguir   to get, to obtain
contar   to count, to tell
contar con   to depend on, to count on
contestación f.   answer, reply
contestar   to answer, to reply
contra   against
contraseña f.   password
contraventana f.   shutter
control m.   control; **control de seguridad** m.   security check
contusión f.   bruise
copia f.   print (photo)
copos de jabón   soap flakes
corazón m.   heart
corbata f.   necktie

correa f.   strap; **correa de ventilador** f.   fan belt
correo m.   mail, post office; **correo aéreo** m.   air mail; **correo electrónico** m.   e-mail; **correo urgente** m.   special delivery
correr   to run
corriente de aire m.   draft (current of air)
cortar   to cut
corte de pelo m.   haircut
cortés   polite
cortesía f.   politeness, courtesy
corto   short
cosa f.   thing
costilla f.   rib
creer   to believe
crema f.   cream; **crema de afeitar** f.   shaving cream
cremallera f.   zipper
cruce m.   crossroad
cuadra f.   block (city)
cuadrado m.   square (shape)
cuadro m.   picture
cuál   which?, which one?
cualquier, cualquiera   any; **en cualquier caso, de cualquier modo**   in any case
cuándo   when?
cuánto   how much?; **¿cuánto tiempo?**   how long?
cuántos   how many?
cuarenta   forty
cuarto   room, quarter; **cuarto de baño** m.   bathroom; **cuarto tocador** m.   powder room
cuatro   four
cubierta f.   deck (ship)
cuchara f.   spoon
cucharada f.   spoonful
cucharadita f.   teaspoonful
cucharilla f.   teaspoon
cuchillo m.   knife
cuello m.   neck, collar
cuenta f.   bill (restaurant)

cuentagotas m. dropper (eye)
cuerda f. rope, cord, string
cuero m. leather, hide
cuerpo m. body
cuidado m. care; **con cuidado** carefully; **tener cuidado** to be careful; **¡Cuidado!** Be careful! Watch out! Attention!
cura m. priest

D

danés Danish
dar to give; **dar las gracias a** to thank; **dar un paseo** to take a walk
darse prisa to hurry
de of, from
debajo de under, beneath
deber to have to, to owe
débil weak
décimo tenth
decir to say, to tell
dedo m. finger
dejar to let, to permit, to leave behind
demasiado too much
dentadura f. denture
dentro inside, within
depósito m. tank
derecho right (opposite of left); **todo derecho** straight ahead
derechos de aduana m. pl. customs duties
desayunarse to have breakfast
desayuno m. breakfast
descansar to rest
descolorante hair bleach
descuento m. discount
desde since; **Desde luego.** Of course.
desear to wish
desechable disposable
desembarcar to land (from ship)
desodorante m. deodorant
despacio slowly

despejarse to clear up (sky)
despertador m. alarm clock
despertarse to wake up
después (de) after, afterward, later
destinatario m. addressee (on packages or letters)
destornillador m. screwdriver
desviación f. detour
detrás de back of, behind
devolver to return, to give back
día m. day; **por . . .** by the day; **buenos días** good morning, good day
diablo m. devil; **¡Qué diablos!** What the devil!
diarrea f. diarrhea
diecinueve nineteen
dieciocho eighteen
dieciséis sixteen
diecisiete seventeen
diente m. tooth
diez ten
difícil difficult, hard
digital digital
dinero m. money; **dinero contante m.** cash
dirección f. address, direction; **dirección única f.** one-way traffic
dirigir to direct
disco m. compact disc
disparate m. nonsense
dispensar to excuse, to pardon
Dispénseme usted. Pardon (excuse) me.
distancia f. distance; **¿A qué distancia?** How far?
doblar to turn, to fold
doce twelve
docena f. dozen
dolor m. pain, ache; **dolor de cabeza m.** headache; **dolor de estómago m.**

stomachache; **dolor de garganta m.** sore throat; **dolor de muelas m.** toothache
domingo m. Sunday
donde where
dormir to sleep
dormitorio m. bedroom
dos two; **dos veces** twice
droga f. drug (illegal)
ducha f. shower
dulce sweet; **dulces m. pl.** candy
durar to last
durazno m. peach
duro hard, tough

E

elástico m. rubber band
ellas f. they
ellos m. they
embrague m. car clutch
emparedado m. sandwich
empastar to fill a tooth
empaste m. filling (tooth)
empezar to begin, to start
emplear to use, to hire
empleo m. use (purpose), job
empujar to push
en on, in, at; **en casa** at home; **en casa de** at the home of; **en seguida** at once, immediately, right away
encaje m. lace
encendedor m. cigarette lighter
encender to light
encendido m. car ignition
enchufe m. jack (electrical)
encías f. pl. gums
encima (de) above, over, upon
encontrar to find, to meet
encrucijada f. crossroad
encurtidos m. pl. pickles
enchufe m. electric outlet
enero m. January
enfermedad f. illness

enfermera f. nurse
enfermo ill
engranaje m. gears
engrasar to grease, to lubricate
enhorabuena f. congratulations
enjuague m. mouthwash
ensalada f. salad
enseñar to teach, to show
entender to understand
entrar to enter, come in
entre between, among
entrega f. delivery
entregar to deliver, to hand over
entremés m. appetizer, hors d'oeuvre
enviar to send
envolver to wrap
equipaje m. baggage
equivocarse to be mistaken
esa, ese, eso that; **a eso de** at about, approximately (a certain hour)
esas, esos those
escalera f. stairs
escalofrío m. chill
escaparate m. display window
escape m. exhaust (car), leak
escarpado steep
escoger to choose, to select
escribir to write
escuchar to listen to
escuela f. school
escupir to spit; **prohibido escupir** spitting forbidden
esmalte m. nail polish
espalda f. back (of body)
español Spanish
esparadrapo m. adhesive tape, bandage
espejo m. mirror
esperar to hope, to expect, to wait for
espeso thick
espinaca f. spinach
esposa f. wife

esposo m.   husband
esta, este, esto   this
Está bien.   All right, okay.
estación f.   season; **estación de ferrocarril** f.   railroad station
estacionar   to park; **se prohibe estacionar**   no parking
Estados Unidos de América m. pl.   U.S.A.
estanco m.   cigar store (Spain)
estar   to be; **estar de pie**   to be standing; **estar de vuelta**   to be back
estas, estos   these
este   east; this
estancia f.   stay
estofado m.   stew
estómago m.   stomach; **dolor de estómago** m.   stomachache
estrecho   narrow, straight
estrella f.   star
esquina f.   street corner
etiqueta f.   label, etiquette; **traje de etiqueta** m.   evening dress
euro m.   euro
evitar   to avoid
extranjero m.   foreign, foreigner

F

facturar   to check (baggage)
faja f.   girdle
falda f.   skirt
farmacia f.   pharmacy
faro m.   headlight
farol m.   street lamp; **farol delantero** m.   headlight; **farol trasero (de cola)** m.   taillight
favor m.   favor; **Por favor.**   Please.; **Haga el favor.**   Please.

fax m.   fax
febrero m.   February
fecha f.   date; **fecha de hoy**   today's date
¡Felices Pascuas!   Merry Christmas!
felicitaciones f. pl.   congratulations
feliz   happy; **¡Feliz Año Nuevo!**   Happy New Year!; **¡Feliz Navidad!**   Merry Christmas!
feo   ugly
ferrocarril m.   railroad
fiambre m.   cold cuts
ficha f.   token (for bus or phone)
fiebre f.   fever
fieltro m.   felt
fila f.   row (theater), line
filmadora f.   movie camera; **filmadora de video**   video recorder
fin m.   end
flor f.   flower
fonda para estudiantes f.   youth hostel
fósforo m.   match
francés   French
frenos m. pl.   brakes
frente m.   front, f. forehead
fresa f.   strawberry
fresco   fresh, cool
frijol colorado m.   kidney bean
frío m.   cold; **hacer frío**   to be cold (weather); **tener frío**   to be cold (person)
frito   fried
fuego m.   fire
fuente f.   fountain
fuera   out, outside
fuerte   strong
fumador m.   smoker
fumar   to smoke
función f.   performance
funda f.   pillowcase
furgón m.   baggage car

G

gabán m. overcoat
gafas f. pl. eyeglasses
galería comerical f. shopping mall
gana f. desire; **tener ganas de** to feel like
ganado m. cattle
gancho m. hook
ganga f. bargain sale
ganso m. goose
garganta f. throat; **dolor de garganta** m. sore throat
gasa f. gauze
gastar to spend
gasto m. expense, expenditure; **gasto mínimo** cover charge
gato m. cat, car jack
gay m. gay
gemelos m. pl. twins, cuff links, binoculars
gente f. people
gerente m. manager
ginebra f. gin
giro postal m. money order
goma de recambio f. spare tire
gorra f. cap
gorro de baño m. bathing cap
gracias f. pl. thanks, thank you
grande big, large, great
granizar to hail (weather)
granizo m. hail (weather)
griego Greek
grifo m. tap, faucet
gris gray
grueso thick, stout
guante m. glove
guardar to keep
guardabarros m. fender
guía m., f. guide; guidebook
guiar to drive
guisado m. stew
guisante m. pea
gustar to like, to be pleasing

gusto m. taste, pleasure; **con mucho gusto** gladly

H

habichuela f. string bean
habitación f. room; **habitación para dos personas** f. double room; **habitación individual** f. single room
hablar to speak, to talk
hace ago
hacer to do, to make, to pack (baggage); **hacer cola** to stand in line
hacerse to become
hacia toward
Haga el favor. Please.
hallar to find
hasta until, even; **Hasta mañana.** See you tomorrow.; **Hasta la vista.** Good-bye. Till we meet again.
hay there is, there are
hecho a mano handmade
helado m. ice cream
herida f. wound
herido wounded
herir to wound, to hurt
hermana f. sister
hermano m. brother
hermoso beautiful
hervido boiled
hielo m. ice
hierro m. iron
hígado m. liver
higo m. fig
hierba f. grass
hilo m. thread, string
hinchado swollen
hinchar to swell
hoja de afeitar f. razor blade
hombre m. man
hombro m. shoulder
hongo m. mushroom

hora f. hour, time; **¿Qué hora es?** What time is it?; **por hora** by the hour
horario m. timetable
horno m. oven; **al horno** baked
horquilla f. hairpin
hoy today
hueso m. bone
huevo m. egg; **huevo duro** m. hard-boiled egg
húngaro Hungarian

I

idioma m. language
iglesia f. church
imperdible safety pin
impermeable raincoat
importar to be important, to import; **No importa.** It doesn't matter.
impuesto m. tax
incómodo uncomfortable
indicar to indicate
infierno m. hell
informes m. pl. information
inglés English
internet m. Internet
interruptor m. electric switch
invierno m. winter
ir to go; **ir a casa** to go home; **ir de compras (de tiendas)** to go shopping
irse to go away, to leave, to depart, to get out
izquierdo left (opposite of right)

J

jabón m. soap; **copos de jabón** m. pl. soap flakes
jamás never
jamón m. ham
jaqueca f. migraine
jarabe m. syrup; **jarabe para la tos** m. cough syrup

jardín m. garden; **jardín zoológico** m. zoo
jefe m. chief, leader, head; **jefe de camareros** m. headwaiter; **jefe de estación** m. stationmaster
joven young, young person
joya f. jewel
joyería f. jewelry, jewelry shop
joyero m. jeweler
judío Jewish, Jew
juego m. game
jueves m. Thursday
jugar to play
jugo m. juice
julio m. July
junio m. June

L

labio m. lip; **lápiz de labios** m. lipstick
lado m. side; **por otro lado** on the other hand
ladrón m. thief, robber
lámpara f. lamp
langosta f. lobster
lápiz m. pencil; **lápiz de labios** m. lipstick
largo long; **el largo** m. length
lástima f. pity; **¡Es lástima!** Too bad; **¡Qué lástima!** What a pity!
lastimar to hurt, to injure, to bruise
lata f. can (noun)
lavabo m. sink, washroom, lavatory; **lavabo de señoras** m. ladies' room; **lavabo de caballeros** m. men's room
lavandera f. laundress
lavandería f. laundry
lavar to wash (something)
lavarse to wash (oneself)
laxante m. laxative
leche f. milk
lechuga f. lettuce

leer to read

legumbres f. pl. vegetables

lejos far, distant, far away

lengua f. tongue; language

lentamente slowly

lente m. lens

lento slow

letra f. letter, bank draft

lesbiana f. lesbian

letrero m. sign, poster, placard

levantar to lift

levantarse to get up, to stand up, to rise

libre free

librería f. bookstore

libro m. book

liga f. garter; **liga de goma f.** rubber band

ligero light (adj.)

lima de uñas f. nail file

limpiar to clean

limpieza a seco f. dry-cleaning

limpio clean

lindo pretty

línea aérea f. airline

lino m. linen

linterna f. flashlight

lista list; **lista de correos f.** general delivery; **lista de platos f.** menu; **lista de vinos f.** wine list

litera f. berth; **litera alta (litera de arriba) f.** upper berth; **litera baja f.** lower berth

llamada f. telephone call; **llamada local f.** local phone call; **llamada a larga distancia** long-distance phone call; **llamada conferencia f.** conference call

llamar to call, to knock, to ring; **llamar por teléfono** to phone

llamarse to be named, to be called; **¿Cómo se llama usted?** What is your name?

llanta f. car tire

llave f. key; **llave inglesa (llave de tuerca) f.** wrench

llegada f. arrival

llegar to arrive

llenar to fill, to fill out; **¡llénelo usted!** Fill her up!

lleno full

llevar to carry, to wear, to take a person or thing somewhere

llover to rain

lluvia f. rain

loco crazy

lograr to obtain, to get to

luego then, afterward; **Desde luego.** Of course; **Hasta luego.** See you later.

lugar m. place, spot, site

luna f. moon

lunes m. Monday

luz f. light; **luz de parada f.** stoplight; **luz de trafico (luz de tránsito) f.** traffic light

M

madera f. wood

madre f. mother

maíz m. corn

mal bad, badly; **estar mal** to be ill

maleta f. suitcase, valise, bag

mandar to send, to order, to command

mandarina f. tangerine

manga f. sleeve

mano f. hand; **de segunda mano adj.** secondhand

manteca f. lard, fat, butter

mantel m. tablecloth

mantequilla f. butter

manzana f. apple, block (of houses)

mañana f. morning, tomorrow; **por la mañana** in the morning; **Hasta mañana.** So long (until tomorrow).; **pasado mañana** the day after tomorrow

mapa m. map; **mapa de carreteras (de automovilista) m.** road map

maquinilla f. hair clippers; **maquinilla de afeitar f.** safety razor

mar m. sea

mareado seasick

mareo m. seasickness

marido m. husband

mariscos m. pl. seafood

martes m. Tuesday

martillo m. hammer

marzo m. March

más more

masaje m. massage

mayo m. May

medianoche f. midnight

medias f. pl. stockings

medicamento m. drug (legal)

médico m., (adj.) doctor; medical

medidas f. pl. measurements, measures

medio half; **medio crudo** medium rare

mediodía m. noon

mejilla f. cheek

mejillón m. mussel

mejor better, best

mejores saludos m. pl. best wishes

melocotón m. peach

memoria f. memory

menos less, least, fewer; **al (por lo) menos** at least

mente f. mind

menudo small, minute; **a menudo** often

mercado m. market

mes m. month

mesa f. table, plateau

meter to put in, insert

miedo m. fear; **tener miedo** to be afraid, to fear

miércoles m. Wednesday

mil thousand; **mil millones** billion

minusválido handicapped

mirar to look, to look at

mismo same; **ahora mismo** right now; **hoy mismo** this very day

mitad f. half (n.)

moda f. fashion, style

modo m. way, mode, manner

mojado wet

mojarse to get wet

molestar to bother, to annoy; **No se moleste.** Don't bother.; Don't trouble yourself.

moneda f. coin; **moneda corriente f.** currency; **moneda suelta f.** change

morada f. stay

morado purple

moreno brunette, dark-complexioned

mosquitero m. mosquito netting

mostaza f. mustard

mostrar to show

mozo m. porter, waiter

muchacha f. girl

muchacho m. boy

mucho much, a great deal of, a lot of

muchos many, lots of

muelle m. pier, dock, wharf

muerte f. death

muerto dead

mujer f. woman, wife

muleta f. crutch

multa f. fine (n.)

muñeca f. wrist, doll

muro m. (outside) wall

museo m. museum

muslo m. thigh

muy very

N

nacer to be born

nada nothing; **De nada.** You're welcome.; Don't mention it.; **nada más** nothing else

nadar to swim

nadie no one, nobody

naranja f. orange

nariz m. nose

navaja de afeitar f. razor

Navidad f. Christmas

necesitar to need

neumático de repuesto m. spare tire

nevar to snow

niebla f. fog

nieve f. snow

ninguno none

niño m. child

noche f. night; **Buenas noches.** Good evening. Good night.

nombre m. name

norte m. north

noruego Norwegian

nos us, ourselves

nosotros we, us

novela f. novel

noveno ninth

noventa ninety

nube f. cloud

nublado cloudy

nuestro our, ours

nueve nine

nuevo new; **de nuevo** again, anew

nuez f. walnut

número m. number

nunca never

O

occidente m. western world

ochenta eighty

ocho eight

octavo eighth

ocupado busy, taken

ocurrir to happen

oeste m. west

oficina office; **oficina de cambio f.** exchange office; **oficina de informes f.** information bureau; **oficina de objetos perdidos f.** lost-and-found

oído m. ear (internal); **dolor de oídos m.** earache

oír to hear

ojo m. eye

olvidar, olvidarse de to forget

once eleven

óptico m. optician

oreja f. ear (external)

oro m. gold

ostra f., ostión m. oyster

otoño m. autumn, fall

otra vez again

otro other, another

P

padre m. father

pagar to pay, to cash

página f. page

país m. country (nation)

paja f. straw

pájaro m. bird

palabra f. word

pan m. bread

pañales m. pl. diapers

panecillo m. roll

paño m. cloth

pantalla f. screen

pantalones m. pl. trousers, pants

pañuelo m. handkerchief

papa f. potato

papel m. paper; **papel de cartas (de escribir) m.** writing paper; **papel de envolver m.** wrapping paper; **papel de seda m** tissue paper; **papel higiénico m.** toilet paper

papelería f. stationery store

paquete m. packet, package, parcel; **paquete postal** m. parcel post

par m. pair

para for; **Es para usted.** It's for you.

parabrisas m. windshield

parachoques m. car bumper

parada f. stop; **señal de parada** f. signal sign; **parada intermedia** f. stop-over; **parada ordinaria** f. scheduled bus stop

paraguas m. umbrella

parar to stop, to stall (car)

pardo brown

parecer to seem, to appear

pared m. inner wall

párpado m. eyelid

parrilla f. grill; **a la parrilla** broiled

partida f. game

pasado past, last; **el mes pasado** last month

pasajero m. passenger

pasar to pass, to happen, to spend (time)

pasear, pasearse to take a walk, ride; **¡Pase usted!**; Come! Come in!

paseo m. ride, walk; **paseo en coche** m. drive

paso a nivel m. railroad crossing

pastel m. pie

pastilla f. tablet, cake (of soap), candy

pato m. duck

peatón m. pedestrian

pecho m. chest

pedazo m. piece

pedernal m. flint

pedir to ask for; **pedir prestado** to borrow

peinar to comb, to set hair

peine m. comb

película f. film

peligro m. danger

peligroso dangerous

pelo m. hair

pelota f. (bouncing) ball

peluquería f. barbershop

peluquero m. barber

pendiente m. earring

pensar to think, to intend

pensión completa f. American plan (hotel)

peor worse, worst

pepino m. cucumber

pequeño small, little

pera f. pear

perder to lose, to miss (a train or boat)

¡Perdón! Pardon me!

perdonar to pardon, to excuse

perfumería f. perfume shop

periódico m. newspaper

permiso m. pass, permit

permitir to permit, to allow

perno m. bolt

pero but

perro m. dog

persa Persian

pertenecer to belong

pesado heavy

pesar to weigh

pescado m. fish (when caught)

peso m. weight, monetary unit

pestaña f. eyelash

pez m. fish (in water)

pila f. battery (electronics)

pie m. foot; **a pie** on foot

piel f. skin, fur, leather

pierna f. leg (of body)

pieza f. play (theater)

piezas de respuesto f. spare parts

píldora f. pill

pimienta f. black pepper

pimientos m. pl. peppers

piña f. pineapple

pinacoteca f. art gallery

pinchazo m. puncture

piscina f. swimming pool

piso m. apartment, suite, floor

pista f. plane runway

pitillera f. cigarette case

placer m. pleasure
plancha f. flat iron
planchar to iron, to press
planilla f. form, document
plata f. silver
plátano m. plantain, banana
platillo m. saucer
plato m. plate, course (meal);
  plato del día m. today's
  special
playa f. beach
plaza f. square (n.); **plaza de
  toros** bullring
pluma f. pen; **pluma fuente
  f.** fountain pen
poblado m. village
pobre poor
poco little; **un poco** a little;
  poco asado (hecho) rare
  (steak)
pocos few, a few
poder to be able
policía m./f. police officer;
  policía f. police
polvo m. powder **polvo de
  talco m.** talcum powder
polvos para la cara m. pl.
  face powder
pollo m. chicken
poner to put, to place
ponerse to put on, to become
por for (exchange), by; **pagar
  por** to pay for; **por aquí**
  this way; **por día** by the day;
  ¿Por dónde? Which way?
porque because
¿por qué? why?
portaequipajes m. trunk (car)
porte m. postage
portero m. doorman, janitor
poseer to possess, to own
postre m. dessert
precio m. price, cost
pregunta f. question, inquiry
preguntar to ask, to inquire
preocuparse to worry; **No se
  preocupe.** Don't worry.
prepagado prepaid

presentar to introduce, to
  present
prestar to lend
primavera f. spring (season)
primero first
primeros auxilios first aid
prisa f. hurry, haste; **darse
  prisa** to hurry
probarse to try on
prohibido prohibited,
  forbidden
prohibir to forbid; **se prohibe
  la entrada** no admittance;
  se prohibe el paso no
  thoroughfare
prometer to promise
pronto quick, quickly, soon
propina f. tip (gratuity)
prostituta f. prostitute
provisionalmente temporarily
próximo next; **el año
  próximo** next year
puede ser perhaps, maybe
puente m. bridge
puerta f. door
puerto m. port, harbor
pulgar m. thumb
pulsera f. bracelet; **reloj de
  pulsera** wristwatch
pulverizar to spray
puro pure, cigar

Q

que that, which, who
qué what?, how?
quebrado broken
quedarse to remain, to stay, to
  be left; **quedarse con** to
  keep
queja f. complaint
quejarse to complain
quemadura f. burn
quemar to burn
querer to wish, to want, to
  desire, to love; **querer decir**
  to mean
queso m. cheese

quién, quiénes (pl.) who?, which?; **¿quién sabe?** who knows?, perhaps, maybe
quijada f. jaw
quince fifteen
quinto fifth
quitarse to take off
quitasol m. parasol
quizá maybe
quizás perhaps

R

rábano m. radish
rabino m. rabbi
radiografía f. x-ray
raíz f. root
raya f. part (of hair); **hacer la raya** to part hair
razón f. reason, right; **tener razón** to be right; **no tener razón** to be wrong
real royal, real
recado m. message
recalentar to overheat
receta f. prescription, recipe
recibir to receive
recibo m. receipt
recién pintado fresh paint, freshly painted
recobrar to recover, to get back
recomendar to recommend
reconocer to recognize
recorder to remember
recuerdos m. pl. regards
rechazar to refuse, to reject
red f. net, train rack
redecilla f. hair net
redondo round
refresco m. soft drink
regalo m. gift, present
rehusar to refuse
reírse to laugh
rejilla f. rack (in R.R. coach)
relámpago m. lightning
reloj m. watch, clock; **reloj de pulsera** m. wristwatch

remendar to mend
remitente m. sender, shipper (mail)
remolacha f. beet
remolcar to tow
repente sudden; **de repente** suddenly
repentino sudden
repetir to repeat
reponerse to recover health
requemado overdone
resfriado cold (health)
resorte m. spring (mechanical)
respirar to breathe
responder to answer
respuesta f. answer
resultar to result, to turn out to be, to prove to be
retrete m. restroom, washroom, toilet
revelar to develop (film)
revisor m. conductor
revista f. magazine
rico rich
rieles m. pl. R.R. tracks
río m. river
robar to rob, to steal
rociar to spray
rodilla f. knee
rojo red
rollo m. roll (of film)
romper to break
ropa f. clothes; **ropa blanca** f. linen; **ropa interior** f. underwear
rosado pink
roto broken
rueda f. wheel
ruido m. noise
ruidoso noisy
rumano Romanian
ruso Russian

S

sábana f. bedsheet
sábado m. Saturday

saber   to know a fact, to know how

sabroso   tasty

sacacorchos m.   corkscrew

sacar   to take out, to extract

saco m.   coat

sal f.   salt

sala f.   living room, hall; **sala de equipajes** f.   checkroom, baggage room; **sala de espera** f.   waiting room

salado   salty

salchicha f.   sausage

salchichón m.   salami

sales aromáticas f. pl.   smelling salts

salida f.   exit

salir   to leave, to depart, to go out

salón   lounge; **salón de belleza** m.   beauty parlor

salsa f.   sauce, gravy

salud f.   health; **¡A su salud!**   To your health!

saludo m.   greetings

saludos m. pl.   greetings, regards; **muchos saludos**   best wishes

salvavidas m.   lifeguard

sandalia f.   sandal

sandía f.   watermelon

sangre f.   blood

sanidad f.   health

santuario m.   shrine

sastre m.   tailor

sazonado   seasoned

se   self, himself, herself, itself, themselves

seco   dry; **limpieza en seco** f.   dry-cleaning

sed f.   thirst; **tener sed**   to be thirsty

seda f.   silk; **papel de seda** m.   tissue paper

seguir   to follow, continue; **seguir a la derecha**

(izquierda)   keep right (left)

segundo   second

seguro   sure, insurance; **seguro de viaje** m.   travel insurance

seis   six

sellar   to seal

sello m.   postage stamp, seal

semáforo m.   traffic light

semana f.   week

sentar   to fit; to seat

sentarse   to sit down

sentir   to be sorry

sentirse   to feel (in health)

señor m.   Mr., Sir, gentleman

señora f.   Mrs., lady, madam

señorita f.   Miss, young lady

séptimo   seventh

ser   to be

servicio m.   service

servilleta f.   napkin

servir   to serve

servirse (+ infinitive)   please (do something); **¡Sírvase hablar más despacio!**   Please speak more slowly!

servirse   to help, serve oneself; **Haga el favor de servirse.**   Please help yourself.

sesenta   sixty

setenta   seventy

sexto   sixth

si   if

sí   yes

SIDA m.   AIDS

siempre   always

siete   seven

significar   to signify, to mean

silla f.   chair; **silla de cubierta** f.   deck chair; **silla de ruedas** f.   wheelchair

sillón m.   armchair

simpático   pleasant, likable

sin   without

sinagoga f.   synagogue

sitio m.   place, spot

smoking m.   tuxedo

sobre   on, upon; **sobre todo** above all, especially

sobrecargo m.   purser

sobretodo m.   overcoat

sol m.   sun

solamente   only, solely

solo   alone, only, sole: **café solo m.**   black coffee

sombra f.   shade; **a la sombra** shade

sombrerería f.   hat shop

sombrero m.   hat

sortija f.   ring

sostén m.   bra, brassiere

su, sus   his, her, its, their, your

suave   mild, soft

subir   to go up, to climb

suceder   to happen

sucio   dirty, soiled

sueco   Swedish

suela f.   sole (shoe)

suelo m.   floor, ground, soil

suelto adj.   loose; **m.**   small change

sueño m.   sleep, dream; **tener sueño**   to be sleepy

suerte f.   luck; **¡Buena suerte!** good luck

suizo   Swiss

sujeto a derechos de aduana dutiable

supuesto   supposed; **por supuesto**   of course, naturally

sur m.   south

suyo   his, hers, yours, theirs, one's, its

T

taberna f.   tavern, saloon

tacones de goma m. pl. rubber heels

talón m.   baggage check, heel of foot

tal vez   perhaps, maybe

talle m.   waist

tamaño m.   size

también   also, too

tapa f.   hors d'oeuvres

taquilla f.   theater box office, ticket office

tarde   late; **la tarde** afternoon; **¡Buenas tardes!** Good afternoon!

tarifa f.   fare, rate; **tarifa nocturna f.**   night rate; **tarifa por hora f.**   hourly rate

tarjeta f.   card; **tarjeta de crédito f.**   credit card; **tarjeta de memoria f.** memory card; **tarjeta postal f.**   postcard; **tarjeta telefónica**   phone card

taza f.   cup

té m.   tea

techo m.   roof, ceiling

teclado m.   keyboard

tela f.   cloth

telefonista m., f.   telephone operator

teléfono m.   telephone

temporalmente   temporarily

temprano   early

tenazas f. pl.   pliers

tenedor m.   fork

tener   to have, to possess; **tener noticias de**   to hear from; **tener prisa**   to be in a hurry; **tener que**   to have to

teñir   to tint

tercero   third

terciopelo m.   velvet

ternera f.   veal

terrorismo m.   terrorism

terrorista m./f.   terrorist

tía f.   aunt

tiempo m.   weather, time

tienda f.   store, shop; **tienda de departamentos f.** department store

tierra f.   land, earth

tijeras f. pl.   scissors

timbre m.   bell

tinta f.   ink

tintorería f. dry cleaners
tío m. uncle
tirantes m. pl. suspenders
toalla f. towel
tobillo m. ankle
tocar to play an instrument
tocino m. bacon
todavía still, yet; **todavía no** not yet
todo all, everything, every, each; **todo el mundo** everybody, everyone
todos everybody, everyone, all
tomacorriente m. electric outlet
tomar to take
tontería f. nonsense
torcedura f. sprain
toro m. bull
toronja f. grapefruit
toros m. pl. bulls, bullfight
torta f. cake
tortilla f. omelet, cornmeal cake
tos f. cough
toser to cough
tostada f. toast
trabajar to work
traducir to translate
traer to bring
traje m. suit (of clothes); **traje de baño m.** bathing suit; **traje de etiqueta m.** evening clothes
transbordar to transfer
transbordo transfer
tranquilo quiet
tranvía m. trolley, streetcar
trece thirteen
treinta thirty
trepar to climb
tres three, **tres veces** three times
tronar to thunder
trueno m. thunder
tuerca f. nut (mechanical)
turco Turkish
turismo m. tourism

U

un, una a, an, one; **una vez** once
uña f. nail (finger or toe)
uno one, someone, people
usar to use
uso m. use (purpose)
usted (Ud., Vd.) you (sing.)
ustedes (Uds., Vds.) you (pl.)
uvas f. pl. grapes

V

vacío empty
valer to be worth
válido valid, good for
variedades f. pl. musical show
varios several
vaso m. drinking glass
¡Váyase! Scram! Go away!
veinte twenty
velocidad máxima f. speed limit
venda f. bandage
vendar to bandage
vender to sell
veneno m. poison
venir to come
venta f. sale
ventana f. window
ventanilla f. train, ticket window; **ventanilla de los certificados f.** registry window
ventilador m. fan
ver to see
verano m. summer
verdad f. truth
verdaderamente really, truly
verdadero true
verde green
verduras f. pl. vegetables
vestido m. dress
vestirse to get dressed
vez f. time (occasion); **una vez** once; **en vez de** instead of, in place of

viajar   to travel
viaje m.   voyage, trip, journey;
   ¡Buen viaje!   Bon voyage!
   Have a pleasant trip!
viajero m.   traveler
vida f.   life
video m.   video
vidrio m.   glass (material)
viejo   old
viento m.   wind; **Hace (hay)
   viento.**   It's windy.
viernes m.   Friday
vino m.   wine
vista f.   view
vitrina f.   showcase
vivir   to live
volante m.   steering wheel
volver   to return, turn
vuelo m.   flight
vuelta f.   turn

Y

y   and
ya   already
yo   I
yodo m.   iodine

Z

zanahoria f.   carrot
zapatería f.   shoe shop, store
zapatillas f. pl.   slippers
zapato m.   shoe
zarpar   to sail
zarzuela f.   musical comedy
zumo m.   juice

INDEX

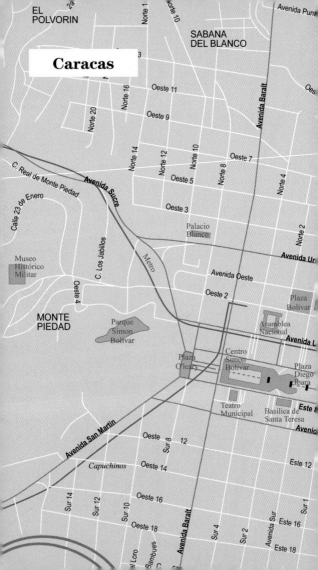

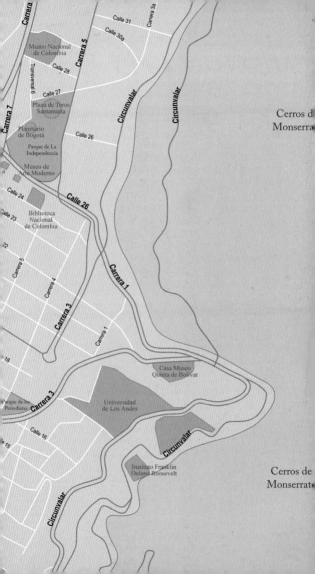

Carrera 7

Carrera 5

Calle 31

Calle 30a

Carrera 3a

Museo Nacional
de Colombia

Transversal 6

Calle 28

Calle 27

Plaza de Toros
Santamaría

Planetario
de Bogotá

Parque de La
Independencia

Calle 26

Museo de
Arte Moderno

Circunvalar

Circunvalar

Cerros de
Monserrate

Calle 24

Calle 26

Calle 23

22

Biblioteca
Nacional
de Colombia

Carrera 6

Carrera 4

Carrera 3

Carrera 1

Carrera 1

18

Casa Museo
Quinta de Bolívar

Parque de los
Periodistas

Carrera 3

Universidad
de Los Andes

Circunvalar

Cerros de
Monserrate

Calle 16

15

Instituto Franklin
Deland Roosevelt

Circunvalar

Circunvalar

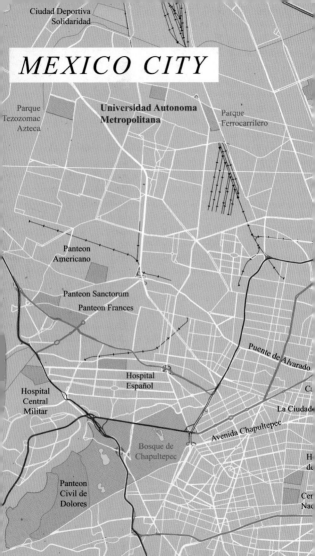

MEXICO CITY

Ciudad Deportiva
Solidaridad

Parque
Tezozomac
Azteca

**Universidad Autonoma
Metropolitana**

Parque
Ferrocarrilero

Panteon
Americano

Panteon Sanctorum
Panteon Frances

Puente de Alvarado

Hospital
Español

Ca

Hospital
Central
Militar

La Ciudad

Avenida Chapultepec

Bosque de
Chapultepec

H
de

Panteon
Civil de
Dolores

Cer
Nac